The international politics
of Central Asia

MANCHESTER
UNIVERSITY PRESS

Regional International Politics series

In memory of
Beverley Thould-Evans (1961–96)
and
Doris Anderson (1905–97)

Contents

Maps

Preface

This book has its origins in my own interest in Central Asia dating back to the early 1980s, and problems that emerged during the early 1990s in teaching courses on post-Soviet politics. Most of the books available at that time focused primarily on Russia and, whilst there were many useful articles, there was no systematic treatment of Central Asian politics. Thus when Richard Purslow, then in Manchester, suggested that I contribute to the MUP regional politics series it seemed too good an opportunity to miss. At the same time it seemed inappropriate to duplicate the glut of books that were then appearing on the 'geopolitics' of the region, and for this reason this text deals primarily with the politics of the region rather than 'international politics' in the strictest sense. Though the book starts and finishes with geopolitics, much of its content is devoted to the politics of the five states that make up Central Asia – Kazakhstan, Kyrgyzstan, Tajikistan, Turkmenistan and Uzbekistan – from the time of the Russian conquest until the present. Yet, as will become apparent in sections on history, economics and nationality questions, domestic and international politics are not easily separated out, with external influences playing a key role in shaping and constraining political development in many of these states. In turn their own foreign policies and relationships with the outside world have been shaped by internal political requirements, notably those relating to economic reconstruction and the guaranteeing of their security and status as independent states.

In many respects this is the classic 'ivory tower' production, coming largely out of work carried out within the confines of British universities. Though useful material has been gathered during earlier visits to Moscow, Tashkent, Bukhara and Alma Ata, the commencement of work on this project was followed by the onset of persistent health problems, making travel to the region impossible. Given the nature of a text of this sort, heavily dependent as it must be on the work of other scholars (credited in the notes and in the bibliography), this has been less of a problem than I had feared, largely thanks to the help given by the librarians of those British libraries still taking Central Asian publications. In particular I am grateful to librarians at the Universities of St Andrews, Glasgow, Birmingham and Essex, and the School of Slavonic and East European Studies in London. During earlier research into Russian involvement in Central Asia, staff at the Russian State Library (formerly the Lenin Library) and the library of the Institute of Scientific Information on the Social Sciences (INION) were especially helpful. Various individuals have provided material, commented on individual chapters and answered questions, including Audrey Anderson, Patricia Carley, Sally Cummings, Felix Corley, Roland Danreutther, Rick Fawn, Asyl Imanalieva and Ali Watson. Above all, the support and love provided by my wife Jill and the boisterous affection of Joseph and Caitlin have, as always, helped to keep my feet on the ground.

Note

In this book we use Russian and Soviet designations for place names and countries when referring to developments prior to independence, and current titles when referring to the independent states. Hence the capital of Turkmenistan is Askhabad during the earlier period and Ashgabat post-1991; in similar vein Kirgiz/Kyrgyz, Alma Ata/Almaty, etc.

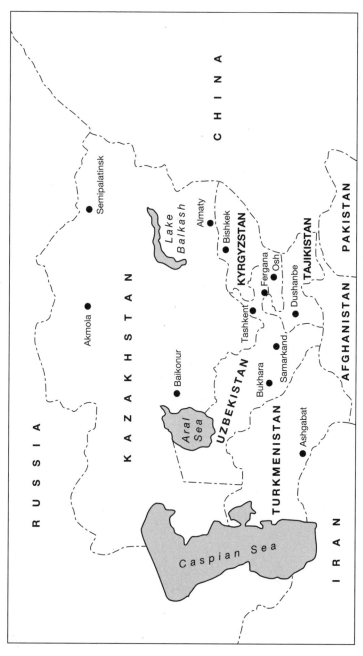

Map 1 The Central Asian states

Introduction

On an unbearably hot day in June 1842 two British officers, Colonel Charles Stoddart and Captain Arthur Connolly, were dragged out into the public square in Bukhara and unceremoniously put to death. They were but the latest, and by no means the last, victims in the so-called 'great game' in Central Asia. Throughout the mid-nineteenth century, as Britain and Russia struggled for influence in the region, numerous soldiers, spies, journalists and assorted adventurers were to meet their end, sometimes in battle but more often as a result of disease and the extremes of climate. By the 1880s the 'game' was effectively over, as Russia made its last conquests and the southern borders of Central Asia were stabilised for over a century to come. A hundred years later the five states of the region created by the Soviet system acquired their nominal independence and, in seeking to make a reality of this status, found themselves seeking new allies and partners to provide political and economic support. This in turn led to talk of a new 'great game' in which various forces, alternatively seen as malign or benign, struggled to influence the political, economic and ideological shape of the emergent states.

This book explores the evolution of Central Asian politics from the time of the Russian conquest to the present. Chapters 1 to 3 focus on the period of Russian dominance, from the 1860s to the late 1980s. Our starting point in the first chapter is the 'great game', as we look at Russia's move into the region which gathered pace following the Crimean defeat and which, despite British displeasure, ended with St Petersburg exercising nominal control over the region. We then turn to the centre's attempt to establish control over the region, a subject that dominates the rest of Chapter 1 and all of Chapter 2. On the surface the picture is one of a gradual and inexorable extension of control but the reality is somewhat different. A series of struggles around the turn of the century pitted Russian administrators against local rulers, whilst both had to face the different threats posed by reformers and revolutionaries, by liberals, nationalists and socialists. At the end of the day it appeared that socialism had won out but, once in power, the Bolsheviks discovered that here at least formal control did not guarantee the successful exercise of authority. Elites were purged, histories rewritten and the economy reshaped so as to breed dependency upon Moscow, yet by the late 1970s it was clear that in many areas central control was a fiction, something recognised by Yuri Andropov and then Mikhail Gorbachev. Nonetheless, until the very end of the Soviet period Central Asia was sold to developing countries as a useful alternative model of development to that offered by the capitalist West.

Gorbachev sought to redefine the relationship of Central Asia to Moscow, in particular by attacking what was described as the corrupt behaviour of local personnel and by calling on the region to become more self-sufficient in the economic sector. Yet his failure to recognise that dependency was as much a product of central policies as local misbehaviour led even the traditionally quiescent Central Asian elites to fight back. Though glasnost bit less deeply here than in other parts of the USSR and independent social organisations were tightly controlled, the leaders of these republics bargained for reductions in central quotas, notably for cotton, called for more investment, and encouraged the cultural revival which predated Gorbachev but had lacked the overt official backing essential if it was to flourish. At the time of the August coup most of these leaders sat on the fence and afterwards, led by Kazakhstan's President Nursultan Nazarbaev, they sought to keep the union together. In December 1991, however, they were forced to recognise the inevitable and accept the not altogether congenial status of independent states.

Chapter 4 introduces some of the political issues that have dominated Central Asia since 1991, pointing to both similarities and differences in the development of each polity. In particular it focuses on the role of the leaders of these states, each of whom has played a key role in shaping the destiny of the young state over which he presides. Two, Islam Karimov of Uzbekistan and Saparmurad Niyazov of Turkmenistan, have opted for an overtly authoritarian approach, the latter's characterised by an extremely colourful personality cult. In both states the press is muzzled and opposition effectively outlawed, all justified in the name of stability, the prevention of 'fundamentalism' and the belief that only with tight control can economic change be effected. Tajikistan has also adopted an authoritarian, often violent form of rule since the partial conclusion of civil war in late 1992, but discussion of this tragic republic is left until Chapter 7. In Kazakhstan and Kyrgyzstan, originally seen as potential beacons of democracy, the more recent trend has been towards a more autocratic presidentialism, especially in the former. Here Nazarbaev dissolved parliament in March 1995 and subsequently pushed through a constitution which concentrated extensive powers in the hands of the presidency. In neighbouring Kyrgyzstan, Askar Akaev, the former champion of democratic order and civil society, has also shifted his position, in February 1996 pushing through constitutional changes that increased the power of the head of state, albeit not to the extent seen in other Central Asian states. Nonetheless, the tiny republic of Kyrgyzstan remains the freest of the Central Asian states, with a restrained but relatively lively press and a wide range of political parties, albeit effectively rendered near impotent by their own actions and official restraints. Yet to examine Central Asian politics purely in terms of formal structures is clearly inadequate, for much of political life in Central Asia remains beneath the surface in an area where loyalties and alliances are often rooted in family, tribal and regional connections. Whilst these remain hard for the outside observer to unravel with any precision, in Chapter 4 and others we seek to point to some of the ways in which traditional and 'modern' styles of political activity interrelate and impact upon the shaping of the orders emerging in the new states.

Chapters 5 and 6 look at key problems faced by the new states in making a reality of their independence. New constitutions, institutions and political orders are all very well, but it is how they resolve key issues that matters. Two issues are of acute concern: rebuilding economies whose stagnation if not decline was accelerated by the break-up of the Soviet Union, and creating a sense of national unity in a region where nation-states have never existed before and where many people's loyalties and identities are essentially sub-national in nature.

Central to the efforts of the states to make a reality of independence have been attempts at economic reconstruction. To this end the states have evolved a variety of strategies, from that of Turkmenistan where economic reform has been slow to evolve, to that of Kyrgyzstan which is rooted, at least rhetorically, in a belief that only a full-blooded transition to the market can solve its problems. In seeking to strengthen their economic positions some of these states are in a better position than others, with Turkmenistan having the third largest reserves of natural gas in the world, and Kazakhstan and Uzbekistan considerable oil potential. Other valuable resources to be found in the region include gold, cotton and, more controversially, opium. Against this one might note that, with the exception of northern Kazakhstan, the area lacks substantial industrial development. In the case of Kazakhstan, the industrial sector is closely tied in with the economy of southern Siberia and is dominated by Slavic and European personnel. In developing its natural assets Central Asia has mainly looked to outside investment, and a number of major deals have emerged to encourage the exploitation of natural resources. At the same time regional leaders have recognised that in the medium term the old relationships with Russia and the Commonwealth of Independent States (CIS) states cannot be ignored, for they depend upon the old interdependent relations for many of their manufactured goods and they rely on their northern neighbour's good will in order to be able to export many of their natural resources. In practice their economic progress can only be described as halting, with considerable economic disruption and decline following independence, and only partial stabilisation apparent by the mid-1990s. Nonetheless, the fears of many commentators that poor economic results and falling living standards would translate into mass social unrest capable of toppling the existing regimes have not been realised.

The second major problem facing Central Asian elites stems from the national demarcation of the early 1920s when the Bolsheviks created embryonic states in the region. In practice this division did not always sit easily with ethnic divisions, left a number of disputed borders and deposited minorities from one ethnic group in the state formation of another. For example, southern Kazakhstan's Chimkent oblast has a large concentration of Uzbeks, as does Kyrgyzstan's Osh oblast and Tajikistan's Leninabad oblast. From the late 1980s these and other tensions on occasion produced bloody intercommunal violence and, though territorial claims have been renounced by the five states concerned, these are problems that could be a destabilising force in the future. In addition attempts to create national unity are hampered by the fact that many of the region's population still think in largely family, communal, tribal and regional terms, as evidenced by the conflict in Tajikistan.

Finally, in seeking to create a real sense of national identity and civic belonging, the states of Central Asia have to address the major problem posed by the presence of large numbers of Russian speakers, especially in northern Kazakhstan. For many of these people the achievement of independence has been nothing less than a disaster, as they have suffered a loss of status, whilst facing new difficulties in private and professional life posed by the adoption of state languages, the perceived Islamicisation of daily life, cadres policies which often exclude them from political power, and a feeling that they are not wanted by many local inhabitants. Though the presidents of each country have stressed the need to treat all citizens equally and some have gone out of their way to persuade Russians to stay, many Slavs have emigrated to an uncertain future in Russia. This is a situation which has implications for both socio-economic life and international relations, for in the short term these states are dependent upon the expertise of Russian speakers in many areas, and alienating this population may negatively affect relations with their large neighbour to the north.

The complexities of forming coherent national identities and deciding upon the proper role of religion in public life was nowhere clearer than in Tajikistan, as is shown in Chapter 7. Formerly one of the most conservative of Soviet republics, the ruling party elite faced a growing challenge to its rule in late 1991 from a coalition made up of Islamic, democratic and nationalist groupings. In May 1992 these elements were taken into a coalition government and for a few months in the autumn of that year held power, before being brutally expelled by armed groups loyal to the old order. Since that time the government of Tajikistan led by Imomali Rakhmonov has sought to establish its authority in the face of persistent pressure from armed oppositionists operating out of Afghanistan. Though originally billed as a struggle between 'fundamentalists' and 'communists', this conflict in fact provided further evidence of the shallow nature of national identities in much of Central Asia. Underlying the struggle were tensions not just between ideologies, but within them – as Muslims took different sides in the struggle –

and perhaps more significantly, between the various regions of the country. Moreover, this was a conflict with international dimensions, drawing in not just the republic's Central Asian neighbours, but also outside powers such as Russia and Afghanistan. In Chapter 8 we return to our starting point, in focusing more explicitly on the relations of the region with the outside world, though eschewing talk of a new 'great game'. Here we examine Central Asia's search for new international partners in the Western, Islamic and Asian world, noting that in most cases the interest or possibilites of involvement by these states is often extremely limited. Equally problematic have been efforts to engender regional cooperation, often hampered by economic inequality within the region, and the personal rivalries and ambitions of Central Asian leaders. Finally we return to Russia whose involvement in the region since the 1860s if not earlier created many of the problems these states now face. For the foreseeable future Russia looks to be the major player in the region and one which the new states can ill afford to antagonise. The struggle for overt control may have ended in 1991 but the contestation for influence would appear to remain as sharp as ever.

1

Russia in Central Asia: the struggle for political control, 1865–1924

Central Asia during the second half of the nineteenth century and the early years of the twentieth provided a stage for a succession of struggles, as imperial powers, native rulers, conservatives, reformers and revolutionaries fought for control of the region. Up until the middle of the century Russia's advance into the region had been spasmodic and unsystematic, more concerned with ensuring the safety of Russian borders and the protection of the growing trade connections with the East through Turkestan (as it was then known to Russian officialdom) than promoting any grand imperial design. Following defeat in the Crimean War, however, some policy-makers in St Petersburg began to look on Central Asia as a region where rivalry with Britain could be more favourably pursued. Over the next two decades what came to be known as the 'great game' reached its climax, as adventurers, travellers and ambitious officers on both sides sought to promote their countries' influence in the region with varying degrees of support from home governments.

Ultimately, political and economic control in Turkestan fell to imperial Russia and by the mid-1880s the southern boundary of the Russian empire was effectively fixed for the next hundred years. Yet as St Petersburg sought to render its control effective and to exploit the natural resources of the region, new struggles emerged. Native rulers backed by Russia never fully reconciled themselves to subordination and continued to assert their independence, often with backing from traditional societies of which the colonial administration had little understanding and which it was unable to penetrate. In turn old-style leaders faced increasingly vocal opposition from small groups of reformers within their own societies who saw in Russia's conquest of the region evidence of the need for a wider social reform that could enable Muslim societies to modernise whilst retaining traditional values. Such people were influenced by the ideas of liberals and revolutionaries within the wider Russian empire who sought to moderate or overthrow tsarist rule. At the end of the day it was the latter who were to triumph and ensure continuing control of the region by Moscow, though they too were to find that formal political dominance could not in itself ensure control over the peoples of the region.

The 'great game' and the Russian conquest

Russia's advance towards and into Central Asia had its roots in the sixteenth century when Ivan the Terrible reversed the historic conquests of the Tatars. Kazan fell in 1552, followed soon after by Astrakhan, and Russia gradually began to advance into Siberia, occasionally using troops but more commonly relying on intrepid merchants or adventurers. Much of this early emphasis was upon trade rather than conquest, with successive tsars and their policymakers concerned to develop links with India and the East.

From the early eighteenth century Russia began to establish control over the Kazakh steppes through a series of forts and towns in southern Siberia and the north of what we know as Kazakhstan – Omsk, Semipalatinsk and Ust-Kamenogorsk (built in 1716–19). From here regional officials sought to exploit clan and tribal divisions amongst the Kazakhs to develop their own influence and provide some degree of protection for Russian caravans crossing the steppes *en route* to the markets of Bukhara and beyond. During the 1730s and and 1740s, individual leaders of the three Kazakh hordes sought Russian protection against rivals and through them partial control of the steppes was established, though this did not always protect Russian traders from the predatory habits of many Kazakh groups. Increasingly Russia developed its own administrative apparatus for the region and stripped away the real powers of the khans. Occasionally Kazakh leaders fought back and for a short while in the late 1830s Kenisary Kasimov of the Middle Horde posed a serious threat to the Russian authorities, but generally such resistance was easily suppressed.

During the later years of the reign of Nicholas I (1825–55) the military presence of Russia in the steppes was strengthened by the building of a series of forts extending southwards towards Turkestan: from Orenburg in the west, through Turgai and Irgiz (1845) to Kazalinsk (1853), and from Semipalatinsk in the east, via Kopalsk (1847) to Vernyi, the future Alma Ata (1853). When Aleksander II came to the throne in 1855 he was to inherit an empire that effectively bordered the khanates of Central Asia and an international situation that appeared to render Russian imperial ambitions more realisable in Central Asia than in Europe or the Black Sea. Moreover, as Mehmet Saray has pointed out, Russia's control of the Caucasus and strong influence in Persia effectively gave it control of the Caspian Sea and provided an opening to Central Asia through the territory of the Turkmen.[1]

Russia's advance into Central Asia during the nineteenth century was motivated by a number of considerations, and took place in the context of wider international struggles. In Westminster some British politicians began to speak of a Russian threat to India, in consequence of the abortive Russian expedition to take Khiva in 1839–40, and the seemingly inexorable advance of Russian troops and administrators into the Kazakh steppes. Seeking further clarification a growing number of British officers and travellers began to visit the region, with or without the approval of their government. Some found fame and glory, but others became Victorian martyrs, men such as Stoddart and Connolly brutally done to death by the Emir of Bukhara in 1842.[2] For their part officials in St Petersburg during the 1830s and 1840s began to talk in terms of a British threat to Russian interests in the region, using as evidence the presence of assorted British adventurers turning up in various Central Asian towns.[3]

In practice Russia's involvement in the region grew as a result of its defeat in the Crimean War and the perceived failure of its policies in Europe. Under the influence of his friend Prince Aleksander Bariatinskii, whom he appointed Viceroy of the Caucasus, Tsar Aleksander II came to believe in the reality of a British threat to Russia's military and commercial interests in Central Asia. Given the impossibility of countering British influence in Europe, Russia's southern neighbours appeared to offer what Lenin might have called a 'weak link'. In view of this a series of exploratory missions were sent to the region during the late 1850s, one of which was to be headed by N. P. Ignatiev, a close associate of Bariatinskii and a keen advocate of a forward policy in Turkestan. Following his trip to Central Asia Ignatiev recommended making a show of force on the eastern shores of the Caspian and taking action against the Kokand khanate, arguing that Britain only respected countries it feared and suggesting that whilst Russia had no pretence to India, the perception that it might have could prove useful in dealings with London.[4] Although his proposals met with opposition from both the Foreign Ministry, fearful of upsetting Britain, and the Finance Ministry, wary of the costs of any major involvement, by the mid-1860s Russia was committed to a more aggressive policy in Central Asia.

Alongside military-strategic factors, St Petersburg was also influenced by economic considerations. Even before the conquest Russia's trading links with the region had expanded considerably, with the value of goods exported from Russia rising from 2,724,820 roubles in 1849 to 16,634,396 roubles in 1962.[5] Yet trade remained difficult, as caravans faced not only harsh climatic conditions, but also the continued uncertainties associated with travel through terrain peopled by hostile tribes and rulers, and discrimination against Christian traders in Central Asian markets. As trade developed Russian merchants were increasingly vocal in calling for the government to take steps to protect their activities and to influence the rulers of the emirates to open up their states. Further pressures stemmed from the evolution of the domestic textile industry, largely dependent upon foreign supplies of raw cotton for its expansion. These needs were exacerbated by the American civil war (1861–65) which raised the world price of cotton more than five times and forced Russia to look elsewhere for its needs. And where better than Central Asia? From 1860 to 1864 imports of cotton from Central Asia rose from 174,059 to 459,391 puds,[6] and increasingly the Russian state saw the economic value of a more direct control of the region. Finally, policy-makers also argued that annexation of the region would provide a place to settle the growing numbers of landless or impoverished Russian peasantry, though most of these were to go to the Kazakh steppes rather than Turkestan proper.[7]

The new advance began in 1864 with the taking of Turkistan, Alie Ata and Chimkent, thus effectively joining the eastern and western lines of forts and thus encompassing the Kazakh steppe. Within days the conqueror of Chimkent General M. G. Cherniaev launched an abortive assault on Tashkent, the economic centre of the Khokand khanate. Dismayed, the ever-cautious Foreign Minister Prince A. M.

Gorchakov called on the tsar to drop ideas of further conquests in Central Asia, but by late 1864 it was clear that his advice was to be ignored. Accepting reality, Gorchakov drafted a memorandum to Russian diplomats abroad, though clearly intended for Western chancellories, stressing that whilst Russia respected the independence of the Central Asian states, it also had a civilising mission in the region comparable to that of other European states in their colonial acquisitions.[8]

In its conquest of Central Asia Russia was greatly aided by ongoing hostilities between the three khanates of Bukhara, Khiva and Khokand, which found it impossible to cooperate for long enough to provide an effective counter to the invaders. In June 1865 Cherniaev successfully took Tashkent. Three years later he took the Bukharan town of Samarkand, effectively turning the emirate into a Russian protectorate, albeit one with considerable internal independence and one whose internal life was little affected in the short term by Russian dominance. By 1873 Khiva had met a similar fate, and in 1876 Russia simply abolished the khanate of Khokand. Having dealt with the settled states, St Petersburg turned its attention to the troublesome Turkmen tribes, culminating in the bloody capture of the Geok-Tepe fortress in 1881. Having seen what had happened here, other Turkmen leaders quickly capitulated and in 1884 Merv was taken without loss of life.[9]

This steady advance southwards alarmed British policy-makers. Within twenty years Russian forces had moved nearly 500 miles closer to India, and Russian railroads to within 200 miles of the strategic Persian town of Herat – with the nearest British railhead some 400 miles away. Questions were raised about Britain's relationship with Persia and Afghanistan and about the impact these developments might have upon perceptions of British power within the region. As George Curzon noted after his travels in Turkestan, Russia's reputation had been raised 'owing to their unchecked and apparently irresistible advance, by the credit that their troops enjoy of being merely the advanced guard of inexhaustible numbers ... It has been noticed ... that while the inhabitants of the regions are amazed at the wealth of England, they are impressed by the numerical strength of Russia'.[10]

Britain responded slowly to the Russian advance, preferring to reinforce its influence and control in India, whilst seeking to avoid confrontation. In March 1885 Russo-Afghan border clashes at

Pendjeh briefly brought the threat of overt conflict, but after that Anglo-Russian rivalry in the region was brought to an effective end, with both sides agreeing on the demarcation of the Afghan border in 1895. Russia's expansion southward had come to a halt and its boundaries set, more or less, for the next century. Of greater concern to St Petersburg now was the consolidation and exploitation of its new territories.

Central Asia as a colony

The administrative integration of Kazakhstan and Turkestan into the Russian empire was to a considerable extent an *ad hoc* process in which military rule became the norm. In the Kazakh region this process culminated with the work of the Steppe Commission of 1865–66 which produced a series of legislative acts dividing Kazakhstan into six oblasts, two subordinate to the Governor-General of Orenburg (Ural'sk and Turgai), two to Omsk (Akhmolinsk and Semipalatinsk), and two to the Turkestan Governor-Generalship established in 1867 and based in Tashkent (Syr Darya and Semirechie).[11]

As more and more areas of Central Asia were brought under Russian control they were subordinated to Tashkent, although the Transcaspian oblast only became part of Turkestan in 1898, having been subordinate to the Caucasus command until 1890, and then the Ministry of War. But St Petersburg remained unwilling to take on excessive responsibilities in the region for this reason, and despite promptings from officers on the spot, declined to annex fully the Bukharan and Khivan Protectorates. These states were permitted to control their own internal affairs, though Russia retained control over their foreign affairs.[12] Elsewhere, the Turkestan region was divided into a number of oblasts, each presided over by a military governor subordinate to the Governor-General in Tashkent, the first of which was General K. P. Kaufman (1867–81).

Though the precise boundaries of the regions were subject to changes over the following decades, and their jurisdictional loyalties were occasionally altered,[13] the basic principle of military predominance remained in place, from Governor-Generalship to *uezd* level. This in turn bred problems, in the early years because General Kaufman and many of his commanders were more interested in pushing forward Russian borders than in the everyday work of administration, and later because military commanders often lacked the requisite skills for handling civil affairs. Moreover, they often had to work with military and civilian officials from the bottom of the administrative pile, people who had blotted their copybooks in the centre and had been more or less exiled to Central Asia. The concern of many of these was less with efficient administration and more with using their positions for personal gain. Even for relatively honest and committed officials such as Kaufman the problems of administering this region were compounded by the difficulties of communication within Central Asia and with the various departments and ministries in St Petersburg, often themselves in conflict as how best to handle these new acquisitions.[14]

At the local level administration was largely left in the hands of native administrators, with customary courts retaining jurisdiction over all but the most serious cases. Yet, as Seymour Becker has pointed out, 'violence was done to traditional conceptions and practices by the Russians' sense of order and administrative regularity'.[15] Thus in the nomadic regions, the rule of clan and tribal leaders was replaced by election, often producing the same elites, but violating tradition in combining different kinship groups within the same electoral district.[16] Moreover, elected native leaders often aroused resentment because, obliged to bribe and corrupt Russian officials, they had to increase the levels of income raised from the local population. When combined with the general unwillingness of Russians to adapt to the local culture, and their air of superiority and assumption that the native would see the virtues of Russian administration, colonial rule engendered hostility and stored up problems for the future.

Despite these trends, the initial inclination of Russia was to leave native customs well alone, on the assumption that this would make Russian rule more palatable. This was evident in the treatment of Islam, with General Kaufman resisting attempts to bring large numbers of Orthodox missionaries to the region,[17] and refusing to interfere in the activities of the numerous religious schools. But as Russian rule became more secure, and especially after Kaufman's resignation in 1881, this more liberal policy was rejected. Religious schools began to be merged with Russian literacy schools, and *waqf* property designed for the upkeep of such schools taken over. From the 1890s the pilgrimage to Mecca was made more difficult by the authorities, and slightly more effort put into spreading Orthodoxy.[18] Yet despite these limitations on religious schools little provision was made for the education of native Central Asians in Russian schools, and as late as 1902 Turkestan had only 52 schools providing places for some 1,582 pupils.[19] At the same time Russian administrators remained suspicious of the 'new method' schools created by reformist intellectuals at the beginning of the century, viewing them as likely to sow the seed of rebellion against Russian rule.

In the economic sphere the integration of Central Asia into Russia was facilitated by the extension of the rail network from the 1880s onwards. During that decade lines were extended from the Caspian Sea to Samarkand, then some years later on to Tashkent, and by 1906 the Orenburg–Tashkent line was complete. Designed initially for military purposes, it was in fact the economic factor that very quickly came to predominate.[20]

Chief among the products shipped along the new railroads was cotton for the Russian textile industry. The area sown was enlarged and production increased rapidly, rising more than eight times during the last two decades of the nineteenth century and continuing to rise, albeit more slowly, during the first fifteen years of the twentieth.[21] With the development of American varieties of cotton, as against the coarser types grown in the Bukharan and Khivan Protectorates, Turkestan provided an increasingly large share of Russia's cotton, supplying more than half her needs by 1891.[22] Simultaneously, by the end of the century cotton ginning and pressing accounted for over 70 per cent of Turkestan's limited industrial production.[23] As more and more effort was poured into the exploitation of cotton, other crops suffered. In the most developed cotton-producing regions such as the Fergana valley where nearly 40 per cent of sown land was given over to cotton, shortages in foodstuffs and grain production began to develop, and had to be met by imports from other parts of the empire.[24] Though silk, fruit, vegetables and the famous karakul wool were also being exported, and the Kazakh steppes provided livestock for northern markets, already the dependency relationship that was to characterise relations with Moscow in the late twentieth century was taking root.

The impact of this on the local economy and population was ambiguous. By providing access to world markets, the Russian conquest opened up new possibilities, especially for elites and the growing band of middlemen who provided finance, seed and expertise to

the peasantry, but inevitably it brought considerable social disloca-
tion as centuries' old patterns of rural life were disrupted. Joining
the world market rendered peasant lives subject to the fluctuations
of cotton and grain prices. Moreover, with the explosion in the
amount of land given over to cotton, the creation of a money economy, the extortions of the middlemen and the pressure on the land
came inflationary tendencies and peasant debt.[25]

Further problems were created for the steppe populations by the
influx of Russian colonists which grew rapidly from the 1890s
onwards. Largely *ad hoc* during the middle part of the century,
immigration was increasingly encouraged by the authorities following the 1891 Steppe Statute and the creation of the Resettlement
Administration in 1896. The former stated that all land 'in excess of
Kazakh needs' was to be given over to the Ministry of State Proper-
ties for redistribution, and in practice this soon meant that whilst
Kazakhs were permitted small amounts of land, much of the best
quality land (and 40 per cent was designated 'surplus') was given
over to Russian settlers.[26] As Russian settlements began to obstruct
traditional Kazakh grazing patterns, pressure was placed upon
nomadic groups to settle and take up farming. By the turn of the
century Russians were increasingly dominating the lands in the
north of Kazakhstan, and by 1911 some 40 per cent of the steppe
population was Russian. Turkestan was less affected, with only 4 per
cent of the population being Russian in this same year, but their predominance in the urban areas served to exacerbate the impression
that they were taking over Central Asian life.[27]

Though Central Asian economic development was stimulated by
its integration into Russia, it was only partially affected by the capitalist development emerging in the centre. Whilst the Russian state
preferred to treat the region as a source of raw materials, Russian
businesspeople did not invest in a major way in industrial development, preferring to focus on trade and the importation of cotton.
Little was done to encourage the creation of a native bourgeoisie or
native industry, with most of the industry created lying in the field
of cotton processing. Nonetheless, Soviet authors writing from the
late 1930s thought it possible to speak of the embryonic development of capitalism in the region and criticise earlier writers such as
P. Galuzo and G. Safarov who downplayed this development. V. I.
Lavrent'ev describing the decade or so before the revolution wrote
that 'in the prewar decade, in the period when capitalist Russia

included itself in the world system of monopoly capitalism as an indissoluble part, Turkestan was transformed into a colony of the most economically advanced and most aggressive Russian bourgoisie'.[28] In practice, Russian businesspeople proved reluctant to invest in locally based enterprises which did not offer quick profits, and in the early years of the century it was often foreign companies which were active, especially in the development of mineral resources. In the oil fields of Fergana and Cheleken it was British companies who carried out exploratory work and sought capital on English stock markets, whilst French companies played a role in some of the newly discovered coal fields.[29]

Revolutionary stirrings

During the late nineteenth century Russian rule met with little concerted resistance, though isolated and elemental outbursts served to remind the authorities that their presence was far from universally accepted. On occasions Russian actions provoked unrest, as happened in Tashkent in 1892 when measures to limit the cholera epidemic were seen as contrary to custom and divine order, and provoked riots.[30] A far greater shock was provided by the Andizhan rising of 1898. Here growing peasant unrest in the Fergana valley was used by religious and secular elites to strike back at the Russian authorities. Eventually repulsed and crushed with considerable ease, those involved were treated harshly and a handful executed. The rising was later presented by Soviet authors as an anti-feudal and anti-colonial revolt, but one whose class character was probably deflected by the 'holy war' slogans utilised by its leader.[31] In general, however, peasant unrest was sporadic and occasional, with resistance tending to take the form of refusals to pay taxes or to undertake agricultural responsibilities, or spontaneous responses to the seizure of land or water channels.

The revolution of 1905–7 left the local population largely untouched, though it played a role in stimulating the activities of reformist intellectuals. Such revolutionary activity as took place was the work of Slavic or Caucasian activists, or elements from the tiny working class emerging during this period. But the size of this latter group, limited to perhaps 30–40,000 people concentrated in the mines and railroads, and the fact that those from the local population were still closely tied to their villages, gave little scope for mass worker militancy.[32] From the mid-1890s there had been occasional strikes on the railroads, largely over pay and conditions, with activism often inadvertently stimulated by the tendency of the authorities to deport troublemakers to Turkestan thus serving to spread revolutionary ideas.[33]

Typical of such exiles was V. D. Kornyushin, exiled from Kazan in 1895, who organised the first social-democratic circle in Tashkent in 1902. Others came voluntarily, people such as Mikhail Morozov, a Bolshevik activist with 15 years of revolutionary activity and periods in exile behind him, who came to Samarkand from Baku in 1902.[34] And in northern Kazakhstan later Bolshevik luminaries such as Mikhail Frunze, Sergei Kirov and Valerian Kuibyshev were to earn their revolutionary spurs. Though by no means influential in the region, these people were all active in seeking to propagate Marxist ideas through newspapers and study circles.

As in other parts of the Russian Empire, 'Bloody Sunday' brought forth a banquet campaign from the liberal intelligentsia which the socialists sought to hijack and give a more explicit anti-tsarist flavour.[35] As 1905 progressed the railways were hit by repeated strikes and in May elements within the Tashkent garrison mutinied. Demonstrations, funeral marches and strikes were often noisy affairs but, not surprisingly given the size of the working class and radical intelligentsia, the numbers involved were generally small and on the whole the native population was noticeable by its absence. Though the scope of militancy again increased after October, the authorities were never seriously threatened, though they remained fearful of the potential impact of unrest on the native population. For example, on 10 October Governor-General Sakharov wrote to General D. F. Trepov in St Petersburg:

> In recent times we have noted a significant strengthening in the Turkestan region of revolutionary elements ... It is to be feared that the natives will doubt the power of the Russian authorities if they see with their own eyes that we are completely powerless to struggle with a handful of young people who ignore the administration and the police. Such doubts are but one step ... from mass outbreaks amongst the native population, amongst whom there are always fanatics waiting for a chance to repeat the Andizhan events of 1898.[36]

When revolution broke out in 1905 socialist groupings in Central

Asia still tended to work together although by the end of the year the social democrats had broken away, holding their first conference in February 1906. Amongst the latter the Mensheviks appear to have been the dominant force, although later Soviet accounts stressed the influence of Bolshevik activists such as Morozov. In practice factional differences had little impact upon the workers who struck in the Fergana oil fields or at the Krasnovodsk docks, nor upon the troops who mutined with increasing frequency, and some 500 of whom appeared before military courts in 1906. These people were open to direction and guidance from revolutionary forces, but the power of such was limited. As repressive activity by the state increased from the winter of 1906–7, organised socialist groups were easily destroyed, with the local press carrying frequent reports of searches, arrests and trials in 1907.[37] Strikes continued on a sporadic basis, as did terrorist activities such as the attempt on the life of the Fergana region's military governor as he left church in February 1907,[38] or the murder of the head of the Central Asian railroad in May,[39] but the back of the revolt had been broken.

Though not at the centre of the revolution, the native population were not untouched by it. Peasant unrest, disputes over land and water, and refusal to pay taxes all became more common during these years. On occasion unrest and brigandage came together, as poverty-struck peasants took to the hills and joined bandit gangs. The most colourful of these was that associated with Namaz Pirimkulov. A convict who escaped from prison in February 1906, Namaz soon acquired a Robin Hood-style reputation in the Samarkand region. Credited by the population with almost miraculous powers, and arousing considerable fear amongst the authorities who suspected he might mobilise a mass following, his activities were followed with considerable excitement by the local press. Though there is no evidence that Namaz put forward any social or political programme, his activities made the authorities extremely jumpy, and there was great relief when he was eventually killed in mid-1907.[40]

Of equal concern to the Russian authorities were the activities of reformers amongst the Central Asian elites. One of the consequences of the Russian conquest had been the opening up of the region to new ideas, stemming from both contact with the West and the opening up of the region to other, reform-inclined Muslims. In the Kazakh steppes and Turkestan, leading aristocrats and merchants had long seen the advantages of sending their sons to be educated in Russia and it was from such groups that many of the supporters of reformist ideas were to emerge.

Central to the spread of new ideas were the activities of Tatar traders and educators, whose inspiration came from the work of Ismail Bey Gaspirali, better known as Gasprinsky (1851–1914). In response to the Russian conquest he and others asked questions about why Islam appeared so weak in the face of aggression. Had Islam's ideas proved false, or did the current situation stem from Islam being bound down by traditions and customs having little to do with it, and from being ruled over by corrupt secular and religious establishments? What was needed according to these thinkers was the modernisation of Muslim societies and the creation of Muslim unity. This entailed not slavish imitation of the West, but a willingness to learn from the best that the West had to offer. To this end Gasprinsky and his associates promoted the spread of secular education and the creation of a common Turkic language. Such ideas were disseminated through a series of newspapers, and via the attempts to create so-called 'new method' (*usul' jadid*) schools, from whence came the word *jadid* to describe these reformers.[41]

Prior to 1905 such ideas had attracted only a tiny minority of the Central Asian elite, and not until 1901 was the first non-Tatar new method school opened in Turkestan. Nonetheless such ideas contributed to later developments, as did Russia's defeat by Japan which pointed to the possibility of defeating colonial power. During the 1905 'dress rehearsal' for revolution, native intellectuals and activists slowly began to organise separately from the Russian revolutionary movement. In the Kazakh steppes the summer of 1905 witnessed agitation for an end to Orthodox proselytisation and the return of land seized from the Kazakhs. In December of that year *Alash Orda* (the Horde of Alash, one of the mythical founders of the Kazakh people) was formed as the first nationalist political party, with a programme similar to that of the Constitutional Democrats in Russia.[42]

During 1905–6 a series of Muslim congresses were held in Russia, in an effort to unite and organise Muslims throughout the empire, though these efforts effectively ceased with the defeat of the revolution. During the embryonic constitutional experiment four Kazakhs were elected to the first duma, whilst four Muslims from the steppes and six from Turkestan were elected to the second duma.

Yet in this quasi-parliament the Muslim deputies were often divided, and the revised electoral law created after the dissolution of the duma deprived Central Asia of any representation at all.

In the years leading up to 1914 Muslim intellectuals tended to adopt an evolutionary approach based upon enlightenment rather than overt political organisation. Over 100 'new method' schools were opened in Turkestan in the years following 1905, although many lasted but a short time. Their position was not helped by the fact that in addition to the suspicion of the tsarist authorities they faced opposition from traditional clerical elites, a Bukharan representative of whom opined that 'in the first year the students will learn to read newspapers, in the second they will demand freedoms, and in the third they will turn his highness from his throne and into prison'.[43] In the emir's territories the so-called 'Young Bukharans', heavily influenced by recent developments in Persia and Turkey, enjoyed a tenuous existence, constantly harassed by the emir's police. Following the Sunni-Shiite riots of 1910 they were effectively forced underground, and turned to the creation of secret societies whose prime objective was the modernisation of the emirate.[44] Later Soviet sources were to dismiss the *jadids* as serving the interests of the merchant class in distracting the workers and peasants from class struggle, and it is true that these groups made only limited efforts to develop contact with the masses. Nonetheless, their commitment to reform and modernisation was recognised by at least some of the Bolsheviks prominent in the early stages of the revolution, people such as Faizulla Khodzhaev, whose own roots lay in the movement.[45]

In the Kazakh regions various activists associated with *Alash* created a series of papers, expressing different viewpoints, the most influential of which was *Qazaq* (1907, 1913–18). Here were developed ideas about Kazakh nationalism based upon respect for the past and acceptance of the need for modernisation. The spread of Islam in the steppes came in for some criticism – insofar as it had led to a denigration of women – and the need for an eventual end to a migratory existence was accepted with the provision that it should be voluntary and that those settling should be given adequate land to farm (something not provided for by the existing legislation).[46]

Though controlled, tensions in Central Asia were never far beneath the surface in these years, and they re-emerged with considerable force after the outbreak of war. To the seizure of land and water, the break-up of nomadic lifestyles, the creation of a landless peasantry and the creation of a class of corrupt administrators were added new burdens. Everyone was subject to war taxes, and higher prices for grain from Russia, though cotton prices remained controlled. The nomadic peoples were forced to send horses and livestock for the war effort, often through middlemen who increased official demands several fold in order to turn a profit. It was in this context that the Mobilisation Decree of June 1916 was brought into force, calling for the drafting of some 250,000 men to carry out war-related duties behind the lines, that is, to support a war in which the enemy included the guardian of the holy places, Turkey.

The authorities were caught unawares by what followed. First to revolt were the settled peoples, provoked more immediately by a mobilisation timed to coincide with the harvest when every hand was needed. In Khojent and the Fergana valley protests took on a religious colouring with 'holy war' declared in some parts. By August these revolts had been put down, but at this stage the Kazakhs and Kirgiz had joined in, initially focusing their attacks on native administrators responsible for implementing the decree. Many Kazakh intellectuals sought to prevent violence, but they were ignored by the masses, who were most likely to be affected by the decree. At times extremely violent the 1916 revolt cost several thousand Russian lives, and far more from the local populations. In addition many lost their homes, and fled to the hills or to China. The revolt failed in part because it lacked coordination or leadership in the face of superior Russian forces. In addition General Kuropatkin, appointed Governor-General of Turkestan in July, combined repression with some effort to meet native grievances on land and water rights. But just as the last traces of revolt were being mopped up in the winter of 1916–17, existing power structures were to be swept aside by the outbreak of revolution.[47]

The October revolution and national resistance

With the collapse of the old regime, many of the developments in the capital were repeated in Central Asia. The Provisional Government created a Turkestan Committee based upon the old governor-generalship, but in both Turkestan and the steppe towns local

soviets soon emerged. In general these brought together representatives of different political groupings, and not until the middle of
1917 did the Bolsheviks become prominent. Following the Sixth
Congress of the party held in Petrograd in late July, the Bolsheviks
withdrew from joint social-democratic activity, and soon after
acquired a majority in the Orenburg soviet whose authority
stretched into the northern steppe territories.

In Turkestan dual power was predominantly Russian in character,
although by the autumn of 1917 it was clear that soviet power was
gaining strength. After winning over the Tashkent garrison, the
soviet formally seized power a week before the Bolsheviks acted in
Petrograd. Proclaiming the establishment of Soviet rule under the
guidance of a Council of Peoples' Commissars, the Tashkent soviet
in practice enjoyed only limited authority outside the confines of
the city of Tashkent. It also did little to change the colonial attitudes
and practices of the Russian population. At the Third Congress of
Soviets (dominated by Bolsheviks) which met in November, there
was no Muslim representation and a resolution was passed which
stated that:

> at the present time one cannot permit the admission of Muslims into
> the higher organs of the regional revolutionary authority, because the
> attitude of the local population towards the soviet is quite uncertain,
> and because the native population lacks proletarian organisation.[48]

Yet in practice the Russian population also lacked such organisation,
for not until 1918 was a proper Bolshevik apparatus established for
Turkestan.[49]

Whilst Russians in general dominated the formal structures of the
soviets and provisional government through most of Russia in
1917, Muslims also took the opportunity to develop their own
organisations. Amongst the key tasks facing them was that of forging some form of unity in the face of ethnic, regional and ideological differences, and in particular to address the question of what
attitude to adopt towards changes in the Russian political system. At
the first All Union Muslim Congress held in Moscow in May 1917
these issues were debated with considerable vigour, as reformers
and conservatives struggled over issues such as the role of women
and whether to seek separation from Russia or autonomy within a
democratic republic. Though some progress was made, the victory
of the Bolsheviks in October raised new questions, whilst the

descent of the country into civil war was to disrupt further attempts at creating unity.

In the Kazakh steppes similar efforts were made to forge some form of Kazakh organisation during 1917, with the intellectuals around *Qazaq* instrumental in re-forming *Alash Orda* in March, with a programme close to that of the Constitutional Democrats.[50] The first All-Kazakh conference, held in Orenburg in July 1917, expressed some support for the Provisional Government, but qualified this by emphasising the need for self-government, a resolution of the land problem – through a cessation of immigration and return of confiscated land not currently in use – the guarantee of legal rights for women, and an end to Christian proselytisation. The third Kazakh conference held shortly after the Bolshevik victory went further in proclaiming Kazakh autonomy and creating nascent administrations for the steppe regions, but once again civil war served to undermine national unity, whilst Kazakh control of the steppe region was nominal at best.[51]

Similar demands for greater autonomy, albeit within a democratic Russian republic, came from various Muslim conferences held in Turkestan during 1917.[52] Here Muslims came up against representatives of the Provisional Government and of the soviets, each committed to maintaining Russian dominance over the region. In response to the rejectionist position of the Tashkent soviet, the Fourth Congress of Central Asia Muslims was held in Khokand in December. This body announced the autonomy of Turkestan and elected a national council to oversee the implementation of its decisions. Though 18 of its 54 members were Russian, its executive, chaired by Mustafa Chokaev, tended to be dominated by Uzbeks. Briefly a dual power situation was created, but in February forces of the Tashkent soviet seized Khokand and massacred many of its inhabitants. For the time being, the idea of Muslim autonomy was dead.

Nonetheless, the harsh, chauvinistic policies of the Tashkent soviet were met with increasing unease by Moscow, which felt that they only served to alienate further the native population. During 1918 tensions between Moscow and Tashkent, and between native radicals and the soviet came to a head. The Peoples' Commissariat of Nationalities sought to moderate the soviet's policies, and encouraged the creation of a Turkestan commissariat of nationalities (within the context of the Turkestan Autonomous Soviet Socialist Republic (ASSR) created in April 1918) to develop means of involving Muslims in party and state administration. Simultaneously efforts were made to entice Muslims into the ranks of the communist party. Yet the Tashkent soviet remained unwilling to shift its policies, and through its forced requisitioning of grain and seizure of land it contributed to the famine of 1918–19 which caused the deaths of up to a million people. It was in this context that the first conference of Muslim communists in Central Asia was held in May 1919, a gathering that witnessed sharp attacks on the authorities in the capital. The problem for Moscow was how to curb the chauvinism of the Russians without encouraging the nationalism of many of the Muslim radicals. Finding a solution to this dilemma was assigned to the Turkestan Commission which was sent to the region in November 1919, and which set about purging many of the Tashkent veterans whilst seeking to create some degree of central control over the activities of the native cadres.[53]

All of these debates and struggles took place in the context of a nationwide civil war whose result was still far from clear. From the summer of 1918 Whites and Reds contested for victory in the steppes, whilst Kazakh nationalists sought to preserve some form of independence. Increasingly, however, White rejection of their claims for autonomy pushed leading figures in *Alash Orda* into the arms of the Bolsheviks. In November 1919 the Military Revolutionary Council issued an amnesty for *Alash* members, and the following month saw the start of formal negotiations. With the vast majority of Kazakhstan in Bolshevik hands by March 1920, the formation of the Kirgiz (Kazakh) ASSR within the Russian Federation was announced in April 1920. By this time most of the *Alash* leaders had joined forces with the Marxists, hoping to preserve something of the national dream within the context of the new Soviet Russia.

In Turkestan proper the Tashkent soviet remained isolated from the Soviet regime and at times controlled little more than the area surrounding the city, but in practice its position was rarely threatened, despite a short-lived coup attempt at the beginning of 1919. In the territory of the Turkmen the situation was more complex. Here a Socialist Revolutionary-dominated Transcaspian Provisional Government invited in a British expeditionary force led by General Malleson, which was originally stationed in Northern Persia, to be ready to respond to any German-Turkish advance through this area.

In Soviet history texts this force gained a certain notoriety through its alleged complicity in the execution of the 26 Baku commissars, but in practice and despite a few clashes with Red forces from Tashkent, British soldiers played a very minor role and, unable to prevent Bolshevik victory, soon withdrew from the region.[54]

A more serious threat was posed by the so-called *basmachi*. In response to the harsh policies of the Tashkent soviet and following the bloody suppression of Khokand autonomy there emerged small guerilla forces, often based upon bandit groupings that had emerged in the chaos of recent years. Prominent yet again was the Fergana valley where the Khokand security chief Irgush led a particularly adept band of fighters. For a while in 1919 most of the Fergana valley was under *basmachi* control, and there were bands active in other parts of Central Asia. They were given a further boost in 1921 when the Turkish leader Enver Pasha sought refuge in Soviet Russia and then promptly offered his services to the rebels. For a brief while he was able to provide a unifying symbol for a movement riven by tribal, ethnic and personal differences, but after his death at the hands of Soviet troops in April 1922 the movement began to wither and die. Lacking coordination or clear goals, except rejection of the Russian occupiers, the *basmachi* were further undermined by Bolshevik concessions to national and religious feelings in 1921–22. Grain requisitioning was ended, mosques and *waqf* property returned, and an amnesty offered to those who had previously fought the Bolsheviks. Though fighting lingered on in some areas into the late 1920s and briefly revived under the impact of collectivisation, by 1922–23 the Bolsheviks had acquired at least formal control over all of Central Asia.[55]

Throughout this period of struggle for power, the Bolsheviks had generally left the Khivan and Bukharan Protectorates alone, albeit providing support for more radical elements amongst the political elite. In September 1920, however, Russia signed an agreement with the Khorezmian Soviet Peoples' Republic (that is, the Khivan republic), formed on the back of Soviet arms earlier in the year, which gave it certain economic privileges, though formally maintaining its political independence. In Bukhara, armed Soviet intervention during the same month led to the overthrow of the emir and the creation of the Bukharan Soviet Peoples' Republic early in 1921. Nonetheless, disruptive elements remained within the new government, as some members maintained links with the emir, some went over to the *basmachi*, whilst others sought to develop closer links with Moscow. But as time went on and opposition was quelled Moscow began to feel more confident and placed increasing pressure on the young republics until in 1924 both were formally included in the Soviet Union.[56]

National delimitation: creating embryonic states

In April 1918 the Fifth Regional Congress of Soviets had adopted a 'statute on the autonomy of the Turkestan ASSR', which proposed considerable restraints on Moscow's power to intervene in local affairs. After considerable debate this draft was turned down and, in September 1920, the Ninth Regional Congress of Soviets approved a document more acceptable to the centre, whilst the Turkestan ASSR formed in April 1921 adopted a constitution which left control of foreign, military and trade affairs in Moscow's hands. This put it on a par with the Kirgiz (Kazakh) ASSR created the previous year. With the winning of the civil war the Bolsheviks increasingly pressed for unity in the region. During 1923 a conference of the southern states (Turkestan, Bukhara and Khiva) adopted a common economic policy tied into that of Russia. One year later the Bukharan and Khivan Peoples' Republics created in 1920 disappeared into history to be incorporated into the new socialist republics that stemmed from the national delimitation of 1924–25.

The work of setting out the boundaries of the new states was assigned to various Central Asian agencies during 1922–24, each of which, according to Geoffrey Wheeler, faced the delicate task of appearing sensitive to local demands whilst carrying out the wishes of Moscow.[57] In this process tensions were inevitable as smaller ethnic groups tried to avoid being swallowed up in the new Uzbek republic, which was seen as a reincarnation of a Greater Bukhara and was strongly promoted by Faizulla Khojaev and other 'Young Bukharans' turned Bolsheviks. By the end of 1925 it appeared that these activists had been successful with the acquisition of the fertile Fergana valley and with Tajikistan being granted a subordinate status within a Soviet Socialist Republic of Uzbekistan.[58] Only Turkmenistan had been granted a similar status, whilst Kazakhstan had to accept the status of Autonomous Soviet Socialist Republic (within Russia), and the Kirgiz and Karakalpak had to accept the status of autonomous regions. In subsequent changes, Tajikistan was granted the status of a socialist republic in 1929 and given parts of the Fergana valley, much to the chagrin of the Uzbek elites, whilst in 1935–36 Kazakhstan and Kirgiziya were to follow suit. Of less concern to us than the details was the fact that this carving up of Central Asia in many areas paid little attention to ethnic geography, and probably could not have done given the complexity of the ethnic map, thus creating potential problems for the future.

Conclusion

By the mid-1920s the project to bring Central Asia under Moscow's rule begun by the tsars appeared to have been completed by their Bolshevik successors. Yet making a reality of this rule was to be far from simple. War, revolution and civil war had seriously weakened the economy of the region, reducing the area of sown land by up to 50 per cent in some parts, leading to the large-scale destruction of livestock, and a depopulation of some 2 million people (that is, 27 per cent of the population) for Turkestan and the steppe regions.[59] Moreover, Soviet rule was resented by many as merely a new incarnation of Russian dominance and one which fundamentally challenged the traditions and ways of life of the indigenous peoples in a way the tsars had never done. Overcoming this distrust and establishing real authority in the region was going to be a difficult task and one that was never fully achieved.

Notes

1   M. Saray, 'The Russian conquest of Central Asia', *Central Asia Survey*, 1:2 and 3, 1982/3, 3; the Russian advance into the Kazakh steppes and Turkestan is detailed in a large number of works including R. A. Pierce, *Russian Central Asia, 1967–1917 – A Study in Colonial Rule* (Berkeley, 1960); S. Becker, *Russia's Protectorates in Central Asia – Bukhara and Khiva, 1865–1924* (Cambridge, Mass., 1968); M. B. Olcott, *The Kazakhs* (Stanford, 1987).

2   An entertaining account of the lives of some of these men can be found in F. Maclean, *A Person from England* (Oxford, 1958).

3   See 'British policy in Central Asia in the early nineteenth century:

The mission of Richmond Shakespear', *Central Asian Review*, 5:4, 1958, 386–98.

4   N. S. Kinyapina, *Vneshnyaya politika rossii vtoroi poloviny XIX veka* (Moscow, 1974), pp. 242–4.

5   A. Aminov and A. Babakhodzhaev, *Ekonomicheskie i politicheskie posledstviya prisoedineniya Srednei Azii k Rossii* (Tashkent, 1966), Chapter 1.

6   Saray, 'The Russian conquest', 8.

7   Amongst Soviet authors there has been some dispute about the relative importance of economic and political factors in motivating the annexation of Central Asia. See the discussion in Kinyapina, *Vneshnyaya politika*, pp. 243–4; N. S. Kinyapina, M. M. Bliev and V. V. Degoev, *Kavkaz i Srednyaya Aziya vo vneshnei politike Rossii* (Moscow, 1984), p. 230.

8   D. Gillard, *The Struggle for Asia, 1828–1914* (London, 1977), pp. 118–19.

9   More detailed accounts of the conquest can be found in Becker, *Russia's Protectorates*, Chapter 1; Kinyapina, *Vneshnyaya politika*, Chapter 3; Pierce, *Russian Central Asia*, Chapter 1; and Saray, 'The Russian conquest', 1–25.

10 G. Curzon, *Russia in Central Asia* (London, 1889), pp. 364–5.

11 Olcott, *The Kazakhs*, p. 78; M. O. Avezov, ed., *Istoriya Kazakhskoi SSR*, Volume 1 (Alma Ata, 1957), Chapter 17.

12 S. Becker, 'Russia's Central Asian empire, 1885–1917', in M. Rywkin, ed., *Russian Colonial Expansion to 1917* (London, 1988), p. 236.

13 On these see Pierce, *Russian Central Asia*, pp. 54–9.

14 See D. MacKenzie, 'The conquest and administration of Turkestan, 1860–1885', in Rywkin, *Russian Colonial Expansion*, pp. 218–19.

15 Becker, 'Russia's Central Asian empire', p. 239.

16 *Ibid.*

17 The absence of proselytisation was a positive feature of Russian rule noted by George Curzon during his visit to the region in the 1880s. Curzon, *Russia in Central Asia*, p. 393.

18 K. E. Bendrikov, *Ocherki po istorii narodnogo obrazovaniya v Turkestane* (Moscow, 1960), pp. 61–102.

19 Reported in the official Russian language newspaper *Turkestanskie vedomosti* 1902, No. 44, 2/15 June 1902.

20 G. S. Kunavina, *Formirovanie zheleznodorozhnogo proletariata v Turkestane, 1881–1914gg* (Tashkent, 1967), Chapter 1.

21 See Aminov and Babakhodzhaev, *Ekonomicheskie i politicheskie posledstviya*, Chapter 3; P. G. Galuzo, *Turkestan – Koloniya* (Moscow, 1929, republished in Oxford, 1986), p. 110.

22 Becker, 'Russia's Central Asian empire', p. 241.
23 V. I. Lavrent'ev, *Kapitalizm v Turkestane* (Leningrad, 1930), pp. 48–50.
24 D. MacKenzie, 'Turkestan's significance to Russia', *Russian Review*, 33:2, 1974, 182.
25 Becker, 'Russia's Central Asian empire', p. 243.
26 Olcott, *The Kazakhs*, p. 87.
27 Becker, 'Russia's Central Asian empire', pp. 244–8; G. Demko, *The Russian Colonisation of Kazakhstan, 1896–1916* (Bloomington, Ind., 1969).
28 Lavrent'ev, *Kapitalizm v Turkestane*, p. 151.
29 M. I. Veksel'man, 'Rossiiskii monopolisticheskii i inostrannyi kapital v toplivnoi promyshlennosti Srednei Azii v kontse XIX–nachale XXv.', in *Istoricheskie zapiski, 113* (Moscow, 1986), 283–304.
30 Becker, 'Russia's Central Asian empire', p. 251.
31 Aminov and Babakhodzhaev, *Ekonomicheskie i politicheskie posledstviya*, Chapter 5; Pierce, *Russian Central Asia*, Chapter 14; A. Sheehy, 'The Andizhan uprising of 1898 and Soviet historiography', *Central Asian Review*, 13:2, 1966, 139–50.
32 Kh. Z. Ziyaev, *Revolyutsiya 1905–1907gg v Srednei Azii i Kazakhstane* (Tashkent, 1985), Chapter 2.
33 Kunavina, *Formirovanie zheleznodorozhnogo proletariata*, Chapter 2; A. V. Pyaskovskii, *Revolyutsiya 1905–07 gg v Turkestane* (Moscow, 1958), pp. 63ff.
34 For an account of Morozov's life see A. I. Mavlani, *Mikhail Vladimirovich Morozov* (Tashkent, 1963).
35 This account is largely based upon the works by Ziyaev and Pyaskovskii cited earlier.
36 Quoted in E. Fedorov, *Ocherki natsional'no-osvoboditel'nogo dvizheniya v Srednei Azii* (Tashkent, 1925), p. 23.
37 See *Turkestanskie vedomosti*, 1907, Nos. 1, 3, 7, 13, 19, 26 and 50 for examples.
38 *Ibid.*, 1907, No. 22.
39 *Ibid.*, 1907, No. 80.
40 *Ibid.*, 1907, Nos. 6, 16, 18, 56, 70 and 81.
41 See J. Landau, *The Politics of Pan-Islam: Ideology and Organisation* (Oxford, 1990), Chapter 3; E. Lazzarini, 'Beyond renewal – The Jadid response to pressure for change in the modern age', in Jo-Ann Gross, ed., *Muslims in Central Asia – Expressions of Identity and Change* (Durham, 1992), pp. 151–66.
42 Olcott, *The Kazakhs*, pp. 111–12.
43 Quoted in Fedorov, *Ocherki natsional'no-osvoboditel'nogo dvizheniya*, p. 28.

44 H. C. d'Encausse, *Islam and the Russian Empire – Reform and Revolution in Central Asia* (English edn, London, 1988; first published in French in 1960), Chapter 6.

45 See the relatively sympathetic if not uncritical approach in F. Khodzhaev, ed., *Ocherki revolyutsionnogo dvizheniya v Srednei Azii*, (Moscow, 1926), pp. 7–12.

46 Olcott, *The Kazakhs*, pp. 116–17; see also A. Bennigsen and C. Lemercier Quelquejay, 'The history of the Kazakh press', *Central Asian Review*, 13:2, 1966, 150–63.

47 On 1916 see E. Sokol, *The Revolt of 1916 in Central Asia* (Baltimore, 1954); A. V. Pyaskovskii, ed., *Vosstanie 1916 goda v Srednei Azii i Kazakhstane – sbornik dokumentov* (Moscow, 1960); B. S. Suleimenov and V. Ya. Basin, *Vosstanie 1916 goda v Kazakhstane* (Alma Ata, 1977).

48 Quoted in H. C. d'Encause, 'Civil war and new governments', in E. Allworth, ed., *Central Asia – 130 Years of Russian Dominance* (Durham and London, 1994), p. 225.

49 Many of the works cited earlier have sections on 1917 in Turkestan and the Kazakh steppes. For a standard Soviet interpretation see Kh. Inoyatov, *Pobeda Sovetskoi vlasti v Turkestane* (Moscow, 1978).

50 For the programme of *Alash* see *Programmnye dokumenty musul'-manskikh politicheskikh partii, 1917–1920gg.* (Oxford, 1985), pp. 49–53.

51 Olcott, *The Kazakhs*, pp. 138–40; S. Zenkovsky, *Pan-Turkism and Islam in Russia* (Cambridge, Mass., 1960), pp. 210–12.

52 Zenkovsky, *Pan-Turkism*, pp. 229–30.

53 For a useful account of these conflicts see S. Blank, 'The contested terrain: Muslim political participation in Soviet Turkestan, 1917–19', *Central Asian Survey*, 6:4, 1987, 47–73.

54 C. H. Ellis, *The British 'Intervention' in Transcaspia, 1918–1919*, (Berkeley and Los Angeles, 1963).

55 On the *basmachi* see M. B. Olcott, 'The basmachi or freemen's revolt in Turkestan, 1918–24', *Soviet Studies*, 33:3, 1981, 352–69; M. Broxup, 'The basmachi', *Central Asian Survey*, 2:1, 1983, 57–81.

56 D'Encausse, 'Civil war and new governments', pp. 241–50.

57 G. Wheeler, *The Peoples of Central Asia* (London, 1966), p. 67.

58 See S. Sabol, 'The creation of Soviet Central Asia: The 1924 national delimitation', *Central Asian Survey*, 14:2, 1995, 225–42; D. Carlisle, 'Soviet Uzbekistan: State and nation in historical perspective', in B. Manz, ed., *Central Asia in Historical Perspective* (Boulder, 1994), pp. 103–26.

59 M. Buttino, 'Study of the economic crisis and depopulation in Turkestan, 1917–20', *Central Asian Survey*, 9:4, 1990, 59–74.

2

Central Asia's Soviet experience

By 1924 Moscow had established *de jure* control over Turkestan and the Kazakh steppes, but it still faced the task of remaking the region in the Bolshevik image. And though the USSR has traditionally been seen as a society and polity in which the central state held tight control over the regions, in Central Asia much of the Soviet period was characterised by an ongoing and by no means always successful struggle to make a reality of that appearance. In this chapter we explore the ways in which the centre sought to establish political, economic and social control in the region and ask to what degree the formal subordination of the region to Moscow disguised a more ambiguous situation and one which, by the time that Gorbachev came to power, had seen some diminution of central control. We then turn briefly to the international dimension of developments in the region, focusing on the ways in which the Soviet state sought to use the Central Asian experience both to 'sell' the socialist path of development and as a basis for evolving better relationships with the Islamic world.

Establishing political control

Despite the creation of nascent national and territorial administrations for Central Asia, in the mid-1920s Soviet rule remained largely nominal in many areas. In much of the region there were insufficient ideologically committed personnel to carry out basic administrative tasks, let alone grandiose plans of social transformation. Party organisations remained weak, most not having been set up formally until the early 1920s, and they often lacked people from the indigenous communities or cadres who understood the peculiarities of the region. In Kazakhstan the party had around 26,000 members in 1922 of whom around a third were Kazakhs, but most of the latter were semi-literate and had little idea about Marxist doctrine. In many areas party organisations and later local soviets served to institutionalise traditional clan and tribal rivalries.[1] In Turkestan recruitment drives which sought to draw in members of the Muslim community meant in practice taking whoever could be persuaded to join, whether intellectuals 'infected' with *jadidism* or ordinary people who saw no incompatibility between party membership and the maintenance of old religious traditions, and who resisted strongly when the party elite attacked Islam.[2]

In Moscow the key word in dealing with the national republics was *korenizatsiya* ('nativisation'). At successive party congresses resolutions stressed the need to draw in native cadres and to provide for the use of national languages in education, the courts, media and administration. In 1920 the Central Committee sent a letter to the Turkestan Communist Party ordering the removal of all those members tainted by 'colonising fever' or Great Russian nationalism, and called for the drawing in of the best labouring elements in the region. Yet as B. T. Olivier points out,[3] native membership grew slowly, in Kazakhstan rising from 8 per cent in 1924 to 38 per cent in 1928, and in Uzbekistan reaching about 40 per cent by 1927. In April 1928 the Uzbek Central Committee adopted a resolution on the 'Uzbekisation' of the government apparatus, with the objective of making this 100 per cent by 1930, but the target achieved was in fact 22.6 per cent. Problems in finding native cadres were accentuated by the low levels of literacy and education that remained until well into the 1930s, so that even in the middle of that decade over 90 per cent of city soviet chairmen in Uzbekistan had only a primary education. In addition many Russian personnel, despite their egalitarian philosophy, had inherited old-style colonial attitudes which often produced resistance to centrally imposed efforts to promote Muslim cadres.[4]

As Rakowska-Harmstone has suggested, *korenizatsiya* was based upon the assumption that drawing Muslims into the power structure would eventually lead to class loyalties overriding older emotional and traditional ties to group and religion. Yet it soon became clear that such ties remained strong, even amongst the well-educated elites. In 1920 many of the latter were faced not with the possibility of national independence, but with making a difficult choice between the communists and their opponents. Given the latter's tendency to reject almost all aspirations to national autonomy, it was perhaps inevitable that reformist elements would look to the Bolsheviks with their promises of national self-determination.[5] Members of *Alash* and the Young Bukharans entering the communist party sought to ensure that national interests were protected and that Soviet rule was not simply Russian rule with a red flag. In practice this meant that they opposed centralising policies, attempted to dissuade Moscow from immediate and radical assaults on traditional lifestyles, and on occasion sought to organise regionally based groups within the communist party to promote what Moscow saw as nationalistic ends. At the Fifth Regional Conference of the Communist Party, Turur Ryskulov, a leading Kazakh communist who had joined the party very early on, argued quite explicitly for the creation of a pan-Turkic republic and a Turkic Communist Party, a plan firmly rejected by Moscow.[6]

Along with other Turkic leaders Ryskulov was involved in various discussions of what came to be known as 'national communism', whose essence lay in efforts to create a socialist model suitable for Eastern conditions. Its best-known exponent was Mir Said Sultan Galiev, a leading member of the Commissariat of Nationalities who was to feature prominently in later Soviet demonology. Sultan Galiev, pointing to the failure of the revolution in Europe, argued that the heart of revolutionary struggle would move eastwards and would be led by the peasantry and national bourgeoisie of the 'proletarian nations'. Within the USSR he argued for leaving traditional elites in place, for the abandonment of notions of class struggle, and for an effort to bring Marxism together with the more progressive elements of Islamic teachings. Like so many, Sultan Galiev was to disappear into Stalin's purge machine, but his ideas were shared by many Central Asian leaders of the time.[7]

Tensions between national elites and the centre surfaced over a variety of issues. In Kazakhstan, former *Alash* members, often stronger in the southern party organisations, argued for the redistribution of land seized by Russian settlers to Kazakh family groups and protested the brutality that often accompanied the settlement of traditionally nomadic groups. In Uzbekistan, Faizulla Khojaev, chairman of the republic's Council of Peoples' Commissars and a veteran *jadid*, appears to have resisted efforts to impose a cotton mono-culture. His disillusionment with Soviet rule was accentuated by the *khudzhum* of 1927, which overnight sought to transform the position of women, and the assault on religion which was reactivated at the end of the decade.[8] Above all it was the drive for collectivisation which convinced most representatives of the nationalist elite that Soviet and national goals could no longer be combined. Efforts to halt this drive led to a series of purges, initially based on the division of elites, as in Kazakhstan where the more aristocratic representatives of *Alash* lost power from about 1927 whilst the earlier Bolshevik supporters, often from lower class origins, tended to last into the early 1930s.[9]

By then, with collectivisation in full swing and centralisation the order of the day, concerns for the efficiency and political reliability of cadres overtook the need for ethnic representation.[10] National party organisations were subject to thorough purges, as in Tajikistan where membership was reduced from 14,329 in January 1933 to 4,791 two years later.[11] In Central Asia, as in other parts of the USSR, Kirov's murder in 1934 gave the purges a murderous colouring. The charges levelled against national elites became increasingly harsh, with accusations that they had only joined the Bolsheviks in order to sabotage socialist rule. Even Russian elites in the regions were unsafe, for as early as 1932 Kazakh First Secretary F. I. Goloshchekin had been removed for failures that had 'fed' nationalism.[12] In 1937–39 most of the leading nationalists were arrested and executed, alongside the remaining old communists. The centrepiece was the trial of Uzbek First Secretary Akhmal Ikramov and Faizulla Khojaev alongside Nikolai Bukharin in 1938. Khojaev confessed that he had sought to undermine the fulfilment of cotton production targets and that he had hoped to create an independent Uzbek economy.[13] Simultaneously a series of trials took place throughout Central Asia, with the local press reporting their almost inevitable outcome – 'death by shooting'.[14] Within a very short period the native elites of the region had been decimated, and a new generation began to take its place, a younger generation with a technical rather than humanitarian education, schooled to the hard realities of Soviet rule.[15] Nonetheless, to ensure control as well as make good the deficiency caused by the purges and the shortage of educated personnel, Moscow also appointed numerous Russians, whether local or 'parachuted' in, to key positions in the region.

The years following the war witnessed further central efforts to make good the shortfall in local cadres by investing heavily in education so as to provide the specialists needed to man economic and administrative posts. The representation of the titular nationalities in republican party organisations grew rapidly in three of the Central Asian republics – in 1945–70 rising from 42.7 per cent to 54.9 per cent in Uzbekistan, rising from 39.7 per cent to 55.3 per cent in Turkmenistan, and rising from 42.1 per cent to 47.9 per cent in Tajikistan.[16] In Kazakhstan and Kirgiziya, where there were a larger number of Russians, indigenous membership remained below 40 per cent until well into the 1970s.[17]

For all these changes Slavs retained dominant control positions in administrative, security and industrial sectors, though in the latter sphere this may have stemmed as much from the shortage of trained personnel as from deliberate policy choice. Decrees issued by the Central Committee in the 1950s and 1960s continued to complain about the failure of Central Asian party organisations to find young, competent officials from the local population, and noted the failure of these organisations to adapt their work to the needs of the local situation. Yet the same documents also attacked the fact that even when put forward local cadres often failed to break with negative aspects of ancient traditions, for example, maintaining an ambiguous attitude towards 'religious survivals'.[18]

Such comments pointed to one of the major problems facing the Soviet state in its dealings with Central Asia, and one that had reared its head in the 1920s. On the one hand the Soviet state needed to promote local cadres who would enjoy legitimacy within the region and would not appear to be instruments of Russian rule, but on the other hand there was always the danger that once in place such people would act in ways contrary to Moscow's desires. In particular they might inject patterns of behaviour typical of traditional societies into the working of the communist party, and seek to promote the interests of their region rather than that of the union as a whole. The national communist bogey was ever present.

The 'threat' of regionalism was also strong. Writing in the 1970s, Rakowska-Harmstone noted that officials at all levels:

> based their selection, distribution and transfer of personnel on traditional, familial, friendly, religious and cultural obligations, and on the need to secure followers ... They attempted to create 'family groups' for the mutual advantage of all local elements concerned. These

groups maintained a united front, intended to frustrate the efforts of a higher authority to impose controls and to atomise local structures. In the tug of war between the local and the central authority, family groups appeared and were solidified and then destroyed in a continuing cycle.[19]

In many areas traditional regional and tribal alliances underlay the internal politics of republican party organisations. Donald Carlisle has pointed to the ways in which leadership in Uzbek politics may have swung between a Tashkent–Fergana based elite with a more pro-Moscow position, and a group of leaders whose career backgrounds and loyalties lay with the southern periphery and towns such as Samarkand and Bukhara. Under the latter grouping, led from 1959–83 by First Secretary Sharaf Rashidov, Uzbekistan moved increasingly outside of Moscow's control. Leaders promoted relatives, friends and colleagues, and built alliances (often reinforced by marriage), which in turn conspired to cover up economic failings and persistently withheld information from Moscow.[20] In similar vein one could point to the political dominance of the Leninabad elite within Tajikistan, to the prominent role of northern tribes in Kirgiz politics, or to the role of the traditionally dominant Tekke tribe (and even clans within it) in the Turkmen Communist Party.

Such developments were not, of course, incompatible with loyalty to the Soviet system or promotion of the union, as is evident from the career of Sharaf Rashidov. First Secretary of Uzbekistan for 24 years, he was a keen promoter of the alliance with Russia and of the importance of Russian language and culture.[21] Nor did such groups have to be mono-ethnic, for in Kazakhstan it appears that Brezhnev loyalist D. Kunaev created his own patronage networks which drew in Russian as well as Kazakh personnel.[22] In many cases such practices were effectively permitted by the centre which was content so long as republican bosses maintained political control and met the required production targets. Increasingly, however, it appeared that for all the formal structures of control, these elites were treating their territories as feudal fiefs and that by the Brezhnev era even the loyalty of local Russians could not be taken for granted, as such people could be coopted, bribed or intimidated into supporting traditional modes of rule.

Establishing economic control

In the economic sphere the new Soviet authorities, after a few disastrous experiments, hung back from radical change. Lacking in
both personnel and clear ideas, and fearful of jeopardising political
control, they sought to placate a largely rural society in which class
conflict was, in the main, absent. As a result of war, revolution and
civil war, the old empire's internal market had been virtually
destroyed, with the consequence that steppe dwellers could not sell
their cattle, could not therefore afford to buy fodder, and were
forced to slaughter their animals in large numbers. Worse was to
follow as 1920–21 brought famine and the deaths of up to 1.5 million people. Most of Central Asia witnessed some land redistribution in the early 1920s as land belonging to the old rulers and to
religious institutions was spread amongst the poorer peasants, but
attempts to divide villages along class lines met with limited success
and there was little local enthusiasm for dispossessing alleged
'kulaks'.[23]

In Kazakhstan the land question became a major political issue,
with local elites arguing for the return of land taken by Slavic settlers. Simultaneously, the New Economic Policy had the effect of
reviving traditional economic relations as tribal and clannic rivalries
reasserted themselves in the context of the new institutions. There
were efforts to sovietise the *aul* (the migratory, clan- and family-
based unit of the nomadic Kazakhs), reduce nomadism and push for
more cooperative forms of agriculture but until the late 1920s resistance to such policies remained possible.[24] The effect of the more
liberal policies of the mid-1920s was to raise the level of agricultural
production in Central Asia to levels that began to approach pre-war
levels. In Kazakhstan the number of cattle increased greatly, for
example, the number of sheep and goats rose from 17.9 million in
1921 to 27.2 million in 1929.[25] For all this problems remained, with
backward techniques and impractically fragmented land holdings
typical in much of Central Asian agriculture being inimical to the
larger needs of the Soviet state.

By the late 1920s it was becoming apparent that the central state
was contemplating a new turn. In 1928 grain requisitioning came to
Kazakhstan, and in November 1929 the campaign for collectivisation was launched, alongside a campaign to complete the sedentari-
sation of the nomads. The latter was as much political as economic

in aim, for the summer migration of Kazakh and other nomads took them away from administrative and socialisation centres and reinforced patriarchal and clannic authority.[26] Within six years it was claimed that around 90 per cent of Kazakh households had been collectivised, but the cost was great. Over a million Kazakh lives were lost as a direct or an indirect result of collectivisation, and the quantity of livestock decimated, with the number of sheep and goats falling from 27.2 million in 1929 to 2.3 million in 1934. Only in the 1960s was the earlier figure reached again.[27] The southern Central Asian republics experienced much the same during these years though the loss of life was far less, and their populations continued to grow during these years – from 6 per cent for the Turkmen to 27 per cent for the Karakalpaks in the years 1926–39.[28] In Uzbekistan collectivisation was accompanied by a propaganda assault on the 'kulaks' and further attempts to divide village communities along class lines. But such pressures often served to create solidarity which on occasion led to the revival of *basmachi* activity in some parts of the country.[29]

The impact of the collectivisation campaign was at best ambiguous, and in terms of agricultural production disastrous. Production fell in virtually every sector as peasants put up resistance, directly or indirectly, and as repression often carried away the most productive individuals in the village community. And even collectivisation's political aims were not fully met for, as Rakowska-Harmstone has pointed out, the effect of collectivisation was often to create units populated by representatives of single ethnic groups, tribes or clans, rather than encouraging any melting-pot in which Muslims and Slavs worked shoulder to shoulder. In practice the heads of collective farms were barely literate let alone conversant with Marxist-Leninist ideas, and there are many stories of farm chairmen turning to former landlords or to mullahs for advice on how to deal with specific problems. More importantly, collectivisation created a legacy of bitterness which subsequent economic developments could not entirely overcome.[30]

During the same period there was some effort to bring industry to the area, although it remained clear that in the regional division of labour favoured by central planners Central Asia was to remain primarily an agricultural producer. Prior to 1928 there was very little industry beyond cotton processing and handicrafts and, as Nove and Newth suggest, this gave subsequent high growth figures a somewhat inflated appearance. For example, Kirgiz industrial output rose by 736 times in the years 1913–38, as opposed to Ukraine's which grew by 7.3 times, yet this still left Kirgiz per capita output at around three-quarters of that for Ukraine.[31] Industrial development was further stimulated by the war as whole industries were taken eastwards and as planners became aware of the possibilities of exploiting the natural resources of the region, in particular, coal, oil and gas. From the 1940s to the 1960s industrial growth tended to outstrip that for the USSR as a whole, but under Brezhnev capital investment in industry declined and during the late 1970s growth slumped considerably. Individual projects were established, for example the South Tajikistan Territorial Production Complex, involving the creation of a major aluminium plant, and the Nurek Hydro-Electric station, but these ran into numerous difficulties, took years to complete and performed poorly once commissioned.[32]

Despite industrial development – which remained important only in northern Kazakhstan – agriculture remained at the heart of Moscow's vision for the four southern republics and for much of Kazakhstan. During the war the mobilisation of half a million or more Central Asians, and the need for foodstuffs, had led to a reduction in the amount of land sown to cotton, whilst many had taken advantage of the removal of party controls to change their mix of crops. During the late 1940s this trend was reversed and cotton once again became the dominant crop. At the same time it was becoming apparent that agricultural productivity remained low throughout the USSR and in 1953, under Khrushchev's guidance, the Virgin Lands campaign was launched. In northern Kazakhstan where no crops had been sown and the soil was in prime condition, little pre-cultivation was needed to grow wheat, and the large fields were suitable for mechanised agriculture. In a four-year period the acreage sown grew nearly three times, and through much of the 1950s produced a rapid increase in crops. Only in the early 1960s did output fall as a result of poor harvests, poor organisation and over-use of soil, though up until the end of the Soviet period this area remained a major grain producer, if not the saviour hoped for by Khrushchev.

For all this cotton remained king in much of the region. Figures vary slightly, but it seems that by the late 1970s Central Asia produced something like 95 per cent of the USSR's cotton and fibres, and that in Uzbekistan 'white gold' accounted for something like 65 per cent of republican output and employed the services of around 40 per cent of the labour force.[33] During the years 1928–79 cotton output increased some eleven times as against grain production's two and a half times in the four Central Asian republics proper.[34] From Moscow's point of view cotton was a perfect crop, as it suited the region's climatic conditions, was labour-intensive in a labour surplus part of the country, and provided valuable income from exports. Yet this emphasis on a single crop had a disastrous impact upon the social fabric of the region and made little economic sense. In particular the practice of taking 95 per cent of the crop to other parts of the USSR for processing stunted domestic economic growth, whilst mono-culture created dependency on other republics for basic foodstuffs. Alongside these consequences there developed major environmental and public health problems as diminishing returns in the 1970s led to the excessive use of chemical fertilisers and the draining of scarce water resources. And at the end of the day it also forced local elites to engage in production-reporting practices that would lead to charges of corruption under Andropov and Gorbachev.[35]

By the mid-1970s the Central Asian economies were running into difficulties as capital investment failed to keep up with dynamic population growth, and as the population became ever more dependent upon the private sector, legally or otherwise, to supply its basic needs. In Uzbekistan, for example, the 0.7 per cent of land officially registered as private plots produced something like 40 per cent of milk and vegetables, and 46 per cent of meat.[36] With a growing population that was increasingly under-employed, officialdom tended to adopt a more liberal attitude towards private activity than in other parts of the USSR, and this was helped by the fact that in the four southern republics collectivisation had not so fully wiped out the peasant mentality as elsewhere.

Above all, however, it was the population problem that seemed likely to create the greatest long-term difficulties for Soviet policy-makers. From 1939 to 1979 the 'Muslim' population of the union as a whole grew from 20.7 million to 43.8 million, and it was projected by some that it would rise to well over 60 million by the end of the century. As the Russian birth rate declined from 24 to 19 per thousand in the years 1959–70, that for Uzbekistan fell only from 41 to 39 per thousand. Particularly dynamic was the rural population which was estimated to have increased by around 80 per cent in the years 1970–87. The implications of this included a rapid expansion in the work force which would lead to more under-employment if not unemployment, greater demands upon the centre for the provision of welfare and other services, and the pos-sibility of ethnic conflict because in conditions of economic slow-down there were no longer sufficient jobs for all suitably qualified people. Whereas Slavs and Muslims had previously shared out jobs, often on the basis of cultural preferences, they now increasingly found themselves in competition with each other for the same posi-tions. Simultaneously there was a growing tendency for Central Asians to blame the Russians for the perceived economic deteriora-tion whilst the Slavs, finding themselves to be a decreasing propor-tion of the population in the four southern republics, began to reconsider their positions and to think about emigration. Under Brezhnev none of this erupted into serious manifestations of national unrest, but there were signs that the authorities were wor-ried. For the centre, finding an appropriate response was problem-atic at a time when there there were insufficient funds to increase investment in the region, and when attempts to provide jobs and further support for agriculture through plans to divert Siberian rivers southward to Central Asia were met with fierce opposition within Russia.[37]

Between 1917 and 1982 Central Asia underwent a major socio-economic transformation. For all the problems with infant mortal-ity, poor education and a far from adequate level of health care, it had made major advances in the welfare sector. Yet according to most indices of 'development' and 'modernisation', it still lagged behind the rest of the USSR. Nearly 60 per cent of its population still lived in rural areas in 1986 (34 per cent for the USSR as a whole), half of its population worked in agriculture (compared to 20 per cent), and its infant mortality rate was possibly twice that of the rest of the country. Per capita income measurements, for all their inadequacy, suggested that Central Asian levels remained from half (Tajikistan) to two-thirds (Kirgiziya) of the average USSR figure.[38] Moreover, by the late 1970s the chances of improving on this rela-tive backwardness seemed low. Moscow was unwilling or unable to find large-scale investment funds despite the likelihood of further decline. At the same time it lacked the financial or ideological means necessary to persuade, or the will to coerce, the growing labour surpluses in this region to emigrate to other labour-deficient parts of the USSR. And by transforming Central Asia (excluding Kazakhstan) into 'a specialised (agricultural) component ... incorporated into a wider inter-regional division of labour',[39] or some would say into a 'cotton colony', it was perhaps storing up problems for itself as well as for the future independent states. In effect cotton production was based upon the ethnic division of labour and for that very reason was likely to reinforce ethnic, regional or tribal patterns of administration. As it lacked reliable personnel in the industry, Moscow found it hard to check and control whether what it was told corresponded to the actual situation. Though it would be going too far to suggest that Moscow had lost control of the region, the cotton padding scandals of the early 1980s indicated that there is the potential for independent action by regional leaders in times of system lethargy.

Establishing social and cultural control

In many respects the development of control over social and cultural life was even more problematic than the development of control in the areas already discussed, for here Moscow was taking on a centuries-old way of life of which it had little real understanding. Morover, the new rulers of Central Asia often failed to understand that the region was not a single unity, but one in which differences based upon the degree of Islamicisation, upon lifestyles rooted in nomadic and settled forms of agriculture, and upon openness to outside influence varied considerably. Such factors in turn influenced the degree to which Moscow was successfully able to Sovietise the region.

In the early years of Bolshevik power, grandiose schemes of social transformation had to be shelved in the face of limited material and personnel resources, and had be tempered by the need to conciliate indigenous populations to whom Sovietisation looked suspiciously like Russification under another name. Indeed, many of the communist party's goals such as the emancipation of women and the eradication of Islam threatened traditional lifestyles in a way the tsarist authorities had never done. Thus, after the initial assault on native communities under the Tashkent soviet, the new authorities moved rapidly to placate local feeling. Traditional courts were allowed some say in civil matters, although the Russian Soviet Federal Socialist Republics (RSFSR) Criminal Code of 1924 sought to abolish certain traditional family practices including *kalym* (bride price) and polygamy. Similarly religious schools were allowed to function, some *waqf* lands were restored and Friday was declared the official day of rest in Turkestan.[40]

Many of these concessions were, however, short-lived. In 1927 the traditional courts were finally abolished, and one year later the last religious schools were closed.[41] Simultaneously various steps were taken to extend a modern, secular education system to the region, although this proved difficult given the near-universal illiteracy of the Central Asian population. For example, in 1911 in Turkmenistan (then the Transcaspian oblast) there were only 46 secular schools with just 151 Turkmen students, and literacy was officially put at 0.22 per cent. During the mid-1920s the new authorities put over a third of the Turkmen budget into education, yet as late as 1928 only 4 per cent of Turkmen attended village schools, a number that had risen to 37 per cent by the mid-1930s. Even these figures disguised the fact that many pupils failed to complete a full term in schools, that many children were taken out of school at harvest time, and that women remained largely excluded by their own families and communities. Officially literacy had reached 80 per cent in this republic by the end of the 1930s, but one suspects that 'literacy' was fairly loosely defined.[42] Similar developments could be seen in other republics as the authorities battled with local communities suspicious of the new schools and cultural institutions which appeared to threaten centuries-old customs, which was a correct perception insofar as the authorities did see cultural change as a means of undermining traditional ways of life and the resistance to Soviet rule they engendered. This was clear in the language reform and Latinisation of alphabets in the late 1920s which served to limit the power of a clerical group still promoting religion through the Arabic script and to create national languages in the place of predominantly local dialects.[43]

From the late 1920s a new series of campaigns began to impact upon Central Asia. In March 1927 the *khudzhum* (advance) was launched in an effort to encourage female emancipation. In great public ceremonies women removed and burnt their veils, with over 9,000 reported to have done so in Uzbekistan during the first two months. This campaign also targeted a whole variety of customs associated with the oppression of women and sought to draw women more fully into social production. Though officially recognised as a success, the *khudzhum* was increasingly played down as it brought into the open traditional resistance to Soviet policies, leading to the murder of numerous female activists and confirming the suspicion of some that Soviet concessions to communal feelings were but temporary tactics.[44]

The other main campaign of the late 1920s, not unrelated to the effort to emancipate women from traditional customs, was the assault on religion launched throughout the Soviet Union in 1929. During the subsequent decade the vast majority of mosques were closed, imams and mullahs found their way into the camps and execution cellars in their thousands, and public manifestations of religious life were punished.[45] Of course, religious figures were but one section of a wider traditional elite that suffered particularly during the years of the purges, when representatives of the former ruling groups, surviving members of the land-owning classes, and leading intellectuals disappeared. Alongside the purge of individuals ran the purge of culture, language and history. In accordance with the tenets of Stalinist historiography, the Russian conquest of Central Asia was increasingly portrayed as a positive development because it brought with it capitalism and the influence of Russian culture, as well as revolutionary ideas. This history was in turn written not only in Russian, but also in indigenous languages from which every effort had been made to remove Persian and Arabic borrowings and to which had been added many Russian loan words. Moreover, it was a language written from around 1940 in the Cyrillic script, so as to move it closer to Russian and to reduce the ability of indigenous populations to read literature emanating from Turkey or Iran.[46]

The war brought some easing of pressure, especially on the Muslim religion. Anti-religious propaganda more or less ceased, mosques were reopened, a small amount of religious literature was published, and four religious boards were opened to oversee religious life in various parts of the Soviet Union. Of these the most important was that for Central Asia and Kazakhstan. In practice these boards were instruments through which the state sought to control officially recognised religious life and personnel, but their very existence implied that for the time being at least the state was not going to persist with campaigns ostensibly aimed at the eradication of religion. Once the war was over, atheist propaganda resumed, but the level of militancy of the 1930s was never to be achieved again. The Khrushchev anti-religious campaign of 1958–64 led to the closure of some mosques and to the reduction of legally functioning places of Muslim worship in Central Asia and Kazakhstan to around 150. There were also harsh attacks on illegal 'holy places' in many parts of the region.[47] Yet many officials pursued this campaign with little enthusiasm, and much of the available evidence suggests that as soon as Khrushchev fell, anti-religious work halted for good in many parts of Central Asia, despite reports to the centre on thousands of measures being carried out to reduce religious influence.[48]

Under Brezhnev the anti-religious front remained rather quiet until the late 1970s, despite occasional campaigns such as that launched against the payment of *kalym* which was undertaken in Turkmenistan in the mid-1970s. Nonetheless, from the late 1970s Moscow appears to have become more concerned about the continued survival of Islam as a cultural force in the region and with the potential influence on Soviet Muslims of developments within the wider Muslim world. In looking at this one needs to exercise a certain interpretative caution, for much of the material in the press with its tirades against unregistered mosques, holy places, self-appointed mullahs, the religious education of minors and so forth can be found throughout the Soviet period. Yet it is clear from both published speeches and archive sources that there was a renewed sense of anxiety caused by 'the efforts of international reaction to utilise Islam in the struggle against socialism, which was especially clear in connection with the events in Iran and Afghanistan'.[49]

Domestically, this concern may have been exacerbated by the growing awareness of the demographic problem in the region which was outlined earlier. If the Soviet development model and official ideology failed to meet the needs of a growing population, to where might they turn for alternative ideas and models of development? Though there was no immediate 'threat' in the sense of a religious or nationalist movement capable of bringing the system down, events in Iran suggested that even a modernising regime backed by a superpower could fail in meeting the aspirations of its people and be toppled. This potential may have been further brought home by scholarly work done within the USSR which suggested that the forces of 'tradition'[50] remained extremely vibrant in much of Central Asia. Here more than perhaps anywhere in the

Soviet Union, the phenomenon of the 'dual personality' prevailed, as society was modernised and paid lip-service to Soviet ways and yet people lived their daily lives within an informal substructure dominated by an alternative *modus operandi*. The state destroyed traditional institutions in many areas, gave the population a secular education and sought in other ways to 'modernise' Central Asia. Inevitably such measures did serve to change and remake that society, but this was a dynamic transformation in which Soviet culture and 'traditional society' met and impacted upon each other. Official pronouncements encouraged the spread of the Russian language, and census returns from 1970 to 1979 reported a steady growth in the use of Russian as a second language. Yet on occasion these figures were falsified or were based on an extremely loose understanding of 'knowledge' of the language – as in Uzbekistan which reported an increase from 14.5 to 49.2 per cent, as opposed to the rest of the region's growth from around 14 to 29 per cent.[51] But this growth in Russian language 'knowledge' disguised the fact that indigenous languages retained their dominance in everyday life – except in Kazakhstan where by the 1990s it was reported that perhaps half of Kazakhs under 40 functioned better in Russian than Kazakh – and held on to a near monopoly of usage in the predominantly rural areas where most Central Asians lived and where the forces of 'tradition' remained strong.[52]

In many areas of life the seeming destruction of traditional modes of organisation provided no guarantee that they would not reappear in new guises. In the cities the neighbourhood *mahallas* lost their economic functions and were often physically uprooted, and yet they resurfaced in the modern apartment block with its neighbourhood committee regulating many aspects of life in conjunction with mullah, sheikh and *bibiotun* (a cross between a female mullah and a wise woman, who served to educate women and children and ensure the maintence of ancient customs). In the countryside, where Slavs were often non-existent, the force of tradition remained stronger still, reinforced by collective and brigade organisations rooted in family or tribal groupings. The survival of tradition was perhaps also strengthened by the fact that many in the elite were still closely connected to the villages from which they originated and had broken with traditional life to a far lesser degree than their counterparts in the west of the USSR. In such circumstances they were unlikely to launch serious attacks against practices which many saw as intrinsic to their ethnic or group identity. And this was particularly so by the late 1970s when local elites were allowed more space for independent action and at a time when many within the national intelligentsia were looking again at their heritage and finding much to be admired in the past.

For many Central Asians the preservation of tradition was the only possible path of resistance in Soviet conditions. As Janice Baker has noted in the context of the treatment of women in Kazakhstan, the preservation of traditional ways of life hampered female emancipation, but at the same time such customs provided a stable personal and communal landmark following the turmoils of collectivisation. With the very nation under physical threat, at least so it appeared in the Kazakh case, the preservation of tradition became central to the survival of any sense of identity.[53] Less clear was the extent to which these identities were predominantly ethnic in nature, despite Soviet attempts to create socialist nations. Prior to 1917 identities tended to be 'sub-national', focused primarily on tribe, region, clan or family, or supra-national, centred on some sense, however vague, of belonging to a wider Muslim community or, in the case of a few intellectuals, to some vision of a pan-Turkic homeland. In 1924 Moscow created new nation-states and, over a period of 70 years, gave these states formal languages, cultures and administrative structures. Yet it remained uncertain to what extent the inhabitants of the regions now thought of themselves primarily as Uzbeks, Kazakhs, Kyrgyz, Tajiks or Turkmen. Equally the state had hoped to witness the development of a new Soviet identity, something which may have been taken on board by some within the elite so long as the state delivered economic growth and positions, but seems unlikely to have been that well developed amongst the predominantly rural communities of the region. Our evidence on all these questions is extremely limited, and it is the experience of independence, discussed later, that will indicate some of the ways in which regional identities developed during the twentieth century.[54] What does seem clear, however, is that the ambiguity of identities in the region, and the continued strength of close communal ties, militated against the establishment of a degree of social and cultural control comparable to that which seems to have been achieved in some other parts of the USSR.

The international significance of the Central Asian experiment

Though our concern in this chapter has been with the ways in which the Soviet state sought to establish domestic control of Central Asia, it should also be noted that Moscow hoped to use the region in pursuit of its foreign policy goals during the post-war years. Lenin had been aware of the revolutionary potential of the East and the 1920 Baku conference had sought to harness nationalist feeling to the anti-imperialist struggle. In the mid-1920s Stalin had greeted the new Tajik Autonomous Soviet Socialist Republic (ASSR) with an appeal to turn it 'into a model republic of the Eastern countries',[55] yet with the failure of the European revolution and the retreat into building socialism in one country this interest in the 'third world' had largely disappeared.

In the post-Stalin years, as Soviet elites became more aware that many of the newly independent countries were adopting an anti-imperialist stance, Moscow began to look to the 'south' as a new stage for East–West competition. Here the 'Central Asian model of development', which appeared to combine the possibility of economic advance whilst avoiding capitalism, and to offer a solution to regional and national conflict, was seen as a useful propaganda tool. Third World leaders could be brought to the region to see the achievements made under the socialist system, whilst the costs of social transformation could easily be concealed.[56] Under Khrushchev, and then from the late 1960s with more conviction, official Muslim spokesmen from the USSR were increasingly drawn into this effort, making numerous visits abroad where they sang the praises of Central Asian economic development and stressed that this had been managed without any infringement on the rights of believers.[57] From 1968 the Muslim Spiritual Board of Central Asia and Kazakhstan published a glossy journal *Muslims of the Soviet East*, eventually published in six languages, which portrayed the life of Soviet Central Asia in glowing terms and reported extensively on the foreign connections of religious leaders. During the following decade, Soviet Muslim leaders were also far more active in visiting the outside world, hosting foreign religious delegations, and organising large international conferences in the USSR. These generally brought together large assemblages of Muslim dignitaries from around the world who joined in denouncing Zionism or imperialism and in praising peace.[58]

Yet these connections had at best ambiguous results, for the thousands of foreign students who studied in Tashkent must have become aware of some of the darker sides of Soviet life, whilst the much smaller numbers of Soviet Muslims allowed to train in Egypt or Libya would have had their eyes opened to other ideological currents in contemporary Islam. And, as Fred Halliday has pointed out, however much Third World elites might have admired the development model suggested by Central Asia, it is far from clear that they were taken in by the proclamation of freedom of religion in the USSR or that they were going to take anti-American or anti-Israeli positions just because of Soviet Muslim propaganda.[59] In other words, the activities of Soviet Muslims may have reinforced existing pro-socialism and anti-Western positions but they could rarely create them. Indeed Moscow may have been less concerned to turn foreign Muslim states into slavish followers of its line than to neutralise potential opponents and keep them from taking pro-Western positions at international gatherings.

During the 1970s Soviet ideologists fought hard to come to terms with Islam, which had long been portrayed as the most reactionary of religions, but which was also the dominant religion in regions where the USSR was developing growing interests. In the late 1970s and early 1980s this led to an attempt to distinguish between reactionary and progressive elements within the international Muslim community. Thus the Iranian revolution came to be depicted in an essentially positive light because it had led to the overthrow of a US-backed regime on the Soviet Union's borders and a reinforcement of the anti-imperialist bloc.[60] Yet such a stance, which appeared to depict progressive Islam in terms of its support for Soviet foreign policy, proved unconvincing, especially after the invasion of Afghanistan in December 1979. This new war in which the USSR found itself embroiled led to complications in Moscow's use of Islam. Almost immediately it brought condemnation from the vast majority of Muslim states and in many cases led to a temporary cessation of contacts with the Soviet Union. This effect was especially noticeable in the religious sphere, with a major Tashkent conference scheduled for 1980 attracting very few participants from the wider Muslim world. Equally unconvincing was the Central Asian mufti's condemnation of foreign involvement in the Afghan conflict which omitted to mention that Moscow was the major sinner in this matter.

Questions also arose during this period as to the possible effects of the conflict on developments within Central Asia, as local conscripts were called upon to fight their co-religionists, and often co-ethnics, in the bitter war that evolved during the early 1980s. Though it is hard to document, it does appear that developments in Afghanistan served to undermine further Moscow's legitimacy, something already under threat from economic failure and the perception of falling living standards. Though contacts between Moscow, Tashkent and the Muslim states were somewhat gingerly resumed in late 1982, the Soviet model of development had experienced another blow to its prestige.

Even without Afghanistan it was far from clear that the Soviet path of development had in fact achieved more than alternative paths. In terms of literacy and welfare provision, there were some suggestions that Central Asia was better off than comparable Muslim states, but other economic indices were less clear. Comparing the four southern states with Turkey and Iran, Alastair McAuley found little to choose between them in terms of key indices of modernisation such as urbanisation or employment structures, with agricultural and rural life still the norm for the majority of citizens of all those states.[61] Moreover, many within the region were becoming aware by the early 1980s of some of the costs of rapid development, which had created a dependency not unlike that said to characterise much of north–south relations, and at a huge human and environmental price. The Soviet experience had certainly not been without impact nor had it left the region unchanged, but its effect was somewhat ambiguous, with costly social and economic change seeming to have had less impact upon traditional ways of life and patterns of rule than Moscow had perhaps intended. That this was so was to be recognised by Yuri Andropov and Mikhail Gorbachev, though their attempts to change the situation were ultimately to backfire.

Notes

1   M. B. Olcott, *The Kazakhs* (Stanford, 1987), pp. 207–9.
2   J. Critchlow, 'Religious–nationalist dissent in the Turkestan Communist Party: An old document surfaces', in Radio Liberty, *Report on the USSR*, 19 January 1990, 19–21.
3   The figures in this paragraph are taken from B. Olivier, 'Korenizat-

siya', *Central Asian Survey*, 9:3, 1990, 77–98.

4   On resistance in Kazakhstan see S. Blank, 'Ethnic and party politics in Kazakhstan, 1920–24', *Central Asian Survey*, 10:3, 1991, 12–13.
5   A point well made in A. Bennigsen and S. Enders Wimbush, *Muslim National Communism in the Soviet Union* (London, 1979), p. 25.
6   See the profile of Ryskulov in *Kazakhstanskaya pravda*, 20 December 1984, which praises his contribution to the creation of socialism in the republic but notes his mistakes in this area. The same article fails to mention his execution in the late 1930s.
7   Some of Sultan Galiev's writings can be found in *M. S. Sultan-Galiev, Stat'i* (Society for Central Asian Studies Reprint Series No. 1, Oxford, 1984).
8   J. Critchlow, 'Did Faizulla Khojaev really oppose Uzbekistan's land reform?', *Central Asian Survey*, 9:3, 1990, 38–9.
9   Olcott, *The Kazakhs*, p. 210;. cf. H. C. d'Encausse, 'The national republics lose their independence', in E. Allworth, ed., *Central Asia – A Century of Russian Rule* (New York, 1967), pp. 254–65.
10 S. Burg, 'Central Asian political participation and Soviet political development', in Y. Roi, ed., *The USSR and the Muslim World* (London, 1984), p. 4.
11 T. Rakowska-Harmstone, *Russia and Nationalism in Central Asia – The Case of Tadzhikistan* (Baltimore, 1970), p. 40.
12 Olcott, *The Kazakhs*, p. 216.
13 R. Conquest, *The Great Terror* (London, 1971), pp. 516–20; A. Altay, 'Kirgiziya during the great purge', *Central Asian Review*, 12:2, 1964, 97–107.
14 Conquest, *The Great Terror*, p. 389.
15 D. Carlisle, 'The Uzbek power elite: Politburo and Secretariat (1938–83)', *Central Asian Survey*, 5:3, 1986, 100, notes that in Uzbekistan the party first secretary, the head of the Council of Peoples' Commissars and the head of the Tashkent party organisation who replaced the purged leaders were 38, 31 and 34 years old respectively.
16 Burg, 'Central Asian political participation', pp. 56–7.
17 *Ibid.*
18 For example, the Decree of 21 October 1958, 'O rabote s kadrami v partiinoi organizatsii kirgizii', in *KPSS v rezolyutsiyakh i resheniyakh s'ezdov, konferentsii i plenumov TsK, Tom. 9* (Moscow, 1983), pp. 264–70.
19 Rakowska-Harmstone, *Russia and Nationalism*, p. 172.
20 Carlisle, 'The Uzbek power elite', 109–18.
21 G. Gleason, 'Sharaf Rashidov and the dilemmas of national leadership', *Central Asian Survey*, 5:3, 1986, 133–60.

22   Olcott, *The Kazakhs*, p. 244.
23   Critchlow, 'Did Faizulla Khojaev really oppose Uzbekistan's land reform', 32–3; Rakowska-Harmstone, *Russia and Nationalism*, p. 33.
24   Olcott, *The Kazakhs*, pp. 168–70.
25   R. Bideleux, *Communism and Development* (London, 1985), p. 206.
26   L. Dienes, 'Pastoralism in Turkestan – Its decline and its persistence', *Soviet Studies*, 27:2, 1975, 343–65.
27   Bideleux, *Communism and Development*, p. 206; cf. Olcott, *The Kazakhs*, pp. 185–6.
28   A. Nove and J. Newth, *The Soviet Middle East – A Model for Development* (London, 1967), p. 57.
29   'The collectivisation campaign in Uzbekistan', *Central Asian Review*, 12:1, 1964, 40–52.
30   T. Rakowska-Harmstone, 'Islam and nationalism – Central Asia and Kazakhstan under Soviet rule', *Central Asian Survey*, 2:2, 1983, 32.
31   Nove and Newth, *The Soviet Middle East*, p. 39.
32   B. Rumer, *Soviet Central Asia – A Tragic Experiment* (London, 1989), Chapter 3.
33   *Ibid.*, Chapter 4.
34   A. McAuley, 'Soviet development policy in Central Asia', in R. Cassen, ed., *Soviet Interests in the Third World* (London, 1985), p. 310.
35   G. Gleason, 'The Pakhta programme – The politics of sowing cotton in Uzbekistan', *Central Asian Survey*, 2:2, 1983, 109–20.
36   Rumer, *Soviet Central Asia*, pp. 125–6.
37   This paragraph is based upon a variety of sources, including N. Lubin, *Labour and Nationality in Soviet Central Asia – An Uneasy Compromise* (Princeton, 1984), Chapters 1–4; M. Feshbach, 'Trends in the Soviet Muslim population: Demographic aspects', in Roi, *The USSR and the Muslim World*, pp. 63–94; A. McAuley, 'Economic development and political nationalism in Uzbekistan', *Central Asian Survey*, 5:3, 1986, 161–82; Rumer, *Soviet Central Asia*; P. Craumer, 'Agricultural change, labour supply and rural out-migration in Soviet Central Asia', in R. Lewis, ed., *Geographic Perspectives on Soviet Central Asia* (London, 1992), pp. 132–80.
38   Figures taken from A. McAuley, 'The Central Asian economy in regional perspective', in M. Ellman and V. Kontorovich, eds, *The Disintegration of the Soviet Economy* (London, 1992), pp. 137–56.
39   McAuley, 'Soviet development policy', 307.
40   For various decrees and instructions relating to religious life in Turkestan issued in the 1920s see P. Gidulianov, *Otdelenie tserkvi ot gosudarstva v SSSR* (Moscow, 1926, with 1928 supplement), espe-

cially pp. 35–6, 61–2, 273, 277–80, 375–7, 516–17.

41   Rakowska-Harmstone, 'Islam and nationalism', 26; Olcott, *The Kazakhs*, pp. 171–2.

42   N. Bairamsakhatov, *Dukhovnaya kul'tura naroda i ateizm* (Ashkhabad, 1981), pp. 147–62; Olcott, *The Kazakhs*, p. 171, reports only 10 per cent of Kazakhs literate by 1930.

43   W. Medlin, ed., *Education and Development in Central Asia – A Case Study of Social Change in Uzbekistan* (Leiden, 1971), pp. 75–6.

44   See G. Massell, *The Surrogate Proletariat – Muslim Women and Revolutionary Strategies in Soviet Central Asia, 1919–29* (Princeton, 1974); B. P. Pal'vanova, *Emansipatsiya musul'manki* (Moscow, 1982), pp. 163–201; J. Anderson, 'Out of the kitchen, out of the temple: Religion, atheism and women in the Soviet Union', in S. P. Ramet, ed., *Religious Policy in the Soviet Union* (Cambridge, 1993), pp. 206–28.

45   A. Bennigsen and C. Lemercier Quelquejay, *Islam in the Soviet Union* (London, 1967), Chapters 8–10; Rakowska-Harmstone, 'Islam and nationalism', pp. 29–31.

46   L. Tillet, *The Great Friendship* (Chapel Hill, 1969); Allworth, *Central Asia – A Century of Russian Rule*; E. Allworth, *The Modern Uzbeks From the Fourteenth Century to the Present – A Cultural History* (Stanford, 1990), especially Chapters 7–9.

47   J. Anderson, 'Islam in the Soviet archives: A research note', *Central Asian Survey*, 13:3, 1994, 383–4.

48   On the Khrushchev campaign in general see J. Anderson, *Religion, State and Politics in the Soviet Union and the Successor States* (Cambridge, 1994), pp. 6–67.

49   According to Vladimir Kuroyedov, chairman of the Council for Religious Affairs attached to the USSR Council of Ministers, in a report he sent to the Central Committee in January 1980. Centre for the Preservation of Contemporary Documentation (TsKhSD), f. 5, op. 77, ed.khr. 126, p. 172; a useful essay which deals with some of the problems in interpreting the Soviet press in this area is M. Saroyan, 'Rethinking Islam in the Soviet Union', in S. G. Solomon, ed., *Beyond Sovietology* (New York, 1992), pp. 23–52.

50   This concept of 'tradition', defined in terms of shaping lifestyles according to some ancient, primordial or 'classical' model, was developed amongst others by S. Poliakov in a work translated as *Everyday Islam – Religion and Tradition in Rural Central Asia* (London, 1992). Some of what follows is based upon Poliakov's comments.

51   M. Kirkwood, 'Russian language teaching policy in Soviet Central Asia, 1958–86', in S. Akiner, ed., *Cultural Change and Continuity in Central Asia* (London, 1991), pp. 136 and 145.

52   See Nancy Lubin's reference to strategic assimilation (for example the learning of Russian 'so as to get on'), in 'Assimilation and retention of ethnic identity in Uzbekistan', *Asian Affairs*, 12:3, 1981, 277–85.

53   J. Baker, 'The position of women in Kazakhstan in the inter-war years', *Central Asian Survey*, 4:1, 1985, 100.

54   See the discussion in A. Bennigsen, 'Several nations or one people? Ethnic consciousness among Soviet Central Asian Muslims', *Survey*, 24:3, 1979, 51–64; M. Rywkin, 'National symbiosis: Vitality, religion, identity, allegiance', in Roi, *The USSR and the Muslim World*, pp. 3–15; Anderson, *Religion, State and Politics*, pp. 93–96; M. Atkin, 'Religious, national and other identities in Central Asia', in Jo-Ann Gross, ed., *Muslims in Central Asia – Expressions of Identity and Change* (Durham, 1992), pp. 46–72.

55   Quoted in Rakowska-Harmstone, *Russia and Nationalism*, p. 73.

56   T. Rakowska-Harmstone, 'Soviet Central Asia: A model of non-capitalist development for the Third World', in Roi, *The USSR and the Muslim World*, pp. 181–205.

57   A. Bennigsen, 'Soviet Muslims and the world of Islam', *Problems of Communism*, 29:2, 1980, 38–51; E. Lazzarini, 'Through the contact lens darkly: Soviet Muslims and their foreign co-religionists, 1926–86', in S. Akiner, ed., *Political and Economic Trends in Central Asia* (London, 1994), pp. 153–74.

58   See the discussion in A. Bennigsen, ed., *Soviet Strategy and Islam* (London, 1989), pp. 42–56.

59   F. Halliday, 'Islam and Soviet foreign policy', paper presented at the annual conference of the National Association of Soviet and East European Studies, Cambridge, March 1986.

60   See the essays by Roi and Wienbaum in Roi, *The USSR and the Muslim World*, pp. 149–77 and 226–60; and some of the essays in a special edition of *Voprosy nauchnogo ateizma* (Vol. 31, Moscow, 1983) devoted to Islam.

61   A. McAuley, 'The Central Asian economy in comparative perspective', 137–56.

3

The perestroika years

In November 1986 Mikhail Gorbachev paid a brief visit to Tashkent *en route* to India. Addressing a closed meeting of Uzbek party activists, he upbraided the republican party organisation for its failure to overcome the corruption associated with the cotton industry, to improve agricultural productivity in general or to develop the industrial sector. He was equally critical of personnel policies which he said were all too often based on nepotism and he attacked the tendency of many party officials to turn a blind eye to or even to participate in religious practices.[1] In this one outburst can be found many of the perceptions of Central Asia held by the Moscow elite since the early 1980s, and above all the feeling that under Brezhnev this region had slowly slipped away from central control. Gorbachev's aim was to reverse this situation, yet his policies engendered increasingly negative responses from regional elites and were eventually brought to an end by the collapse of Moscow's formal rule over Central Asia.

Gorbachev changes the rules

During the post-Stalin years the centre had been increasingly content to allow republican party bosses considerable freedom of action so long as they ensured political stability and delivered the planned economic goods. By the early 1980s, however, many central leaders felt that Central Asia – with its far less penetrable society, its close familial and regional ties, and its tendency to coopt those non-indigenous cadres which were supposed to oversee local elites – was only paying lip service to Soviet rule and that age-old patterns of public behaviour were reasserting themselves. As Yuri Andropov came to the fore, and especially after he took over as General Secretary in November 1982, moves evolved to restore that lost control. Under Andropov and later under Gorbachev this new trend focused on combating what was described as 'corruption' amongst the elite, and reducing its measured flirtation with nationalism and other 'survivals of the past' such as Islam. Alongside this came a call for a 'renewal of cadres' and an attempt to involve the region in the general restructuring and reform of the Soviet economy.

It was during the Andropov years that the so-called 'cotton affair' began to unfold, as it was revealed that in order to meet excessive targets for cotton production set by Moscow, Uzbek and other republican elites had been involved in over-reporting actual production. This led Moscow to send special investigators to the region, of whom the most notorious were to be N. Ivanov and T. Gdlyan, who began to unravel, by means of often doubtful legality, a web of bribe-taking and nepotism that involved thousands of officials, and led back to senior figures in Moscow including Brezhnev's son-in-law. At the height of the investigation in late 1983 Uzbek party boss Sharaf Rashidov died of a heart attack (or at his own hands according to some accounts), and many other officials were retired or arrested. As James Critchlow has suggested, Andropov and later Gorbachev saw the practices of the local elite as undermining the system and frustrating the centre's long-term goal of social integration, but from the local perspective this was a complete misreading of the situation.[2] In the first place it ignored the fact that it was the centre's forcing of the region into narrow economic specialisation and the setting of unreal targets which made 'illegal' practices essential if the system were to work at all. In addition it failed to take into account differential perceptions of what practices were 'corrupt' or otherwise – in many contexts it might be 'corrupt' not to give a brother or son preference for a job, whilst 'gifts' were essential to facilitate many business transactions.

Nonetheless Moscow persisted in its attack on Central Asian corruption and this intensified under Gorbachev as glasnost developed and allowed more detailed, if often highly prejudicial, reporting of corruption scandals in the central press. In various speeches delivered in the winter of 1985–86 Gorbachev appeared to be singling out Uzbekistan and Turkmenistan for assorted 'violations of socialist legality', 'padding and deception', 'bribery' and other crimes. These themes were in turn taken up by local party leaders who sought scapegoats amongst past leaders or picked on regions within their own republics that had notoriously bad records. Thus Turkmen First Secretary S. Niyazov singled out the Tashauz oblast elite for basing personnel selection on kin or regional basis, and sacked many key officials.[3] This campaign continued throughout Central Asia in the mid-1980s, with the public denigration of numerous officials and the replacement of hundreds. Yet many of those 'sacked' soon reappeared in other posts and in Uzbekistan, I. Usmankhodzhaev, Rashidov's replacement and Moscow's ostensible scourge of corruption, was himself removed in early 1988, along with other key officials, and later imprisoned for his own role in the 'cotton affair'. Indigenous leaders who took part in this attack on corrupt colleagues were not always popular. In February 1986 Kazakh Prime Minister Nursultan Nazarbaev criticised local officials who siphoned off construction funds into prestige projects or built themselves bigger and better apartments, and found himself the subject of a whispering campaign initiated by other members of the republican elite.[4] Moreover, this assault on 'corruption' launched by Moscow may have backfired insofar as it strengthened local elites who could portray themselves as victims of the centre's 'older brother' syndrome which paid little attention to regional sensitivities.

Alongside the attack on economic corruption came a renewed critique of what might be called cultural deviation. Especially in Uzbekistan under Rashidov, there had been a measured and cautious reassessment of the past, with particular attention paid to the rich cultural heritage of the region prior to its contacts with Russia. And inevitably this had entailed some recognition of the contribution of Islam to the region's development. Though institutional Islam had been fundamentally weakened by 70 years of Soviet antireligious policies, most of Central Asia's population retained a loose connection with Islamic practices in their everyday life (*byt*'). From the late 1970s the centre had encouraged a renewed propagandist assault on Islam, but most Central Asian leaders had done little more than go through the motions. Under Gorbachev, Moscow once more called for an end to any compromise with religion and the Central Asian press started to carry a large number of articles attacking Islam's pretensions to be organically linked with national identities, criticising many party leaders' compromises with religion, and detailing what appeared to be a revitalisation of Islam in at least some parts of the region – notably the Fergana valley and parts of Tajikistan.[5] Central concern with Islam was also indicated by an unpublished Central Committee decree issued on 18 August 1986 calling for more anti-Islamic activity, and in Gorbachev's call for a decisive struggle against religious survivals whilst visiting Tashkent in November of that year.[6] Yet though Islam provided the focus of attack, Gorbachev's prime concern appears to have been with religion as a symptom of the localism that to some extent had taken the day-to-day running of the region out of central control during Brezhnev's tenure.

The centre's response to these perceived failings initially took the form of the mass replacement of republican elites and an attempt to redress their ethnic balance which was seen to have swung too far in the direction of indigenous nationalities. Donald Carlisle notes that from Rashidov's death in late 1983 to January 1985 some 40 out of 65 oblast secretaries were replaced in Uzbekistan, including 10 out of 13 first secretaries, and that at the party congress in January 1986 only 34 of 177 Central Committee members were retained whilst only 2 buro members survived from 1981.[7] In 1983–86 all five republican party first secretaries were replaced, though the last change involving Kazakhstan was to provoke the first signs of substantial resistance within the region. This new policy was given shape at the Twenty-seventh Party Congress in February 1986, when Yegor Ligachev suggested that the time had come to re-think aspects of personnel policy. If regionalism and localism were to be combated, it was necessary to promote an 'inter-regional exchange of personnel, an exchange of experienced workers between the republics and the centre'.[8] Though designed primarily with efficiency and control considerations in mind, this policy reflected a failure to understand both the way in which Soviet society had developed in recent decades and the realities of the situation on the ground in Central Asia. Inevitably this policy engendered hostility from indigenous groups which felt that they had gradually been pushing back long-lived Russian dominance of the region. More practically, it was not made clear how Slavs and others 'parachuted in' from outside were to function effectively in a region so culturally different from their own, and one whose language and customs they were completely ignorant of.[9]

The limitations of this policy were brought home to Moscow in December 1986 when Kazakh party boss D. Kunaev was replaced by G. Kolbin, a Russian who had previously worked as a regional party boss within the Russian federation. Within hours of the announcement there were demonstrators on the streets of the Kazakh capital Alma Ata and in the following days violent clashes left at least three people dead and many injured. Unrest appears to have affected many other parts of Kazakhstan in the following days, and in subsequent months hundreds of students lost their places in educational establishments, many party members were expelled and hundreds of those allegedly involved were subjected to administrative or criminal penalties. Though official sources blamed events variously on hooligans inflamed by drink or on corrupt supporters of Kunaev, the official report produced by a Kazakh parliamentary commission in 1989 saw the events of December as the culmination of Kazakhstan's long history of socio-economic exploitation and political domination by Moscow which had rendered the centre insensitive to local needs. In this version such violence as did occur was the product of an over-reaction by the authorities and occurred despite the efforts of local leaders such as Nazarbaev to calm the situation.[10] The longer-term effect of this first major sign of ethnic unrest in Gorbachev's Soviet Union was the bringing to an end of the policy of the inter-republican exchange of cadres and in practice the curtailment of Moscow's efforts to restore control in the region through personnel policy.

The second plank of Gorbachev's policy relating to Central Asia stemmed from the need to overcome the major socio-economic difficulties facing the region which appeared to require a fundamental re-thinking of economic policy. Like the rest of the USSR, the region was hit by declining economic growth and general stagnation, but in this region the problem was compounded by the demographic dynamism of the population. For example, in Uzbekistan official figures recorded that economic growth had fallen from 8.6 per cent in 1971–75 to 3.0 per cent in 1981–85,[11] yet the population had risen by 15.4 per cent in 1979–85. Similarly high growth rates were being recorded in other Central Asian republics. What this meant in practice was that, according to some estimates, from 1985 to 2000 Central Asia was going to have to create upwards of seven million new jobs – or encourage around the same number of local inhabitants to emigrate to labour-deficient parts of the USSR.[12]

At republican party congresses during Gorbachev's first year in office party leaders repeatedly pointed to the failure of many regions to meet their planned targets for industrial and agricultural production, and it was becoming increasingly apparent to many that the over-emphasis on cotton production was undermining broader prospects for economic improvement. Even cotton was proving a far from successful crop as water resources declined and cotton quality decreased, thanks to land exhaustion and over-use of fertiliser. In Uzbekistan the cotton harvest fell short of target by 300,000 tons in 1985, despite the centre's reduction of the target from 6 million to 5.7 million tons.[13] And although the authorities did not publish the statistics till much later, it was becoming clear that the economic decline–population growth mismatch was producing *de facto* unemployment: 25.7 per cent in Tajikistan, 22.8 per cent in Uzbekistan, 18.8 per cent in Turkmenistan and 16.3 per cent in Kirgiziya in 1986.[14]

It was in this context that Mikhail Gorbachev came to power committed to a revitalisation of the Soviet economy. The problem was that in his drive for greater efficiency he paid little heed to many of the difficulties created by his predecessors. For example, in August 1986 he made the rational decision to drop the controversial water diversion scheme which aimed to redirect water from the Siberian rivers southward to Central Asia.[15] On economic and environmental grounds this made perfect sense, but it left many Central Asians aggrieved as their chances of economic revitalisation seemed slim without additional water, and some pointed out that it was Moscow's choice of economic priorities for the region that had created the problem in the first place. Moreover, the more positive elements of the decree ending the scheme which stressed the need for the region to find ways of reducing their water usage by 15–20 per cent over the next five years pointed to the centre's new emphasis on republican self-reliance. Gorbachev had already made this clear at the Twenty-seventh CPSU Congress when he attacked the attitude of 'living at the expense of others' and had suggested linking 'the volume of resources allocated for social needs to the efficiency of the regional economy'.[16] Various decrees issued in 1986–87 reallocated responsibilities for economic management to the republics, and stressed the need for them to make better use of existing resources.

Problems were also created for Central Asia by the new leadership's approach to investment. The new emphasis on intensive rather than extensive use of investment resources worked against the region's need for the creation of large-scale employment opportunities and, as Boris Rumer has pointed out, the emphasis on investment in existing industrial capacity would favour the European parts of the Russian Soviet Federal Socialist Republics (RSFSR) and maintain Central Asia's role as supplier of raw materials.[17] From the first year of Gorbachev's tenure it became clear that Moscow was no longer willing to extend what it saw as 'affirmative action' in the region, with capital investment for the region being cut during the mid-1980s. Some concessions to the region were made, notably in the successive reductions in the cotton targets in 1985 and 1987 which led to the meeting of objectives in 1988, albeit at the cost of the ruthless exploitation of the soil and a reversion to child labour in that year. In early 1989 Uzbek First Secretary Rafik Nishanov asked Moscow for a further reduction in his republic's targets so that more food could be grown, but this failed to reduce growing demands within the republic for an end to the cotton mono-culture.[18]

Overall, Gorbachev's redefinition of economic priorities did little to improve the situation of Central Asia and much to aggravate the region's sense of grievance. Having created a dependency relationship based upon a single crop, Moscow was now asking the region to be self-sufficient. Yet as the all-union economy continued to decline, the likelihood of Moscow providing substantial help to the region was further reduced. On top of this, the centre's talk of administrative reform caused anxiety amongst republican elites, for major retrenchment would create large-scale unemployment amongst the administrative class. All of this meant that even in traditionally quiescent Central Asia there began to be stirrings of discontent and resistance to Moscow during the late 1980s.

Central Asia's response

For many in Central Asia Moscow's assault on corruption appeared to be a singling out of the region in a way that reflected colonial if not racist attitudes on the part of the Slavic population. Although regional elites were to prove amongst the more conservative during the Gorbachev era, they gradually began to fight back against

Moscow's policies and insinuations. As elsewhere, the intelligentsia played a key role in airing grievances, although in much of Central Asia the debate was very much a licensed one as party bosses proved slow to permit the level of glasnost in the media that came to prevail at the centre and in some of the other Soviet republics. Even before 1985 there was developing a subtle and cautious critique of Moscow's treatment of the region in the communications media produced in the local languages, publications which Russian-speaking elites paid little heed to and which even when literally understood could convey alternative messages to those at home with the language.[19]

Under Gorbachev this critique began to be more openly developed though here we can only point to a few of the key issues that were raised from about 1987 onwards. As elsewhere in the Soviet Union, the first subjects to be explored were in the relatively 'safe' area of culture, with a discussion of purged writers, banned works and a reassessment of past history taking place. Notable here was the rehabilitation of writers within the *jadid* tradition such as Cholpan and Fitrat in Uzbekistan and, perhaps more controversially, the reassessment of the 'father of *jadidism*', Ismail Bey Gaspirali. The discussion of these writers questioned their past depiction as counter-revolutionary elements and stressed their democratic and reformist commitment to progressive change in the Russian empire and young Soviet state.[20] More attention was also paid to the Russian conquest of Central Asia, described since the 1930s as a voluntary union, but now spoken of as the action of a colonial power. Events such as the 1898 Andizhan uprising were portrayed as anticolonial revolts rather than as the result of feudal intransigence or religious fanaticism, whilst indigenous resistance to the Bolsheviks in 1918–20 received a more favourable coverage than hitherto.[21] In Kazakhstan July 1989 witnessed the publication in the main republican papers of a round-table discussion of the 1918–19 *Alash Orda* government, in which some participants sought to deny that it was particularly nationalistic, noting the substantial number of non-Kazakhs in its council, and stressing that its prime goal was a just redress of anti-colonial grievances.[22] Though none of these discussions directly questioned the region's inclusion in the USSR, they implicitly raised questions not just about past but also about present colonial attitudes and policies.

Two other issues were to prove equally damaging to Moscow's

rule in the long run. First there was the question of religion, with considerable discussion of the actual place of religion in Central Asia. From the mid-1980s central and republican sources printed a large amount of material which suggested less the disappearance of religion but rather its continued strength, not just amongst the old and the female, but also amongst the younger and the better educated Central Asians. There was a critique of the dishonesty of much anti-religious writing, with the Director of the Tashkent Institute of Scientific Atheism pointing out the tendency of reporting only studies which supported the cause and of ignoring those which showed widespread participation in religious rites.[23] There was also considerable criticism during 1988 of the fact that at a time when the Orthodox Church was gaining concessions in the run-up to the millennium celebration, Islam was still under attack, something that reinforced the image of Central Asia as somehow more backward than the rest of the USSR.

The other cultural issue that was to emerge, and be potentially more destructive for central control, was the discussion of the language issue that began to take place in 1988–89. Small groups of intellectuals began to call for a greater role to be given to indigenous languages, and from 1988 most of the Central Asian republics witnessed growing public demands for reform of the language systems. In the early 1920s each of the local languages had seen its script changed from the Arabic to the Latin alphabet, and then just before the war further changes had transformed these Turkic and Persian languages into Cyrillic. Simultaneously local vocabularies had seen numerous changes, as Slavic or European words were substituted for indigenous ones or added where there was no existing word, as was the case in many technical areas. Before Gorbachev's accession there had been a gradual effort to return many lost words to daily speech, but perestroika gave new impetus to this struggle. In December 1988 some 600 students at Tashkent University held an unofficial Uzbek language festival and collected signatures for a petition arguing that Uzbek should become the state language. Though the regime sought to ban future demonstrations on this subject, in February 1989 Uzbek First Secretary Rafik Nishanov announced that the issue was to be discussed by the republican Central Committee's ideological department.[24]

Alongside these broad cultural issues, the public debate focused heavily on the issue of the cotton mono-culture with all its implications for the regional environment and the population's health, but also as the ultimate symbol of colonial rule. By late 1987 the press had greatly extended its coverage of the issue, with the question of the Aral Sea exciting particular attention. The gradual disappearance of this inland water had increased regional temperatures, shortened the frost-free growing season, and impacted negatively upon local infant mortality rates. Alongside the problems stemming from the over-use of fertilisers and the depletion of water resources, the depletion of the sea only served to accentuate the economic downturn and led many in Central Asia to begin to question the value of Russian-imposed economic priorities.

All in all, glasnost in Central Asia as elsewhere allowed the fuller airing of the problems and grievances that were already well known to elites and intellectuals. Though the regimes in these republics remained cautious and prevented the debate from becoming too extensive, they were unable to quash the discussion completely and indeed, as we shall see, found it useful to utilise it for their own purposes in pursuit of concessions from Moscow which would help to legitimate their own position *vis-à-vis* domestic audiences. Yet for all this, once some discussion was permitted it became likely that more nationalistically-inclined groups and individuals would seek to use these issues to focus attention on the larger question of Moscow's right to rule in the region.

Despite the disastrous socio-economic situation in Central Asia, and the existence of many grievances *vis-à-vis* the centre shared with all the republics, informal groups and nationalist movements developed slowly in the region. In part this stemmed from the lack of any real tradition of political organisation or overt dissent, but other factors also played a role. Of all the Soviet republics these were the most rural, with the mass of the population dependent upon party and collective farm chairmen for their livelihood and tied into traditional patronage networks which they were unlikely to challenge. These patterns of social organisation, relying very much on regional allegiances and reaching right up into the party structures of the republics, created problems for those seeking to organise along nationalist lines. In general the population in these republics lacked any strong sense of national belonging, with self-identification being a far from simple matter. Thus an Uzbek peasant might see himself or herself as a farmer, a member of a specific farm or geographical region, as belonging to a specific family or tribe, as an Uzbek or as a Muslim, depending upon the context in which the question was asked. This situation was further complicated because each republic had substantial numbers of ethnic minorities, especially in Kazakhstan where the titular nationality only made up around 40 per cent of the population. In addition to these factors, popular movements received little support from Central Asian party elites who did not follow the example of some other republican leaders in making common cause with nationalists. Instead they took up some of the same grievances whilst seeking to promote them through traditional within-system bargaining. At the same time they kept the activities of nationalist groups under tight control.

As elsewhere in the USSR the first informal organisations to appear focused on 'single issues' such as the environment – always the easiest to develop within the approved parameters of perestroika. Typical of these were the various intellectual groups associated with the campaign to save the Aral Sea, or the Nevada-Semipalatinsk group set up by poet Olzhas Suleimenov in Kazakhstan. This latter group created in early 1989 used its first meeting to provide documentary evidence suggesting that past nuclear experimentation had led to a radical increase in the number of radiation-related health problems in the region, and called for an end to testing at Semipalatinsk. Later in the year the movement issued appeals to Presidents Bush and Gorbachev calling for a complete cessation of testing.[25]

Attempts to create popular fronts along the lines seen in the Baltic states proved more problematic in Central Asia, though there were various attempts to do so. In April 1989 Turkmen First Secretary Niyazov noted an effort to create one in his republic but dismissed it as being motivated by personal ambition.[26] And when the *Agzybirlik* (Unity) Movement was eventually set up, activists found it difficult to garner support or appeal to the masses in this tightly controlled republic. More surprising was the failure to set up such a movement in Kazakhstan, although again the divided ethnic nature of the country and the perhaps mutually incompatible aims of the two major communities may have had something to do with this. Nonetheless, Kazakhstan was the first to see the creation of explicitly nationalist political parties such as *Zheltoksan*, *Azat* and *Alash*, all committed to the reduction of the communist and Russian presence in the government.[27] To the south in Kyrgyzstan protest

centred on the increasing problems of homelessness and unemployment as young rural males congregated in the capital Frunze and
began setting up squatter camps. Though the republican leaders initially responded harshly, these developments were to lead to the
establishment of a number of informal groups and political movements.[28]

The most significant attempt to create such a movement was
undoubtedly the formation of *Birlik* (Unity) in Uzbekistan. Having
its roots in various discussion groups formed in 1988, the Movement to Protect the National, Spiritual and Material Wealth of
Uzbekistan was unveiled to the public at a Tashkent language
demonstration in April 1989. Its founding congress held several
months later adopted a charter setting out *Birlik*'s goals. Here it
argued for making 'all power to the soviets' a reality, and called for
genuine Uzbek sovereignty 'within the USSR', the promotion of
Uzbek as the state language and a serious effort to tackle the socio-
economic and environmental problems created above all by the
cotton mono-culture. In pursuit of these goals it would abide by
democratic means and seek cooperation with all government and
social organisations. Rejecting ethnic exclusivity, the charter
described membership as open to all Uzbek citizens committed to
the goals set out in the charter.[29] Though *Birlik* initially enjoyed
some success in drawing crowds on to the streets, the more con-
frontational style associated with the charismatic physicist A. Pula-
tov was not to the liking of all council members and by early 1990
the movement had split, with the more moderate elements led by
poet Muhammed Salih setting up *Erk* (Will). This group also
expressed the hope of dealing with the government, though this
feeling was not always reciprocated, and its social basis was largely
confined to intellectuals in Tashkent and a few other cities.[30]

During the early summer of 1990 representatives from popular
movements in all the republics except Turkmenistan met in Alma
Ata to discuss common concerns and the possibility of cooperation.
Springing from the anxieties aroused by recent outbreaks of inter-
ethnic violence in the region (see below), many of the delegates suggested that the way forward might be the creation of an economic
union and a common Central Asian parliament. Even here there
were divisions between those seeking functional cooperation and
those with grander aims, for example, the creation of a greater
Turkestan.[31] Nonetheless, there existed by mid-1990 embryonic

political movements in all of the republics, enjoying varying degrees of success in organisation and, as we shall see, meeting different responses from republican authorities.

The year of troubles

Central Asia had witnessed a variety of disturbances in the early years of perestroika, notably the Alma Ata events of 1986 and a series of petty outbursts of what were officially described as 'hooliganism' in subsequent years.[32] Yet these were as nothing compared to the bloody communal violence that was to rock the region between mid-1989 and mid-1990, events that were to have a major impact upon the regional elites and in part would explain their subsequent concern with stability at almost any cost.

In late May 1989 an incident between an Uzbek and a Mesketian Turk, allegedly over a punnet of strawberries, in a market in the Fergana valley town of Kuvasai, led to a fight and a death. Just over a week later the town of Tashlak erupted and within several days a number of towns in the region had been taken over by marauding mobs bent on destruction, with violence directed primarily against the Mesketians settled there as a result of Stalin's war-time deportations of Caucasian peoples. Within days the troubles had spread, affecting all three regions within the Fergana valley and going well beyond the control of the authorities who at the local level often proved unwilling to intervene.[33] With armed mobs of up to ten thousand in some places it took tens of thousands of Interior Ministry troops to restore order, and the situation remained tense for several months. As a result of these disturbances over 100 died, about two-thirds of whom were Mesketians, over 1,000 were injured, and 700 buildings were destroyed. Within a month over 30,000 Mesketians had 'voluntarily' left the republic.[34]

Hardly had the Fergana disturbances begun to subside than there were reports of unrest in the Kazakh oil town of Novy Uzen. Traditionally an area populated by nomadic pastoralists, the development of the oil industry in the 1960s had brought with it an inflow of Russians and Caucasians, and it was the latter that provided the focus of local Kazakh hostility in late June. Though the violence was not on the scale seen in Fergana, clashes between Kazakhs and Caucasians left at least three dead and many injured as youths went on

the rampage through the town, protesting rationing, unemployment, high prices in cooperatives and the allegedly higher wages
paid to immigrants. As the disorders spread to other parts of the
Mangyshlak region, some protestors made more explicitly nationalistic demands, of both a negative kind, for a removal of the Caucasians, and a more positive kind, for an improvement in the status
of indigenous peoples, symbolised in the call made by demonstrators in Shevchenko for the renaming of their town as Aktau.[35] Three
weeks later the backcloth for unrest shifted to the Kirgiz-Tajik
borders as a long-standing dispute over land and water use came to
a head, with demonstrations, the filling in of canals, bloodshed, and
the eventual imposition of martial law.[36]

The rest of the year remained relatively peaceful, but in early
1990 tensions returned with major unrest in the Tajik capital
Dushanbe in February following the spread of rumours that numerous Armenian refugees from the conflict with Azerbaijan over the
disputed Caucasian territory of Nagorno–Karabakh were to be
given priority for housing at a time when many Tajiks lacked basic
housing facilities. With tens of thousands on the street calling for
the resignation of the political leadership, events took an ugly turn
after troops fired and killed a number of demonstrators. With hind-
sight it appears that groups seeking to change the balance of power
within the elite manipulated the genuine grievances of elements
within the population, but the end result was to strengthen the hand
of the existing authorities who appeared to be the only people capable of guaranteeing order.[37]

This year of troubles ended in June 1990 when perhaps the most
violent clashes of all took place in the most southerly Kirgiz region
of Osh. Here local Uzbeks and Kirgiz came to blows as a result of
tensions engendered in part by the Uzbeks' perceptions that they
were unrepresented in local government and the Kirgiz view that
the Uzbeks took all the best jobs in the retail and consumer sector.
Events in Osh unfolded with particular cruelty as local Kirgiz were
told to paint their doors red if they were to avoid the destruction of
their property and possibly the loss of their lives at the hands of
rampaging mobs. At the end of the violence, well over 200 people
had died.[38]

If one takes this year of troubles as a whole, a number of points
stand out. Though at various times the central authorities sought to
find culprits – whether fundamentalists, criminal groups or oppo-

nents of perestroika – and though in many cases a particular event appeared to have been manipulated by political elites, such events also had deep social roots. As already noted, the region faced severe and growing economic difficulties, with the Fergana valley, criss-crossing three of the republics, experiencing particular difficulties, with a reported 250,000 unemployed young people and many families on the edge of real poverty.[39] In each case it appears to have been unemployed young men who formed the bulk of the rioters, and who proved willing to take their hostility towards minorities to the point of murder. In this they were often inflamed by alcohol or drugs, which were supplied, according to conflicting reports, by one of the following: nationalists, criminals, party workers or KGB officers. Yet for all the genuine problems and grievances, it does seem clear that in each case there was some organisation behind the events, with Yaacov Roi noting that before each outbreak there developed a surge of rumours which often alleged privileges for minorities, and that in each case the rioters were able to locate their victims with considerable efficiency. In most cases the authorities made political capital out of the events, using them as a pretext for undermining the informal groups which could be linked to the violence and also as a justification for introducing tough legislation to ban public meetings and generally tighten up political and social control.[40] At the same time the authorities were able to use these disturbances to persuade the centre to provide them with increased funds for the alleviation of social problems, in the Uzbek case inducing Soviet Prime Minister Nikolai Ryzhkov to promise a major investment effort to bring production and employment opportunities to the region.[41]

The road to independence

In the face of Moscow's renewed attempt to restore control during the mid-1980s the Central Asian elites resorted to the classic tactic of evasion and non-implementation. In part this meant that whilst some officials were disgraced, many of those who lost their jobs in the purges of 1983–88 soon reappeared in other posts. Equally, the centre's attempt to restore ethnic balance in leading organs was quickly halted following the Alma Ata events, and from around 1989 most of the Central Asian party executives, apparats and republican Council of Ministers came to be dominated by Central Asians, a trend that became even more prominent when presidential apparats were created.[42]

More significantly, republican elites began to take up some of the grievances that were being brought to the fore in the press, or to encourage their broad discussion. This was clear in the area of culture and tradition where from early 1989 more scope was given to age-old customs such as the new year festival of *Navruz*, with its religious connotations no longer hidden. Equally, Islam was no longer treated as an opponent, but rather as a force to be utilised and drawn upon in reforming society and overcoming what was seen as its moral decline. This trend was given institutional recognition by the opening of new mosques and the election of the Central Asian mufti Muhammed Sadyk to the USSR Congress of Peoples' Deputies in March 1989.

It was also in this year that republican elites latched on to the public demand for language reform, though they varied considerably in their enthusiasm for real change. April 1989 witnessed the publication of the Tajik draft state language law which gave Tajik priority status whilst recognising Russian as the language of inter-ethnic communication and promising protection for the languages of all groups within the republic. Here as elsewhere it was intended that Tajik should become the language of administration and education, but with provision for translation in the short term and a designated transition period.[43] Similar developments took place in other Central Asian republics in 1989–90 with all five adopting new language laws establishing the indigenous languages as those of the state, and setting timetables for acquisition of those languages in administrative and educational life. In each case the authorities trod carefully, mindful that in many areas Central Asians often spoke Russian better than their own language, and fearful that such laws would spark off Russian resistance, lead to tensions with the centre, or encourage the emigration of a Slavic population that was still necessary for the economic well-being of these republics.[44] In Kazakhstan, for example, the draft law provided for an immediate transition to Kazakh in those areas where Kazakhs formed over 70 per cent of the population, and gave predominantly Russian areas until 1994 to effect the change. This was later modified in a 1990 compromise which postponed full implementation until 2000.[45]

At the same time Central Asian leaders sought to pressurise the centre for greater socio-economic help, both through the traditional means of discrete, behind-the-scenes bargaining, but also more openly as perestroika created new fora for public discussion. Especially important here was the first meeting of the Congress of Peoples' Deputies in late May to early June 1989. Here Uzbek First Secretary Nishanov paid brief attention to the struggle with corruption but then went on to attack the ridiculous situation whereby his republic's production of raw materials and half-finished products had reached 60 per cent of output, with only 10 per cent of Uzbek cotton being processed in the republic. The consequence of this, he told assembled delegates, was the utter exhaustion of land and water resources and an over-chemicalisation of the land, which had severely affected the peoples' well-being.[46] Similar complaints were also made by Turkmenistan's Niyazov who attacked critics of Central Asia, pointing out that his republic met 100 per cent of the demands of other republics, whilst many failed to deliver their assigned output. Along with Makhamov of Tajikistan he accepted the need for economic change but suggested that it had to take into account existing circumstances, for example, the rural nature of the region which meant that declining investment would have a particularly adverse effect. The Tajik party boss and other deputies from the region argued that reform must include the setting of realistic prices for the raw materials emanating from Central Asia, and 70 deputies submitted a memorandum calling for cotton prices to be raised by 50 per cent. Alongside the issue of cotton the region's parliamentarians raised other questions, including nuclear testing in Kazakhstan, the fate of the Aral Sea, and the illegalities evident in the Ivanov-Gdlyan investigations of alleged corruption in Uzbekistan. Many delegates criticised the central media's gloating over the 'Uzbek affair' and rejected the depiction of the region as a bastion of 'conservatism'. Nonetheless Kirgiziya's First Secretary Absamat Masaliev appeared to reinforce the latter perception when he devoted his speech to attacking the breakdown in order which had allowed extremists to surface and expressed his concern as to whether this new-fangled Moscow-based talking shop had the ability to resolve the country's problems.[47]

This tough approach was evident within many of the republics, for whilst elites were willing to bargain for greater rights *vis-à-vis* the centre, they preferred to maintain a tight rein at home. Informal groups in most of them met with official hostility until at least 1990, and beyond this year in some. In Uzbekistan there developed a distinction between what were described as 'positive' informals and those of an 'extremist character' such as *Birlik*. Addressing an Uzbek Central Committee plenum in May 1989, Nishanov described the activities of the nationalist groups as stemming from personal ambition,[48] whilst the following day the republican paper carried a Brezhnev-era-style article on the work of the KGB in conditions of glasnost which sought to link nationalist groups to foreign intelligence agencies.[49]

Nonetheless, by late 1989 there was increasing evidence of change in the stance of the two largest Central Asian players, Uzbekistan and Kazakhstan. In June Nursultan Nazarbaev was appointed as first secretary of Kazakhstan, and he was to prove a firm critic of Moscow's exploitative relationship with the region whilst simultaneously recognising that the maintenance of the union was probably essential for stability. In the same month, Rafik Nishanov was replaced as Uzbek first secretary by Islam Karimov, who was to take a similar line to his Kazakh counterpart, bargaining hard for his republic but within the framework of the union. Addressing his Central Committee in August, Karimov outlined in far greater detail than hitherto the problems facing Uzbekistan, stemming from its dynamic population growth, inadequate social provision, limited industrial base, the over-specialisation of the economy and its orientation to the production of raw materials which created many of the other problems.[50] The following spring this critique was taken a great deal further by Prime Minister S. Mirsaiddov in his maiden speech to the newly elected Uzbek parliament. Here he not only depicted the economic relationship with the centre in terms of exploitation but claimed that Moscow had manipulated the statistics to make it appear that it was subsidising Uzbekistan. He argued that in future all buildings, assets and natural resources located in Uzbekistan should be considered republican property and that henceforth the relationship should be based on mutual and equitable economic contracts, not on state orders. As James Critchlow has suggested, this was part of a wider move under Karimov to bring the republic under local control, which was evident, for example, in the replacement of several key Slavic officials brought in from outside by 'local' Russians, and also in the development of a more ambiguous relationship with informal groups which eventually led to the temporary registration of some.[51]

Other signs of changing attitudes could be found in the gradual development of inter-regional links. This was evident in a relatively informal meeting of Central Asian leaders in Alma Ata which took place in 1989 where they talked about reducing their dependence on Moscow and about economic survival in a situation in which all-union ties were breaking down.[52] A more formal meeting held in June 1990 witnessed discussion on a state-to-state rather than a party-to-party basis and various agreements of intent were signed and a decision taken to set up institutional structures.[53] Simultaneously many of these republics were looking further afield, seeking foreign investment and exploring links with major Western businesses in order to better utilise or develop existing resources, notably oil and gas.

All of this culminated with declarations of sovereignty by Uzbekistan in June 1990 and Kazakhstan in October of that year. In Kazakhstan, this followed prolonged controversy as Russian legislators expressed their fears as to what this might mean for the 6 million-plus Russians living there. These developments also took place in the context of negotiations between the republics over a renewed union treaty which both maintained the rights of the centre and guaranteed republican sovereignty. In these debates the Central Asian leaders generally supported Gorbachev's position that some form of union must be maintained, but the first drafts failed to satisfy their aspirations for greater autonomy and in effect maintained Moscow's leading role. A key role here was played by Nazarbaev who, following Kazakh debates over the language law and sovereignty declaration, came to recognise the fragility of the ethnic balance in his republic and the consequent need for good relations with Moscow, as well as the necessity of a single economic space at least until a more balanced economy could be created. For this reason he was to play a key role in the Novo-Ogarevo negotiations which were to lead to the creation of a new union treaty in mid-1991 and, along with other Central Asian leaders would argue for a 'yes' vote in the March 1991 referendum which asked Soviet voters whether they wanted a renewed federation as proposed by Gorbachev.[54] And when this took place the continued ability of Central Asian leaders to control the popular vote was evident in the old-Soviet-style massive majorities for the proposition recorded in most of the region.[55]

On the eve of the August coup Central Asian leaders met once more, this time in Tashkent, to sign an agreement setting up a consultative council and then, just two days before the attempted seizure of power, Russian President Yeltsin visited Alma Ata to discuss with Nazarbaev the need to maintain a single economic space within the proposed Union of Sovereign States. When the Extraordinary Committee sent tanks on to the streets of Moscow, only Kirgiziya's President Askar Akaev offered immediate support to Yeltsin. Nazarbaev called for calm and after a brief hesitation described the coup attempt as unconstitutional. In the other republics the declarations of the coup leaders were published in the press, though Uzbekistan's President Karimov and Turkmenistan's President Niyazov sat out events, waiting to see which way the wind would blow. Only in Tajikistan did the party leadership warmly applaud developments in Moscow, which were seen as a chance to restore order in the USSR.[56] Yet this action which was intended to save the union in effect hastened its demise, and within days of its collapse most of the republican parties had left the Communist Party of the Soviet Union, party organisations had been banned from state and legal organs, and most had issued or promised declarations of independence – though Kazakhstan held back on its independence proclamation until December.[57] During the autumn three regional presidents sought to bolster their legitimacy by seeking a popular mandate – previously they had been elected by their parliaments. Yet it was perhap ironic that in the two more pluralistic republics, Kazakhstan and Kyrgyzstan, the leaders stood unopposed and received majorities of over 90 per cent, whereas in the more conservative Tajikistan Rahmon Nabiev had to face an opponent and even with a partially manipulated vote was only able to achieve a 57 per cent majority.[58]

In the months that remained to the USSR, Nursultan Nazarabaev played a central role in seeking to preserve some form of union, in early September opening a session of the Congress of Peoples' Deputies with a statement from Gorbachev and the leaders of ten republics which put forward a programme for holding the union together on a voluntary basis. All five Central Asian leaders backed the Treaty of Economic Association proposed in October, and even in early December most continued to publicly affirm their commitment to union.[59] All of these hopes were dashed following the meeting of the three Slavic states in Belarus on 8 December which ushered in the creation of the Commonwealth of Independent States (CIS). Though irritated by the lack of consultation, a hastily convened gathering of Central Asian leaders in Ashkhabad recognised that they had little choice but to seek entry, though it was argued that they must be treated as equal and founder members. Moreover, Nazarbaev suggested that any declaration must contain some recognition of the territorial status quo and that member states must commit themselves to a rapid signing of an economic agreement.[60] In consequence, on 21 December 1991 eleven heads of state meeting in Alma Ata signed the declaration setting up the CIS, committing themselves to build democratic, law-governed states whose relations were built on respect for the sovereignty, equality and borders of each, and which would be governed by international norms.[61] In effect over one hundred years of inclusion in a Russian-governed empire had come to an end for Central Asia, though breaking the links developed in these years and making a reality of independence was to prove problematic for all five of these states.

Notes

1   A very cursory account of his speech can be found in *Pravda vostoka*, 25 November 1986.

2   J. Critchlow, *Nationalism in Uzbekistan: A Soviet Republic's Road to Sovereignty* (Boulder, 1991), p. 49.

3   See the discussion in B. Brown, 'Political developments in Soviet Central Asia: Some aspects of the restructuring process in Turkmenistan, Kirgiziya and Kazakhstan', in S. Akiner, ed., *Political and Economic Trends in Central Asia* (London, 1994), pp. 62–74.

4   N. Nazarbaev, *Without Right or Left* (London, 1992), pp. 90–3.

5   See *Pravda vostoka*, 31 January 1986; *Kommunist Tadzhikistana*, 31 August 1986.

6   J. Anderson, *Religion, State and Politics in the Soviet Union and the Successor States* (Cambridge, 1994), pp. 144–5.

7   D. Carlisle, 'Power and politics in Soviet Uzbekistan: From Stalin to Gorbachev', in W. Fierman, ed., *Soviet Central Asia: The Failed Transformation* (Boulder, 1991), pp. 115–16.

8   *Pravda*, 28 February 1986.

9   J. Critchlow, 'Prelude to independence: How the Uzbek party apparatus broke Moscow's grip', in Fierman, *Soviet Central Asia*, pp. 144–6.

10   The future president Nursultan Nazarbaev's account of the December events suggests that the replacement of Kunaev may have been

correct but was achieved by undemocratic means and after absolutely no consultation with the Kazakh elite. Nazarbaev, *Without Right or Left*, pp. 100–4. The fullest documentary record of events and the work of the parliamentary commission can be found in A. Ponomarev and S. Dzhukeeva, eds, *Dokumenty i materialy o sobytiyakh 1986 goda v Kazakhstane* (Moscow, 1993).

11　S. Thompstone, 'Uzbekistan's economic prospects', in Akiner, *Political and Economic Trends*, pp. 102–13.

12　A. Bohr, 'Current trends in Central Asian labour distribution', in Radio Liberty Research, RL508/87, 22 December 1987.

13　A. Sheehy, 'Uzbek cotton harvest falls short of target', in Radio Liberty Research, RL414/85, 12 December 1985.

14　*Pravda*, 31 December 1989.

15　*Pravda*, 20 August 1986.

16　G. Shroeder, 'Nationalities and the Soviet economy', in L. Hajda and N. Beissinger, eds, *The Nationalities Factor in Soviet Politics and Society* (Boulder, 1990), p. 61.

17　B. Rumer, *Soviet Central Asia – A Tragic Experiment* (London, 1989), pp. 178–80.

18　J. Critchlow, 'How solid is Uzbekistan's support for Moscow?', in Radio Liberty, *Report on the USSR*, 10 February 1989.

19　Critchlow, *Nationalism in Uzbekistan*, pp. 29–30.

20　See J. Soper, 'Uzbek purge victims Cholpan and Fitrat finally rehabilitated', and A. Sheehy, 'Rehabilitation of Ismail-Bey Gaspirali, the father of Jadidism', in Radio Liberty Research, RL 28/88, 18 January 1988 and RL 69/88, 12 February 1988.

21　Critchlow, *Nationalism in Uzbekistan*, Chapter 7 on the reassessment of history.

22　*Kazakhstanskaya pravda*, 19 July 1989.

23　*Nauka i religiya*, 1988/4, 43–4.

24　Radio Free Europe/Radio Liberty, *Report on the USSR*, 10 February 1989, 21–2.

25　See *Pravda*, 8 August 1989; on the associated health problems see H. B. Paksoy, ed., *Central Asian Reader* (New York, 1994), pp. 177–83.

26　*Turkmenskaya iskra*, 29 April 1989.

27　B. Brown, 'New political parties in Kazakhstan', Radio Free Europe/ Radio Liberty, *Report on the USSR*, 31 August 1990.

28　For more detail see E. Huskey, 'Kyrgyzstan: The politics of demographic and economic frustration', in I. Bremmer and R. Taras, eds, *Nations and Politics in the Soviet Successor States* (Cambridge, 1993), pp. 404–6.

29　*Komsomolets Uzbekistana*, 30 September 1989; one Russian-speaking Belorussian Sergei Orlov, was coopted on to the *Birlik* council, but he expressed some unease that the organisation might opt for an excessively nationalist programme, especially with regard to language, that might drive Slavs from the republic in the long term. *Komsomolets Uzbekistana*, 16 September 1989.

30 See W. Fierman, 'The Communist Party, *"Erk"*, and the changing Uzbek political environment', *Central Asian Survey*, 10:3, 1991, 55–72.

31 *Russkaya mysl'*, 29 June 1990.

32 For example, student unrest in Dushanbe in late 1987, language rallies in the same city in February 1989 at which some carried anti-Russian and anti-Jewish banners, the use of 'patriotic slogans' by rowdy youths in Ural'sk, Kazakhstan, in May 1989, and during the same month disorders in Nebit Dag and Ashkhabad in Turkmenistan, where cooperatives were looted and anti-Armenian slogans chanted. See *Sotsialisticheskaya industriya*, 18 January 1989; *Kommunist Tadzhikistana*, 24 February 1989; *Pravda*, 3 May 1989 and 12 May 1989 and *Komsomolskaya pravda*, 12 May 1989.

33 See the early reports on events in *Pravda vostoka*, 6 June 1989 and 9 June 1989; *Pravda*, 7 June 1989 and 10 June 1989; *Komsomolskaya pravda*, 7 June 1989; and *Izvestiya*, 8 June 1989 and 9 June 1989.

34 See Uzbek First Secretary Rafik Nishanov's report on the events and their consequences in *Pravda vostoka*, 17 June 1989.

35 *Izvestiya*, 21 June 1989; *Daily Telegraph*, 21 June 1989; Ann Sheehy, 'Inter-ethnic disturbances in Western Kazakhstan', in Radio Free Europe/Radio Liberty, *Report on the USSR*, 7 July 1989.

36 *BBC Summary of World Broadcasts*, SU/0510. B/1-2, 17 July 1989.

37 See *BBC Summary of World Broadcasts*, SU/0718, B/12, 21 March 1990; *Pravda*, 10 May 1990.

38 T. Razakov, *Oshskie sobytiya – na materialakh KGB* (Bishkek, 1993).

39 See the letter from Mohammed Salih arguing that the Fergana events were a provocation but one that played upon real social distress. *Pravda vostoka*, 10 June 1989; on the social background see *Komsomolskaya pravda*, 17 June 1989 and 7 July 1989; *Moskovskie novosti*, 18 June 1989; and Nishanov's report to party activists reported in *Pravda vostoka*, 17 June 1989.

40 Y. Roi, 'Central Asian riots and disturbances, 1989–90: causes and contexts', *Central Asian Survey*, 10:3, 1991, 21–54; a useful account of the Osh events can be found in the Almaty paper *Karavan*, 26 January 1996, which suggests that the Kyrgyz authorities had received security reports indicating the likelihood of violence as early as January 1990 yet had not acted to reduce the possibility.

41 *Pravda vostoka*, 2 August 1989 and 4 November 1989 touches on Uzbek demands and the USSR Council of Ministers' response.

42 Critchlow, *Nationalism in Uzbekistan*, pp. 139–42.

43 *Kommunist Tadzhikistana*, 14 April 1989.

44 See *Pravda vostoka*, 16 April 1989 and 21 July 1989; and on the impact of the language law on Russian speakers in Uzbekistan see *Trud*, 30 October 1989.

45 M. B. Olcott, 'Kazakhstan: a republic of minorities', in Bremmer and Taras, *Nations and Politics*, p. 320.

46 *Pravda vostoka*, 31 May 1989.

47 Extracts from some of these speeches can be found in O. Glebov and J. Crowfoot, eds, *The Soviet Empire – Its Nations Speak Out* (New York, 1989), pp. 137–57.

48 *Pravda vostoka*, 20 May 1989.

49 *Pravda vostoka*, 21 May 1989.

50 *Pravda vostoka*, 23 August 1989.

51 J. Critchlow, 'Obduracy of Uzbek cadres casting shadow on nationalities plenum', in Radio Free Europe/Radio Liberty, *Report on the USSR*, 30 March 1989.

52 Nazarbaev, *Without Right or Left*, p. 121.

53 *Kazakhstanskaya pravda*, 23 and 24 June 1989.

54 See Olcott, 'Kazakhstan: a republic of minorities', p. 324.

55 J. Anderson, 'Saving the union: The Soviet referendum of March 1991', in A. Macartney, ed., *Asking the People: The Referendum and Constitutional Change* (Edinburgh, 1992), pp. 47–53.

56 B. Brown, 'Central Asia: mixed reactions', in Radio Free Europe/Radio Liberty, *Report on the USSR*, 6 September 1991.

57 *Izvestiya*, 2 September 1991 and 17 December 1991; *Pravda*, 2 September 1991 and 9 September 1991.

58 On Kyrgyzstan see *Pravda*, 14 October 1991; on Tajikistan and Kazakhstan see *Izvestiya*, 24 November 1991 and 2 December 1991.

59 *Izvestiya*, 6 December 1991.

60 *Pravda*, 12 December 1991 and 14 December 1991; *Izvestiya*, 12 December 1991.

61 *Izvestiya*, 23 December 1991.

4

Rebuilding the political order[1]

The five states of Central Asia were somewhat reluctant converts to independence, a status that their leaders had sought to forestall in the last months of 1991. Each was acutely aware that making a reality of their new-found freedom would necessitate overcoming a series of problems, from economic reconstruction to nation-building, and that each of these if handled badly could lead to their own loss of power. Given this, they had to make political choices about the type of order that they were to build. Would the preservation of their new-found independence, as well as their personal positions, be best served by the creation of a democratic or an authoritarian order, or something in between? In searching for new models of political development, should they look to their past (traditional or Soviet) for inspiration, to the West, to the Middle East or to Asia? How they responded to these questions is the subject of this chapter, with the first section focusing on the centrality of leadership in shaping the political orders emerging in four of the five Central Asian states – Kazakhstan, Kyrgyzstan, Turkmenistan and Uzbekistan. We then turn to the response of 'civil and political society' to changes taking place within the region, looking at the role of both traditional or 'organic' social networks, and then at the faltering rise of more modern associations such as interest groups and political parties. The third section examines the growing trend of the mid-1990s towards the concentration of political power in executive hands. This in turn raises questions about the nature of the political processes taking place in the region and the chapter concludes with a brief discussion of the dynamic relationship between elite choice, institutional design and political culture in shaping the politics of the new Central Asia. In subsequent chapters we shall examine the ways in which these new (or not so new) political orders have sought to resolve some of the key economic and ethnic problems facing the region.

The importance of leaders

The leaders of the eleven states who came to Alma Ata to form the Commonwealth of Independent States (CIS) on 21 December 1991 pledged themselves to the creation of democratic and law-governed states.[2] Such a commitment was rather hollow in the context of Central Asia where, despite the ready acceptance of democratic rhetoric, political practice rarely conformed to the requirements for 'polyarchy' set out by Robert Dahl and others.[3] Moreover, in this region the crucial role in shaping the new political order during the first few years of independence was to be played by the elites inherited from the collapse of the USSR.

The situation in which the region's leaders came to power was hardly propitious for the emergence of a democratic order in each state. With the partial exception of Kyrgyzstan's President Akaev, all the leaders had risen to power through the nomenklatura and had learned the art of governance within the constraints of the Soviet system. Turkmen President Saparmurad Niyazov had been appointed republican party first secretary by Gorbachev in 1985, whilst Kazakhstan's Nursultan Nazarbaev and Uzbekistan's Islam Karimov had been put in place by the centre in 1989. In two cases the republican leaders at the time of independence had started their rule as compromise candidates: Karimov was a technocrat with no strong political base who, according to Donald Carlisle, was put forward by a Tashkent elite who saw him as controllable,[4] whilst Askar Akaev, an academician, was elected president by the Kyrgyz parliament in October 1990 after it failed to support the officially backed candidature of communist leader Absamat Masaliev.[5]

The traditional and cultural context within which these leaders operated was also less than conducive to democratic rule, though one might contrast Turkmenistan and Uzbekistan, heirs to the emirates of Khiva and Bukhara, with the formerly nomadic areas that came to make up Kazakhstan and Kyrgyzstan. In the latter, at least according to modern myth-makers led by Askar Akaev, there was some tradition of consultation within the community in the context of the tribal assemblies of earlier days. Khiva and Bukhara, on the other hand, were despotic emirates in which the lives of the citizenry was very much in the hands of the ruler and his leading servants. The more psycho-analytically inclined might also want to note that the two most authoritarian leaders, Niyazov and Karimov, were brought up in state orphanages and thus lacked the close tribal and communal links of many of their leading contemporaries. This factor, which may have made them attractive to a Moscow leadership keen to eradicate what it saw as the scourge of tribalism and nepotism, may have required from these leaders harsher patterns of rule if they were to maintain their positions in the post-Soviet era.

In power these leaders presided over considerable continuity in institutions and personnel. The old apparatus of the communist party remained important in Turkmenistan and Uzbekistan. In mid-December 1991 the Turkmen Communist Party held its last congress which saw the creation of the Democratic Party of Turkmenistan (DPT). Proclaiming its commitment to the democratisation of all areas of public life, the DPT was to be open to all citizens and run on the principles of 'electivity, glasnost and collegiality'.[6] Though the leaders of the party claimed that many of its members had never belonged to the old party, in practice the DPT appears to have taken over the same role as the communist party with the additional brief to act as a support agency for the president.[7] Similar developments took place in Uzbekistan where the party became the Peoples' Democratic Party of Uzbekistan (PDPU), though in 1994 the party was to claim that 70 per cent of its 340,000 members had never been members of the communist party.[8] These states witnessed even less change in personnel than the other Commonwealth of Independent States (CIS) states, with very few replacements of bureaucrats at any level and the appearance of many leading party workers within the ranks of the limited private enterprise that emerged in the region. Indeed, one of the remarkable features of Central Asian life in general over the last hundred years or so has been continuity in patterns of rule, despite the cadre policies of the Soviet state. Thus representatives of the Tekke tribe have continued to dominate Turkmen political life throughout the period,[9] whilst members of the Greater Horde have remained dominant in Kazakhstan. These patterns survived Soviet rule and seem set to continue into the independence era, although in Tajikistan a serious challenge to the traditional dominance of the northern

Khojent elites was to lead to a civil war and a partial redistribution of political power.

Central to developments in all these states has been the key role of the chief executive in shaping the emerging political orders, with their preferences reinforced to a considerable degree by the constitutional and institutional choices made by the states during 1992–93. In Turkmenistan and Uzbekistan the option was for authoritarianism, with the former's choice embodied in the personalist rule of President Saparmurad Niyazov. Following the August coup he moved swiftly to consolidate his position, declaring the departyisation of all state institutions and supplanting the power of local soviets with presidential administrators sent in to enforce his will. Following the adoption of a new constitution in May 1992 Niyazov put himself forward for popular election and in an uncontested campaign won 99.5 per cent of the vote. Around the person of the new president there soon emerged a personality cult of Stalinist proportions, as streets, farms and towns were named after the president. Increasingly referred to as *Turkmenbashi* (father or leader of the Turkmen),[10] Niyazov justified his position as meeting the needs of the state for 'in the transition period there must be one leader. Multi-power centres would engender anarchy'.[11]

Like Niyazov, Uzbekistan's Islam Karimov justified his authoritarian rule in terms of the overriding need for political stability in his much larger country. Even though selected as a compromise candidate in mid-1989, Karimov moved swiftly to consolidate his position, replacing nearly 80 per cent of personnel in the republican party apparatus during his first eighteen months in office.[12] At the same time he appointed a leading Tashkent politician Shakrullah Mirsaiddov as his prime minister. In December 1991 he easily won a presidential election with 86 per cent of the vote, as against 12 per cent for his only rival Muhammed Salih, the leader of opposition movement *Erk*. Once Uzbekistan became independent, Karimov turned on the secular and religious opposition, and removed Mirsaiddov, by then his vice-president. This striving for complete control and the removal of opposition was given added impetus by developments in Tajikistan during 1992 which raised the spectre, skilfully used by Karimov, of Islamic 'fundamentalism' threatening the survival of the current regimes in Central Asia.

Kazakhstan's new political order also emerged in part as a response to fears of instability, although these stemmed from ethnic

rather than religious 'threats'. Kazakhstan only declared independence on 16 December 1991 and, as Martha Olcott has pointed out,
previous debates over sovereignty and language laws had alerted
President Nursultan Nazarbaev to the fact that preserving political
and ethnic consensus was likely to prove problematic in the light of
the ethnic make-up of the country and the north–south divide.[13]
Caught between Kazakh nationalists seeking to remove the 'occupiers' and Russians either side of the border openly discussing the
possibility of redrawing existing boundaries so as to take account of
population distribution, Nazarbaev began to preach a mixed political system. Whilst stressing the long-term need for a democratic
polity with a strong civil society, he made clear his belief in the need
for strong executive power capable of opposing vested interests and
ethnic extremism. Following the example of other CIS states he
effectively neutered local soviets, transferring power to presidentially appointed administrators in every oblast.[14] Under this new dispensation there remained some scope for political pluralism, with
the emergence of a range of political parties and interest groups,
many with their own small publications, and formally enjoying considerable freedom of action. At the same time Nazarbaev early on
sought to marginalise critical voices, denouncing both Kazakh and
Russian nationalists as extremists,[15] and putting his weight behind
attempts to create broad-based political movements.

Kyrgyzstan's President Akaev was keenly aware of the vulnerabil-
ity of his republic and its relative unattractiveness to international
investors. Under these circumstances he seems to have taken the
view that only a full-blooded commitment to democratic reconstruction would garner support for his country in the outside world.
In consequence, Kyrgyzstan quickly developed a degree of social
and political pluralism not to be seen in most of the region. With a
lively and often critical press, a multiplicity of political parties and
a parliament which provided an ongoing critique of the president
and those around him, Kyrgyzstan seemed on its way to creating
some semblance of democracy in early 1992. Yet this tiny republic
faced numerous problems, with ethnic and regional differences
underlying many political conflicts, and an economy that declined
more rapidly than that of all but two of the Soviet successor states.
When pluralism failed to bring much substantive change and the
same old bureaucratic faces reappeared in the most important state
and business positions, it was little wonder that the initial euphoria

felt by many of the political classes in Kyrgyzstan rapidly dissipated or that public enthusiasm for democracy remained half-hearted.[16]

These executive inclinations were partially reinforced by the constitutions that were produced during the first two years of independence. The first state to adopt a constitution was Turkmenistan (May 1992), followed by Uzbekistan (December 1992), Kazakhstan (January 1993) and Kyrgyzstan (May 1993). The beleaguered state of Tajikistan took a little longer, adopting its constitution following a referendum in November 1994 – the other four states had used parliament to approve their fundamental laws. In each case the period preceding the adoption of the constitution witnessed a public debate, more heated in Kyrgyzstan and Kazakhstan than in the others, as to the merits of the document or sections of it. Three broad issues raised particularly fierce controversy: the distribution of political power, the status of the Russian language, and the extent to which the new constitutions could guarantee the extensive array of socio-economic rights promised in the old Soviet constitutions. The latter two debates are dealt with elsewhere and our concern here is with the distribution of power.

Formally all the documents described the new constitutional order as based upon a separation of powers, but much of the public discussion focused on the perception that far too much power was being placed in the hands of the head of state. Addressing local officials in November 1992, Kazakh President Nursultan Nazarbaev justified this in terms of 'the transitional character of our epoch, the complexities of the lengthy socio-economic transformation, the huge territory of our state and its ethnic composition'.[17] Not all were convinced by this argument, reminiscent as it was of the views of Russian conservatives through the centuries, and some expressed fears that the concentration of power could be lethal in the wrong hands. There was particular concern that the constitution appeared to place the president above the constitution, with B. Irmukhanov suggesting that Article 85 of the Kazakh draft be reformulated so as to make the constitution rather than the president the guarantor of citizens' rights.[18]

Two issues relating to presidential power raised special concern. In Turkmenistan a number of writers expressed unease over the proposal that judges be appointed by the president and suggested that it might be better to elect them for fixed terms.[19] This was but a part of a wider debate over the judiciary, with fear that the power of the courts, especially that of the constitutional courts, was insufficiently spelled out and that their independence was not properly guaranteed in existing drafts. The second issue related to local administration, where the post-Soviet trend had followed that of other CIS countries in curtailing the powers of local soviets and transferring the power to presidentially appointed prefects in each region and district. In Kazakhstan the draft spoke of the 'appointment or election' of local administrative heads, and a number of letter-writers argued for election as the more democratic means of selecting leaders and one that would guarantee the appointment of genuine defenders of local interests. In addition two parliamentary deputies proposed giving more rights to local soviets, including control over local budgets, as a means of strengthening local democracy.[20]

Many contributors to these debates suggested that the most effective way of constraining potential abuses would be to create strong parliamentary bodies alongside powerful presidencies. This was the argument put forward by activists in Tselinograd who called for a two-chamber parliament made up of elected deputies in the lower house and 'specialists' in the upper house. In this way legislation could be examined by people with both popular legitimacy and expertise.[21] Needless to say, the most vehement proponents of a greater role for parliament were deputies in the existing legislative assemblies. Others, more sceptical about the democratic commitment of the region's legislators, suggested making a reality of people power. In Kyrgyzstan, T. Aleksandrov suggested that in this small republic the requirement that 300,000 signatures be collected to hold a referendum was far too large and that this should be reduced to 100,000. Equally, the number necessary to propose a legislative initiative by parliament should be only 5,000.[22]

Alongside these arguments about presidential power went those of a technical nature relating to the selection of a president. Should there be an age limit, or requirements as to length of residency in the republic? Should the election of a president necessitate a much higher degree of support from the population than was needed for the election of parliamentary deputies? One Kyrgyz writer argued for a 70 per cent turnout from which the winning candidate had to achieve 75 per cent of the vote.[23] Most controversial of all was the debate over whether the president had to be a member of the titular nationality. In Turkmenistan the draft of Article 3 suggested that the head of state 'should be a citizen of Turkmenistan from amongst the Turkmen'.[24] Whilst this phrasing was retained in the Turkmen version, the other states opted to allow any citizen who met certain residency requirements and knew the state language to stand for the highest post.[25]

Whilst the arguments and the motives of those involved varied, as did the possibility of voicing criticism, in all five of the Central Asian republics there emerged a common concern that presidential power was open to abuse and needed to be constrained in some way by the constitutional drafts. The final constitutional texts made few concessions to the critics on the issue of political power. Only Turkmenistan explicitly described the republic as a 'presidential republic' (Article 1), and here extensive powers were given to the holder of the chief executive post. Turkmenistan was also the only state where the president took the position of head of the Council of Ministers (Article 75). Though here and in Uzbekistan there existed formal procedures for removing the president, the controlled nature of the membership of parliamentary or consultative bodies made such a process unlikely.[26]

The Kazakh situation was more complex. Here there was some scope for the exercise of independent prime ministerial power, although the government was described as 'accountable to the president' rather than to parliament. Whilst there was no provision for the impeachment of the president, there was equally no constitutional means for the president to dissolve parliament. Parliament also had the right to approve the budget and confirm presidential appointments. Though balanced in some respects, the constitution did not always do justice to *de facto* presidential dominance in Kazakhstan, which was evident in the later campaign waged by the presidential apparat to persuade the parliament to dissolve itself at the end of 1993.[27] Presidential power was most limited in Kyrgyzstan where, despite the existence of broad presidential powers to appoint the prime minister, determine the structure of the government and appoint other key figures, the validity of such powers depended upon parliamentary approval. Moreover, parliament retained the right to override presidential vetoes provided two-thirds of the deputies agreed.[28]

Civil and political society

Though the leaders of the Central Asian states played a key role in shaping the emerging polities, they, like all but the most repressive regimes, could not do so without taking some account of the wishes and needs of their populations or the relatively small politically active public. Though the concept of legitimacy remains problematic, it is clear that all regimes require some degree of public support if they are to survive. In some cases this may be achieved through coercion, with Turkmenistan and Uzbekistan adopting policies towards opposition movements that render dissent costly to those involved. Economic persuasion can also be used to ensure compliance, as in Turkmenistan where for a while during the early 1990s some categories of the population were offered free utilities and bread. At the same time each of these states has sought to reinforce their position through public consultation, with a whole series of elections and referenda taking place in the years 1991–96. Needless to say, many of these exercises have strayed considerably from the criteria generally associated with democratic elections, and in some cases the bodies elected have acted as rubber stamps for executive decisions. Finally, it might be suggested that political passivity and acceptance of existing regimes stemming from the Soviet era may have been reinforced by traditional political cultures in which deference to leaders, whether central or local, remains the norm and in which there has never been any genuinely participatory politics. For all this, political leaders have had to remain sensitive to and operate within the context of 'civil and political societies', whether 'traditional' or 'modern', and it is with this wider society that we are concerned in this section.

Civil society and the importance of informal politics

At the outset we face a major definitional problem, for many would deny that it is possible to speak of 'civil society' in Central Asia.[29] Writing in the context of democratisation, Larry Diamond has described civil society as 'the realm of organised social life that is voluntary, self-generating, (largely) self-supporting, autonomous from the state, and bound by a legal order or set of shared rules. It is distinct from "society" in general in that it involves citizens acting collectively in a public sphere to express their interests, passions, and ideas, exchange information, achieve mutual goals, make demands on the state, and hold state officials accountable.' He goes on to suggest that its prime role lies in the limitation of state power, although this is a symbiotic rather than a stark conflictual relationship, with the state – at least in a democratic polity – providing the legal framework within which civil society operates.[30] Though most scholars would reject any simple causal relationship between civil society and democratisation, the general assumption is that where the former is strong the chances of the latter occurring are heightened.[31]

Under definitions of this type the former Soviet-dominated countries of Central Asia would appear to lack many of the basic organisations that make up a 'civil society'. From the late 1920s onwards the professional guilds and religious fraternities were destroyed by enforced modernisation and their leading members disappeared into the camps and execution cellars. Yet for all this, by the 1970s and 1980s it was clear that many features of traditional society remained in place, having successfully adapted to Soviet rule. Hence the demolished neighbourhood *mahalla* reappeared in the apartment block, the destroyed mosque in the *chaikana* (tea-shop), and the tribal or clan unit in the context of the collective farm.[32] Indeed, it might be argued that a form of civil society was stronger here than in other parts of the USSR, with the cotton scandals of the early 1980s providing vivid evidence of the ability of traditional networks to thwart central commands. If one of the primary roles of civil society is to act as a buffer between the state and the individual or family unit, one could argue that here, as in the Middle East where tribal, communal or religious solidarities are primary, these seemingly unpropitious networks played a role akin to that ascribed to more modern forms of 'civil society' in the West.[33] Although one might accept Ernest Gellner's point that such groups tend to replace the tyranny of kings with the 'tyranny of cousins',[34] the flourishing world of what Gordon White calls 'traditional civil society' cannot be ignored.[35] In Central Asia such groups remain central to political life at a time when more 'modern' elements of civil society have often failed to develop beyond the dreams of individual activists. Whilst this may change with economic development and the emergence of distinctive social interests, a study of Central Asian politics, at the risk of analytical imprecision, has to take the broader view of what constitutes civil and political society.

Gregory Gleason has pointed out that 'Central Asian politics is the outcome of a highly complex and variegated process in which groups are continually contesting for power, frequently competing for advantage, and sometimes cooperating for mutual advancement'.[36] This struggle involves a wide variety of informal networks at all levels of the political system though their precise political significance is often hard to gauge. Much of this stems from the weak sense of national identity in the region and the fact that most politicians have their roots in distinctive regions or political families. With regard to Uzbekistan, Donald Carlisle and others have documented the ways in which national politics have often centred around rivalries between different regional coalitions. In various essays Carlisle has shown how Uzbekistan was dominated by leaders from a Tashkent–Fergana axis for most of the Stalin years, and then replaced by a new political elite based upon the 'family' of Rashidov which came from the Samarkand region. Such political families built broad-based coalitions and sought to place loyalists in key positions, often using means as traditional as marriage to cement alliances. In the late 1980s Moscow sought to break up this system by sending in a relative outsider, Rafik Nishanov, as first secretary, but he was replaced in mid-1989 by Islam Karimov, a native of Samarkand but one without his own political base. He in turn seems to have been put forward by the Tashkent elite, but once his position was consolidated he began to develop his own connections, in particular seeking to acquire the patronage network of Brezhnevite First Secretary Sharaf Rashidov by rehabilitating the old party boss and many of those involved in the 'cotton affair'. Though Karimov was able to end the political career of the Tashkenter Mirsaiddov in early 1992, later developments – including the sacking of the mayor of Tashkent in 1994 and of the Tashkent oblast governor in early 1995 – suggest that he still had to struggle to impose his will on the capital.[37]

The centrality of 'groupism' in Central Asia has created dilemmas for the new leaders. Aspiring to be head of the whole nation, they nonetheless could ill afford to alienate the informal power networks that play such a key role in regional life. In Turkmenistan President Niyazov has sought to ensure that each region is governed by a member of the locally dominant clan yet at the central level has continued past practice in ensuring that most of the key economic and 'power' ministries go to members of the Tekke tribe.[38] In similar vein Nursultan Nazarbaev's cadre policy has perpetuated the dominance of the Greater Horde, though the decision to move the capital from Almaty to Akhmola in traditional Middle Horde territory may be in part designed to break this trend.[39]

Though publicly criticising the blocking of reform by regional and clan networks, Kyrgyzstan's Askar Akaev has not been immune from the need to utilise regional connections. Lacking a strong political base in either the old communist party or any of the newer parties, he has increasingly made use of his home territory of Naryn oblast, in the mid-1990s developing close ties with an old enemy from the same territory, Brezhnevite First Secretary T. Usubaliev.[40] With the help of the latter's networks, Naryn increasingly turned out Soviet-style majorities for the president in both the presidential election of December 1995 and the constitutional referendum held in February 1996. Simultaneously, in a country where tribal networks are broadly speaking divided into northern and southern groups, Akaev has to a considerable degree followed tradition in appointing representatives of the north to key positions. Amongst the more controversial of these was the selection of the northerner Zh. Rustembekov as the *akim* (governor) of the southern Osh oblast in which there is considerable opposition to the president.[41]

In practice, however, it has often proved difficult for central leaders to impose outside candidates on to existing client patron networks in the regions. In Kyrgyzstan, B. Osmanov served as the head of the Jalalabad administration in the early 1990s but was eventually removed for nepotism in 1992. Yet Osmanov's power remained intact as he built up a small empire, allegedly based on drug trafficking, and in February 1995 the centre was unable to prevent him being returned as a parliamentary deputy in the neighbouring Osh region.[42] Those who attempt to resist the workings of such groups often find themselves in trouble, as happened to the imam of one Naryn oblast mosque. Following substantial donations for the rebuilding of the mosque, Mukash Esenaliev expected the public support of the religious leader when he sought election to the Kyrgyz parliament in February 1995. This was not forthcoming and after he failed to get elected Esenaliev used his influence to persuade the leadership of Kyrgyzstan's Muslims to remove the offending cleric from his post.[43]

The place and salience of these groups is extremely hard for outsiders to assess, but one can draw a broad conclusion that in general these networks are able to control local affairs relatively untouched by the centre so long as they do not mount overt challenges to the leadership of the country. To some extent this is recognised in the functioning of electoral systems, as in Uzbekistan where local administrations have the right to nominate parliamentary candidates alongside political parties. Only when regional bosses appear to have larger political ambitions do they face serious sanctions, as happened to K. Orazov, administrator of the Mari region in Turkmenistan, whose name cropped up too many times in connection with elite conspiracies against Niyazov and who was eventually sacked in March 1996.[44] It also appears that at least in some of these states the dominance of any single grouping or coalition of political 'families' or clans is not permanent, especially in Uzbekistan where the 70 years of Soviet rule appeared to be characterised by periodic alternations of power between regional alliances. What is less clear is how the removal of Moscow, to which rival groups could appeal for support, will affect the informal group politics of the region. More importantly for our purposes, whilst these groups may have served as a buffer, protecting Central Asian society from the deprecations of the old centre, their roots in clan connections and tribalism, by definition exclusionary identities, may not be conducive to the evolution of mature and tolerant democratic orders in which difference and disagreement are accepted as part of everyday political life.[45]

The 'modernisation' of societal politics

Though 'traditional' society continues to play a major role in Central Asian politics, the reforms introduced in the Soviet Union under Gorbachev laid the basis for the emergence of a 'modern' civil society in which citizens have certain guarantees of human rights and the media, interest groups and political parties play a key part. Unfortunately, in most of Central Asia the all-union laws promising these things were rendered irrelevant by the unwillingness of most of the republican leaderships to permit glasnost or liberalisation to go too far. Most retained control of the press up to and through the collapse of the USSR, and in Uzbekistan and Turkmenistan censorship was retained, and alternative media outlets effectively banned. Prior to the adoption of the new constitution in Turkmenistan, articles relating to freedom of the press were removed, leaving the much weaker right of Turkmen citizens 'to receive information, so long as it does not contain state, official or commercial secrets' (Article 26). Questioned on this, Niyazov suggested that 'in the first stage of the transition process we will establish firm control over the media in order not to permit the blazing up of inter-ethnic or tribal conflicts'.[46] Here the press were also to play a key role in the adulation of the president, with a parliamentary decree in August 1994 requiring papers to refer to Niyazov as *Turkmenbashi* or risk a fine.[47] In Uzbekistan the last registered opposition paper was closed in 1992 and since then that republic has been extremely sensitive to criticism of the government from any source. Consequently it has not only controlled its own media outlets but also severely curtailed the access of the population to the information systems of other CIS states.

In Kazakhstan and Kyrgyzstan the situation is more complex. The press in Kazakhastan has developed a critical faculty but one that has been constrained to some degree by self-censorship, government pressure in the form of reminders as to who pays the bills, and occasional heavy-handed hints from officials concerning what can be published and what cannot. Under this oblique form of attack, even the financially independent weekly paper *Karavan* began in 1995 to moderate its critical stance after a fire which destroyed much of its newsprint and which occurred after the paper published acerbic commentary on Nazarbaev's dissolution of parliament. Though the official inquiry blamed the newspaper's staff for failing to meet safety standards, that initiated by the paper suggested sabotage.[48]

Of all the republics Kyrgyzstan maintained the liveliest press after the collapse of the USSR, with even the official newspaper *Slovo kyrgyzstana* (formerly *Sovetskaya kirgiziya*) providing fairly broad coverage of different political viewpoints during the early 1990s. During 1994, however, pressures on the press mounted, with the parliamentary newspaper *Svobodny gory* ('Free Mountains') arousing official ire for its attacks on the president as well as for publishing articles that some saw as anti-semitic. In August 1994 the paper was closed down by a regional court on the grounds that it had carried articles insulting to foreign heads of state (of Israel and China) with which Kyrgyzstan had friendly relations. At around the same time Akaev created a body to oversee the media and ensure that it reported 'responsibly', and this body, eventually abolished in

1996,[49] occasionally warned journalists not to write on certain themes.[50] In 1995 it was the turn of the independent Russian language weekly *Res publika* to come under attack when two of its journalists were charged with libel for suggesting the president had houses in Switzerland and Turkey. The journalists were found guilty and given suspended prison sentences, and the paper temporarily became more circumspect, though in late 1995 it printed an article by Vladimir Zhirinovsky which repeated the offending allegations, and during the presidential election campaign in December it maintained a sharp campaign of criticism of the ways in which the electoral process was being manipulated.

In addition to a wide dissemination of information, a healthy civil society is generally thought to include a broad array of groups capable of articulating public interests outside the channels provided by political parties. Little research has been done into such groups in Central Asia, but it is quite clear that as with the media, the development of an associational life is at an embryonic stage. In the later years of perestroika there emerged a number of issue-oriented groups concerned with ecological matters, charity, religion, culture and so forth, which made some demands upon the system.[51] Yet despite provisions for formal recognition, such groups have enjoyed very little exposure or influence in Turkmenistan and Uzbekistan. Throughout the region it is also generally the case that many of the grandly titled committees, organisations and confederations are little more than a room in an apartment manned by an enthusiastic political entrepreneur.

In both Kazakhstan and Kyrgyzstan there are emerging business groups, free trade unions, movements to defend the interests of specific nationalities and professional associations. In Kyrgyzstan a total of 258 social organisations had been registered by the Ministry of Justice by early 1993, a figure that had doubled two years later. Amongst these were to be found 15 political parties or movements, 46 professional associations, 21 'national-cultural' organisations, 41 sporting organisations and 17 creative organisations, though how many of these were functioning or significant public movements is less clear.[52] In all five states the law provides for the creation of trade unions, yet in practice such bodies face considerable problems. In Uzbekistan and Kazakhstan the old official Soviet trade unions still dominate the industrial scene, with membership dues still being deducted in state enterprises. In Kazakhstan and

Kyrgyzstan there have been partially successful attempts to create independent unions, but in Kazakhstan only a small percentage of workers appear to belong. Typical actions in Kazakhstan have included strikes and sit-ins, especially in the mining industry where nearly every year since independence has seen periods during which miners have not been paid for months on end. In Kyrgyzstan the Federation of Trade Unions has been highly critical of government policies, in particular privatisation, and of the dramatic fall in the living standards of most workers. In Kyrgyzstan the activities of trade unions appear to be more acceptable than in other parts of the region and they are able to make demands upon enterprises and strike where they deem it appropriate.[53] For all this, bodies such as trade unions and business associations remain embryonic, with the interests they claim to represent being far from clearly defined and their place in the new order not being fully institutionalised.

If civil society is poorly organised, political society as represented by modern political parties is in no stronger a position. In three of the states (Kazakhstan, Kyrgyzstan and Uzbekistan) presidents have repeatedly stressed the importance of such organisations, and the law allows for their registration and role as nominating agencies during elections, but in practice they have been slow to develop. In Turkmenistan efforts to create overtly political organisations faltered during the late 1980s under government repression. Although leaders of groups such as *Azgybirlik* (Unity) have been able to make contacts with foreign human rights delegations, they have failed to make an impact upon a largely indifferent population. Since 1992 opposition activity has largely been confined to a few activists in Moscow, although demonstrations in Ashgabat during July 1995 suggested that the population was not entirely passive.[54] With the repression of opposition, the only political parties active in Turkmenistan remain the official Democratic Party of Turkmenistan and a regime-backed Peasant Party which registered with the authorities in the autumn of 1992.

A similar situation prevails in Uzbekistan where the regime clamped down upon opposition groups whilst sponsoring a number of other political parties. As already noted, the late perestroika years witnessed the emergence of a variety of political movements in Uzbekistan, of which the most significant were *Birlik*, founded in late 1998 by a group of Uzbek intellectuals, and *Erk* which broke away from it in early 1990. Despite the fact that *Erk*'s chairman

Muhammed Salih was permitted to run against Karimov in the presidential elections of December 1991, Uzbek independence quickly brought to an end the quasi-legal existence of these parties.[55] *Birlik*'s registration was revoked by the Uzbek Supreme Court in early 1993 and its leaders soon driven into exile. Arrests, beatings and imprisonment were meted out to leading members of the dissenting organisations, and in July 1993 six members of the two groups were tried for attempting to create a parallel national parliament.[56] More recently there have been attempts to create a united opposition movement, with disgraced former Vice-President Shakhrullo Mirsaiddov setting up an opposition coordinating centre in Tashkent at the end of 1995, but it seems unlikely that the authorities will tolerate any significant political involvement on its part.[57] All of these efforts have been hampered by a law which requires that there are 3,000 members and an official address prior to registration, something that is easily preventable in a country where the government still controls property ownership and intimidation of dissenters is the norm. At the same time the law denies registration to religiously based political parties, and this excludes the Islamic Renaissance Party and other similar movements. Though mid-1996 witnessed some talk of improvement in the Uzbek human rights record, there was still little sign of Karimov permitting the evolution of genuine opposition parties.

Of the various registered political parties by far the most important is the Peoples' Democratic Party of Uzbekistan, which in the December 1994 parliamentary elections nominated 69 of the 167 elected deputies. The only other party which contested the elections was the Fatherland Progress Party, set up with President Karimov's approval to give the semblance of opposition, and which eventually gained 14 seats – the rest of the elected deputies were nominated by local councils. Following the election, however, two other parties were formed. The Social Democratic Party of Uzbekistan – *Adolat* (Justice) – was formed, quickly gaining around 47 of the deputies nominated by local councils, and the National Revival Party was also started up, with a smaller number of deputies adhering to this. The former quite deliberately took the name of two earlier movements called *Adolat*, the Islamic militia whose activities in the Namangan region had been crushed by Karimov in early 1992, and a second movement of this name set up earlier by Mirsaiddov.[58] In consequence there was created what appeared to be a multi-party system though in practice each provided solid backing for the regime.

Kazakhstan provides a more complex example, with the emergence of numerous parties independent of the government, but with few showing signs of evolving into serious political organisations. Various types of parties have emerged. First, those whose origins lie in the old communist system, notably the Socialist Party which declared itself the reformed heir, and a new Communist Party of Kazakhstan, also claiming the apostolic succession. The latter was denied registration by the authorities until March 1994 on the grounds that it did not accept the new constitutional order and hankered after the old union, with similar suspicions in April 1996 leading to renewed calls for the banning of the party.[59]

Alongside these have emerged a number of nationalist movements and parties, including: *Azat*, committed to a complete decolonisation of Kazakhstan, and combating Russia's imperial mentality, but subject to various splits during the early 1990s; and *Jeltoqsan* and *Alash*, which at various points have advocated the voluntary repatriation of non-Kazakhs, the use of Kazakh as the sole language of communication, and the closure of Russian bases. Whilst *Jeltoqsan* and *Alash* have sometimes put forward pan-Turkic views, *Alash* has also tended to stress the Islamicisation of Kazakhstan to a greater extent than other parties. These bodies, seen by President Nazarbaev as extremist in nature, have found it hard to break through the hurdles facing parliamentary representation and have largely been confined to gesture politics. Enjoying more support have been movements representing the interests of the substantial Russian population which feels under threat in the new Kazakhstan. Their views have been articulated by a number of groups, notably *Lad* which has adopted a more conciliatory approach, stressing the traditional good relations of Kazakhs and Russians. A more provocative position has been taken by the various Cossack groups, notably the Semirechie organisation, at whose meetings suggestions about incorporating the northern territories into Russia can sometimes be heard.

Kazakhstan has also witnessed several attempts to create presidential parties such as the Popular Congress of Kazakhstan sponsored by Nazarbaev and chaired by poet Olzhas Suleimenov and Mukhtar Shakhanov. Designed as a centrist party seeking to appeal to all ethnic groups, the movement increasingly came to be seen as a vehicle for the political ambitions of Suleimenov. The president in turn shifted his backing to the Union of Popular Unity of Kazakhstan (SNEK) and expressed the hope that its creation would engender the emergence of a second opposition party with a clear programme and ideas.[60] Yet none of these movements have evolved into recognisable political parties with extensive organisation throughout the country, programmatic aims or distinctive social bases. The same could probably said of the new wave of parties created in the build-up to the tightly controlled parliamentary elections of December 1995. The most significant of these was the Democratic Party of Kazakhstan, another party supported by the president, which gained 12 seats in the new two-chamber, 102-seat parliament – as opposed to SNEK's 24.[61]

Kyrgyzstan has a similar range of parties, many of them originating in the political activism of the late Gorbachev years. In 1989 a squatters movement which seized land for homeless people around Bishkek took organisational form in Ashar. May 1990 saw representatives of 24 groups meet to form an umbrella organisation, the Democratic Movement 'Kyrgyzstan' (DDK). Formed as a movement, and not becoming a party until 1993, the DDK called for the creation of a sovereign Kyrgyzstan based upon democracy and the free market. In practice, however, it proved an uneasy coalition, undermined from one side by the election of Akaev as president, who promptly took over many of its ideas, and on the other by the ambitions of its chairman T. Turgunaliev. In February 1991 he and O. Tekebaev left to form *Erkin Kyrgyzstan*, a nationalist group which sometimes took a strongly anti-Russian position on issues such as landownership. This organisation split again the following year with Tekebaev creating the more centrist *Ata Meken* party which has expressed its willingness to offer critical support to the government. Alongside these groups one should mention *Asaba*, a fairly radical Kyrgyz nationalist movement formed in 1990, and *Osh Aimagy* (never a registered party), the extremist group of Kyrgyz youth that was involved in the bloody events in Osh during 1990 and which in early 1992 could be heard calling for the creation of armed militias in every village near the Uzbek border to repel the threat of attack.[62]

Despite the rise of various nationalist movements, the strongest single party appears to have remained the revived Communist Party. Claiming 25,000 members in 1994, the party inherited a tradition of organisation and an elite from the Soviet period. In a series of interviews in 1993 leaders of the party developed a critique of the government and its reforms based on the suggestion that the head-long rush for international finance and the creation of a capitalist economy had led to some of the more positive elements of the past being thrown out. For example, why break up large collective farms that were continuing to be more productive than their smaller counterparts in Turkey or Iran? And, adopting a nationalist stance, how could the passing of economic decision-making to the International Monetary Fund (IMF) and other institutions be reconciled with the desire for Kyrgyz sovereignty?[63] By late 1995, under the restored leadership of former First Secretary Absamat Masaliev, the party was to take over 20 per cent of the vote in the presidential elections, despite the best efforts of the incumbent's staff to limit its appeal.

To the nationalist and communist parties one might add various 'modern' parties taking a centrist position and seeking to represent specific interests. Amongst these could be found the Republican Peoples' Party, the Party of Unity of Kyrgyzstan, the Democratic Party of Women, two agrarian parties, two social democratic parties and the moderate Slavic movement *Soglasie* which sought to improve the position of Russians within the republic and thus persuade them to stay.[64] None of these can be described in depth here, but it should be noted that few of the parties mentioned have succeeded in developing mass followings and only one, the Social Democratic Party (SDK) of Kyrgyzstan which is made up largely of regional administrators and businesspeople, gained more than a handful of deputies in the February 1995 parliamentary elections.[65] Though a number of additional parties emerged following this contest there is as yet no evidence to suggest that they will fare any better than existing organisations.

For all the parties sprouting up across Central Asia a proper party system has failed to develop in any of the five countries, something that can be accounted for by reference to four key factors. First, the attitude of the republican elites. In three of the states genuine alternative parties and movements have been simply prohibited upon various specious grounds. In Kazakhstan and Kyrgyzstan the respective presidents have frequently spoken of the need to develop a mature party system and have expressed their concern about its failure to develop. Less clear is whether they would in practice welcome the emergence of one or more strong, well-organised political parties. Moreover, it might be argued that their inclination to stand above the political fray and not contribute substantially to the creation of presidential parties has served to undermine party development.

Secondly, one must look to the parties themselves. Most started life as the creation of a strong personality, often with roots in a specific region of the country. Lacking strong or distinctive ideological programmes, they depend upon the appeal of the individual or upon their roots in specific geographical localities. Many also originated amongst the intellectuals of capital cities and failed to generate proper organisation throughout the country at large. Nearly all have been prone to schism as dominant individuals alienate others and personal ambitions prevent broad coalition-building of the sort necessary to create successful modern political parties.

Thirdly, in pursuing their aims parties are not helped by public opinion which is by and large suspicious of political organisations. Nancy Lubin's survey of attitudes in Uzbekistan and Kazakhstan showed that even those committed to democracy saw 'order' as one of the most important political values, with 40 per cent of 'democrats' in Uzbekistan and 30 per cent in Kazakhstan believing that opposition groups should be limited or banned.[66] Even where parties are free to organise, as in Kyrgyzstan, opinion polls suggest that they have made little impact upon the public consciousness. A succession of polls carried out during 1994 revealed that in the forthcoming elections from 14 per cent to 19 per cent of those surveyed had no intention of voting and that from 36 per cent to 49 per cent would have difficulty in choosing a party. In February of that year only the communists, with 21.6 per cent, were backed by a significant proportion of the population, and by September their prospective vote had fallen to 9.45 per cent, closely followed by the moderate nationalist *Ata Meken* (Fatherland) Party with 8.65 per cent. Particularly striking in the latter poll was the fact that 67.9 per cent had no clear party identification. Moreover, these republican figures disguised considerable regional variations, for whilst in the Naryn oblast just over 60 per cent did express support for specific parties in September, in the capital Bishkek just under 20 per cent could link themselves to a party.[67] And these figures appear to have been borne out by the February 1995 elections in this republic in which only about a third of the elected deputies were associated with political parties.

Finally, one would have to point to institutional design as a major factor inhibiting party development. Though each state has opted for single member constituencies and majority requirements in elections, a system said to favour the simplification of party systems as political movements are forced to create broad-based coalitions if victory is to be achieved, this has in fact not happened in Central Asia. This failure, partially explainable in terms of the continued strength of traditional networks, may also stem from the creation of heavily presidential systems. With legislatures as largely ineffectual bodies there is little incentive to acquire control over them on the part of coherent and disciplined parties. Instead they are treated as simply arenas for self-aggrandisement, whether individual or communal. There have been some attempts to overcome this. The Kazakh electoral law produced prior to the 1995 elections required political parties which wished to contest the election to submit a list of 3,000 signatures which had to come from a minimum of 11 out of 19 regions of the country. Though this could be seen as an attempt to squeeze out opposition parties, in a freer electoral context it could potentially contribute towards the creation of more significant, nationally organised, political parties.[68] Meanwhile in Kyrgyzstan one party leader has suggested that in order to create a proper, preferably two-party system, there should be a poll, with the top two parties in the poll being given state financial backing to develop proper organisational and campaigning structures.[69] For all these debates, as of mid-1996 there remains little indication that coherent party systems were about to emerge in Central Asia.

The growth of executive power

For most citizens of Central Asia formal political participation has been limited to voting in a series of consultative exercises carried out in the mid-1990s. Of these there have been a remarkably large number, including six parliamentary elections, three presidential elections, four referenda on constitutional change, three referenda on extending presidential mandates beyond the constitutionally allotted term, and one *de facto* vote of confidence in the president. Yet inevitably, given what we have already said about the authoritarian nature of politics in much of the region, few of these consultative exercises have resembled free elections. Parliamentary elections held in Turkmenistan in December 1994 saw 50 candidates contest the same number of seats. A similar exercise at the same time in Uzbekistan saw formal contestation, with 634 people contesting 250 places, but in practice all candidates required governmental approval. Both republics have also held referenda on extending the incumbent president's term of office. Due to face re-election in 1997, Niyazov was granted an extension of his term of office until 2002 in a vote in which only 212 people were said to have voted against the proposal.[70] In March 1995 his example was followed by Islam Karimov who also received near-unanimous endorsement from the population.

In Kazakhstan and Kyrgyzstan, on which the rest of this chapter largely concentrates, the situation is more complex. In these republics there remains a formal commitment to pluralism, but this is one which increasingly seems to be taking second place to the needs of nation-building and official perceptions of stability. Though parliamentary elections, and in Kyrgyzstan presidential elections, have generally entailed some degree of contestation, none have matched up to the requirements of genuinely free contests. In all of these cases there were criticisms of the activities of official electoral commissions which acted to prevent the registration of undesirable candidates and were often said to favour those approved by the centre. During the Kyrgyz presidential elections would-be contenders faced considerable difficulty in acquiring the signatures necessary to stand, as local officials obstructed signature collection or refused to verify those collected. On occasions the electoral law put obstacles in the way of candidates, as in Kazakhstan's December 1995 parliamentary poll when contenders had to put up a non-refundable deposit equivalent to 100 times the minimum monthly wage. Other complaints made during the course of these campaigns including gerrymandering so as to exclude opposition or Russian candidates in Kazakhstan, and in both countries exclusion of the opposition from the media, intimidation, bribery, proxy voting by heads of household, voting by dead souls, and inadequate supervision of the count. In addition the increasingly Soviet-style high turnouts were hard to take seriously, especially given earlier opinion polls suggesting voter apathy and the informal reports of observers who recorded low turnouts at some polling stations.[71]

These were clearly not the 'founding elections' that have played such a key role in democratic transitions elsewehere, for they failed to produce legislative bodies that played a central part in shaping the new political order. In addition they produced assemblies that were extremely unrepresentative in the sense that in each case those elected were predominantly male, over-educated and from the indigenous nationality[72] – though in this they differed little from most of the world's legislatures. Nor did they produce powerful decision-making bodies for, as already noted, key policy-making powers were vested in the presidents of Turkmenistan, Uzbekistan and increasingly in Kazakhstan and Kyrgyzstan by the middle of the 1990s. Instead their function should be seen in terms of affirmation, mobilisation and legitimisation of the emerging executive-dominated political orders. The high turnouts produced in presidential elections and plebiscites reflected a desire to be seen to have whole-hearted popular support but may also have genuinely reflected a popular view in these predominantly rural countries that society required strong leadership. There is also the possibility that these elections reflected an informal deal between central and regional interests, with the latter accepting the dominant presidency in exchange for electoral contests which witnessed the return of the leaders or representatives of key patronage networks to parliamentary bodies. These people could then use access to influence in the capital in the interests of 'their' people and at one level the elections could thus be seen as representative insofar as they mirrored the existing distributions of power in the region.[73]

Only in Kazakhstan and Kyrgyzstan were parliamentary bodies created that developed any semblance of independence. In the former republic the old Soviet-era parliament was dissolved in late 1993 following a campaign by the presidential apparatus to persuade deputies to surrender their mandates. New elections were called for March 1994 and it seemed that Nazarbaev was seeking to ensure a more compliant legislature. The electoral commissions acted to limit the number of opposition candidates and 42 of the 177 deputies were to be elected via a presidential list in which all the candidates were approved by the head of state. At the opening session of the new parliament Nazarbaev called on deputies to remember that they represented the country as a whole, not regional or vested interests, and urged them to develop a constructive relationship with the government.[74] Yet at the same session the deputies passed a resolution of no-confidence in Prime Minister

Sergei Tereshchenko's government, and in October continued parliamentary sniping, along with the poor economic performance of the government, led Nazarbaev to ask for his prime minister's resignation.[75] Thus there was a situation in which a body elected with the approval of the president took on a life of its own, not just in defence of vested interests but also in representing, however imperfectly, the very real grievances of a population hit hard by economic decline. In the face of this situation, Nazarbaev, after a brief show of reluctance, was to welcome the March 1995 decision of the Constitutional Court which rendered the elections of the previous year invalid and ended the existence of the parliament.[76]

Though some deputies promised resistance to what they saw as an unconstitutional move, their proposed hunger strike met with public apathy and soon petered out. Nazarbaev's response was to call for a new constitutional settlement, though he was to rule by decree until such an arrangement could be made. In practice this entailed the speedy issuing of much of the legislation that had been blocked by parliament and a move towards curbing opposition activity in the shape of a decree tightening up the procedures for holding public meetings.[77] At the end of April 1995 Nazarbaev followed the example of his Turkmen and Uzbek colleagues in holding a referendum on the extension of presidential power until the end of the century – he was due to face re-election in 1996 – and this proposal was duly approved by a large percentage of the population.[78]

With his legitimacy formally strengthened, the Kazakh president put forward a completely new constitutional draft. Although described as being based upon the constitution of the French Fifth Republic, the document in fact created an extremely powerful presidency which would not have to face the numerous parliamentary, societal and other informal curbs evident in France. The final draft gave the president extensive powers, including the right to appoint the prime minister and other senior governmental figures, to be given law making powers for up to a year by parliament, to dissolve the legislature, and to appoint 7 of the 47 members of the new Senate. A new bicameral parliament was created, the 55-seat Majlis and 47-seat Senate, but its powers were limited in effect to the processing of legislation. Though there were provisions for the impeachment of the president, this required an initial vote by one-third of the lower house, then majorities in both houses, a ruling by the Supreme Court, and then a 75 per cent majority in both houses

sitting together. If the motion was defeated, those deputies who initiated the impeachment process would lose their seats. Other
changes included the replacement of the Constitutional Court with
a Constitutional Council, and a redefinition of the status of Russian
which was now able to be used as an official (still not a state) language in central and local administration. This document was put to
the people in a referendum on 31 August 1995 and approved by
89.14 per cent of the 90.58 per cent of the population taking part.[79]
Three months later elections were held to the new parliamentary
bodies – those to the Senate on the basis of two representatives
chosen by local authority members in each oblast, and those to the
lower house on a single member constituency basis. Though it is
perhaps too early to assess the significance of this body, and despite
its brief resistance to a pension bill proposed by the government in
June 1996,[80] early indications suggest that the new body will provide the president with the more supportive assembly he appears to
desire. Indeed, in his opening speech to the parliament Nazarbaev
gave strong hints that if it failed to do so he would have no hesitation in dissolving parliament.

Constitutional revision has also been on the agenda in Kyrgyzstan
since late 1994. Having engineered the dissolution of his old parliament President Akaev went to the population in October 1994 to
seek approval for the creation of a smaller, professional two-chamber parliament. Following the acceptance of this he summoned a
constitutional convention drawing in representatives of all parts of
the country, political parties and social organisations. Here Akaev
argued that developing democracy in Central Asia was proving
problematic and suggested that Kyrgyzstan would have to go
through a lengthy period of proto-democracy in which the transformation of all spheres of life would take time to develop. Deny-
ing the claims of his critics that he was acquiring ever more powers,
he pointed to the various checks on his position set out in the constitution. Nonetheless he felt that circumstances dictated certain
changes to the constitutional order in a number of areas, relating to
the powers of the president, the position of the legislature, the language issue and private property. He then proposed the speedy
holding of elections to a two-chamber parliament, in which the 35-
member Legislative Assembly would possess the right to legislate,
amend the constitution and impeach the president, and in which the
70-seat Peoples' Assembly would possess broader rights to oversee

the broad lines of state policy and its implementation, and approve the appointment of the prime minister. Taken from parliamentary deputies, however, were their 1993 constitutional rights to approve the appointment of ministers chosen by the prime minister and the determination of the broad lines of domestic and foreign policy, tasks now said to reside with the president. In addition Akaev proposed creating a higher court which could resolve differences between the two chambers and could on the demand of the constitutional court decree the dissolution of parliament.[81]

These proposals, slightly amended, were put to the public for discussion in early January 1995 with public debate to last for a month, to be followed by redrafting and then approval by the new parliament scheduled to be elected on 5 February.[82] This hope was thwarted by the problems that arose following these elections involving numerous charges of irregularity. In addition many, including the president, felt that the electoral system favoured the old elites, regional bosses and criminal elements, whilst leaving ethnic minorities and women severely under-represented. More importantly, the election created new constitutional dilemmas. Of these the most important was the fact that the functioning 1993 constitution made no provision for a two-chamber parliament, an omission which allowed the two bodies to slide into bitter wrangling over their respective spheres of influence and authority. This persistent failure to agree, accompanied by a growing public perception, carefully fostered by presidential spokespersons, that many deputies were only interested in their own privileges, led Akaev to speak of the need for more substantive constitutional changes aimed at increasing his own powers. Following parliamentary rejection of an attempt to extend his mandate, Akaev called a new presidential election for the end of December. Following a brief campaign in which opposition candidates complained of prejudicial media coverage and manipulation of the results, Akaev was reported re-elected with 71.5 per cent of the vote. Though a substantial majority for the president, closer analysis of the results pointed to the ongoing problem of regionalism in Kyrgyz political life, as communist leader A. Masaliev was able, even according to official figures, to garner nearly 50 per cent of the vote in the southern Osh region. This region was proving increasingly resentful of the northern dominance of Kyrgyz politics and was also sceptical about the economic reform programme favoured by the president.[83]

Nonetheless, Akaev took this vote as giving him the authority to push through his ideas on constitutional change. New draft proposals published in the republic's press in January 1996 envisaged a shift in the balance of power between president and parliament. Under these proposals the head of state would be given the power to appoint and retire the government, to appoint judges at all levels and, with the support of the parliament, to appoint people to other key posts such as the head of the procuracy and the constitutional court. Though parliamentary approval was still required for the appointment of the prime minister, if the deputies rejected the president's choice three times he could dissolve the legislature. In addition the president was given the broad right to determine the main outlines of foreign and domestic policy.[84] All this was justified on the grounds that parliament had persistently failed to get on with the task of legislation. For Akaev's critics, these moves, when taken together with the flawed presidential election, the harassment of journalists and the arrest of several opposition activists, signalled a slide towards dictatorship.[85] Supporters of the president rejected this charge, noting that Akaev still had less powers than virtually any other president in the Commonwealth of Independent States (CIS) and stressing that for all these changes parliamentary laws remained superior to presidential decrees.[86] Whatever the arguments, the proposed changes were put to the electorally weary population of Kyrgyzstan on 10 February 1996 and, to nobody's surprise, acquired the support of a massive 94.5 per cent majority of the 96.5 per cent turning out on the day.[87]

Conclusion

Political developments in Central Asia have centred around the relationship between the aspirations of individual leaders, the imperatives of the social structure as evident in the role of informal power networks, and the strivings of 'modern' political society to emerge as a key player in the political system. Each of these has in turn been shaped by the region's heritage, both customary and Soviet, as well as by the context within which the states of Central Asia gained their independence. In particular, the role of leaders has been enhanced by the fact that sovereignty did not come as a result of popular pressure but instead stemmed from the collapse of a larger

empire. Morover, unlike the British in India who, however imperfectly, utilised democratic rhetoric and experimented with native
self-rule prior to independence, Central Asia's Moscow overseers
did little to prepare regional elites for the possibility of self-government, let alone democratic rule. Inheriting a situation of economic
decline and with considerable potential for ethnic conflict as
revealed by outbreaks of communal violence at the end of the Soviet
era, it was hardly surprising that strong central power was to prove
attractive to Central Asian presidents.

One consequence of this perception of the need for strong leadership was the institutionalisation of political systems in which the
president was given extensive powers to shape domestic and foreign
policies, though this may be storing up problems for the future. As
Juan Linz and others have suggested, presidential systems are
inclined to undermine the prospects of democratic development,[88]
though one might suggest that other non-institutional factors have
played a more important role in this region in undermining the
prospects for political pluralism. Nonetheless, it might be argued
that by concentrating power current leaders are undermining their
formal long-term commitment to democracy by habituating the
next generation of political leaders, most of whom will have been
politically educated in independent states, to authoritarianism as a
normal pattern of rule.

Such a pessimistic conclusion would seem to be reinforced by
other features of the region's political system, notably the role of
traditional society which, though providing a buffer against
Moscow's rule, may now encourage exclusivist attitudes intolerant
of others amongst regional or tribal groups who may be seeking
control of the state apparatus. At present there seems to be a sort of
informal deal emerging between the executive and local patronage
networks in many Central Asian states, as the latter are permitted
access to the 'pork barrel' so long as they maintain loyalty and political control of their regions – a relationship not unlike that between
the old Politburo in Moscow and republican first secretaries in the
region. At the same time, heads of state are seeking gradually to
wear down this independence in their efforts to create a sense of
national unity and belonging. Less clear is how much of this is a conscious effort on the part of elites at various levels of the political
system, or how much of it is simply a natural consequence of the situation they find themselves in. That is, the potential for instability

appears to require strong leadership, and this is reinforced by what some regional leaders (and Samuel Huntington) have seen as 'Asian values' which stress community over the individual and consensus over competition. Equally important, strong leadership may be the only way in which vested interests can be tackled and economic reform, to the extent which it is desired, pushed through. Yet should this effort be successful, regional leaders may find, as did their colleagues amongst the 'Asian tigers', that economic change has political consequences. For example, in the latter states, reform created a more complex economy with a richer associational life rooted in distinctive social interests. Such groups in turn began to agitate for political liberalisation and reform, and eventually their systems did begin to change.[89] Whether this scenario might develop in Central Asia, however, is questionable as it is not entirely clear that regional leaders have a very good understanding of the Asian examples to whch they so often refer. At the same time the region continues to face enormous political, economic and inter-ethnic problems, and our concern in Chapters 5, 6 and 7 is to move from speculation about the future evolution of the Central Asian polity to examining how the political systems created in the early 1990s sought to deal with some of these issues.

Notes

1   This chapter draws heavily on J. Anderson, 'Pseudo-elections and political development in Central Asia', *Journal of Communist Studies and Transition Politics* (forthcoming).

2   *Izvestiya*, 23 December 1991.

3   For Robert Dahl there are seven minimal requirements for the establishment of 'polyarchy': elected officials, free and fair elections, inclusive suffrage, the right to run for office, freedom of expression, alternative information and associational autonomy. *Democracy and its Critics* (New Haven and London, 1989), pp. 220–2.

4   D. Carlisle, 'Geopolitics and the ethnic problems of Uzbekistan and its neighbours', in Y. Roi, ed., *Muslim Eurasia – Conflicting Legacies* (London, 1995), pp. 80–1.

5   Tass, 29 October 1990.

6   *Turkmenskaya iskra*, 7 January 1992.

7   *Nezavisimaya gazeta*, 16 November 1994.

8   *Pravda vostoka*, 30 June 1994.

9   See the interview with exiled Turkmen Foreign Minister Avdy Kuliev in *Transition*, 2:10, 17 May 1996, 34–8.

10 *Turkmenskaya iskra*, 2 October 1992.

11 *Moskovskie novosti*, 31 January 1993.

12 D. Carlisle, 'Power and politics in Soviet Uzbekistan: From Stalin to Gorbachev', in W. Fierman, ed., *Soviet Central Asia: The Failed Transformation* (Boulder, 1991), p. 118.

13 See the discussion in M. B. Olcott, 'Kazakhstan: A republic of minorities', in I. Bremmer and R. Taras, eds, *Nations and Politics in the Soviet Successor States* (Cambridge, 1993), especially pp. 322–5.

14 In a speech to local administrators in March 1992 Prime Minister Sergei Tereshchenko described their role as the implementation of government policy and presidential decrees, however unpopular, and pushing through reform. *Kazakhstanskaya pravda*, 11 March 1992.

15 For reports on Nazarbaev's attitudes to political parties see *Nezavisimaya gazeta*, 20 February 1993 and 9 June 1993.

16 For a general overview see I. Pryde, 'Kyrgyzstan: The trials of independence', *Journal of Democracy*, 5:1, 1994, 111–20.

17 *Kazakhstanskaya pravda*, 11 November 1992.

18 *Kazakhstanskaya pravda*, 4 July 1992.

19 *Turkmenskaya iskra*, 4 April 1992 and 14 April 1992.

20 *Kazakhstanskaya pravda*, 8 July 1992; *Nezavisimaya gazeta*, 8 December 1992; for similar concerns in Turkmenistan see *Turkmenskaya iskra*, 16 April 1992.

21 *Kazakhstanskaya pravda*, 15 August 1992; others argued for smaller, professional parliaments with strong committee structures and clearly defined relataions with the executive. *Kazakhstanskaya pravda*, 12 September 1992.

22 *Slovo kyrgyzstana*, 12 February 1993.

23 *Slovo kyrgyzstana*, 24 February 1993.

24 *Turkmenskaya iskra*, 4 April 1992.

25 For example, in Kyrgyzstan the residency period was 15 years and in Uzbekistan, 10 years.

26 For the texts of the constitutions see *Turkmenskaya iskra*, 19 May 1992; *Konstitutsiya respubliki uzbekistana* (Tashkent, 1992).

27 *Konstitutsiya respubliki Kazakhstana* (Alma Ata, 1993).

28 *Slovo kyrgyzstana*, 21 May 1993.

29 See the discussion in chapters on Central Asia by Roger Kangas, Patricia Carley and Rachat Achylova in V. Tismaneau, ed., *Political Culture and Civil Society in Russia and the New States of Eurasia* (New York, 1995), pp. 271–366.

30 L. Diamond, 'Towards democratic consolidation', *Journal of Democracy*, 5:3, 1994, 5–7.

31 'Both political institutionalisation and the progress of liberal economic reform have been most impressive in those countries where civil society is the most robust'. M. Steven Fish, 'Russia's fourth transition', *Journal of Democracy*, 5:3, 1994, 35.

32 See the discussion of the force of tradition in S. Poliakov, *Everyday Islam: Religion and Tradition in Rural Central Asia* (New York, 1992).

33 An argument of this sort appears in Iliya Harik, 'Pluralism in the Arab World', *Journal of Democracy*, 5:3, 1994, 43–56.

34 E. Gellner, 'The importance of being modular', in J. Hall, ed., *Civil Society: Theory, History, Comparison* (Cambridge, 1995), p. 33.

35 G. White, 'Civil society, democratisation and development (i): Clearing the analytical ground', *Democratisation*, 1:3, 1994, 375–90.

36 G. Gleason, 'Uzbekistan: from statehood to nationhood?', in Bremmer and Taras, *Nations and Politics*, p. 331.

37 D. Carlisle, 'The Uzbek power elite: Politburo and Secretariat (1938–83)', *Central Asian Survey*, 5:3, 1986, 91–132; Carlisle, 'Power and politics', pp. 93–130; and D. Carlisle, 'Islam Karimov and Uzbekistan: Back to the future', in T. Colton and T. Rucker, eds, *Patterns in Post-Soviet Leadership* (Boulder, 1995), pp. 191–216.

38 *Transition*, 17 May 1996, at 36–7.

39 *Labyrinth*, Autumn 1994, at 3.

40 *Res publika*, 19 March 1996.

41 On the north–south divide see T. Saidbaev, 'Nationalism in Central Asia', in M. Buttino, ed., *In a Collapsing Empire* (Milan, 1992), p. 303; *Labyrinth*, Summer 1995, at 5; *Res publika*, 27 February 1996. Rustembekov was sacked as *akim* of Osh in July 1996, and was replaced by A. M. Muraliev. *Res publika*, 20–26 August 1996.

42 *Izvestiya*, 27 October 1992; *Nezavisimaya gazeta*, 28 October 1992; on his later career and denial of the drug allegations see the interview with Osmanov in *Slovo kyrgyzstana*, 8 April 1995.

43 *Res publika*, 24 April 1996.

44 On the rumours of elite divisions see *Segodnya*, 2 August 1994 and 4 August 1994; on the sacking of Orezov see *Open Media Research Institute*, 55, 18 March 1996.

45 An argument of this sort is developed further in Rachat Achylova, 'Political culture and foreign policy in Kyrgyzstan', in Tismaneau, *Political Culture and Civil Society*, pp. 318–36.

46 *Turkmenskaya iskra*, 16 December 1992.

47 *Nezavisimaya gazeta*, 9 September 1994.

48 B. Pannier, 'Kazakhstan: A step back from democracy', *Transition*, 1:1, 30 June 1995, 65.

49 *Slovo kyrgyzstana*, 11–12 April 1996.

50 *Nezavisimaya gazeta*, 24 August 1994 and 9 September 1994; US State Department, *Kyrgyz Republic Human Rights Practices, 1995* (Washington, 1996).

51 On the early development of such groups see V. Ponomarev, *Samodeyatel'nye obshchestvennye organizatsii Kazakhstana i Kirgizii, 1987–91* (Moscow, 1991).

52 *Slovo kyrgzystana*, 10 April 1993; this number had reached 520 by late 1995 according to Akaev who was interviewed in *Central Asian Monitor*, 1995/6, at 12.

53 See the State Department Report cited earlier; G. Nekitin, 'Kazakh trade unions', *Demokratizatsiya*, 3:3, 1995, 291–3.

54 *Nezavisimaya gazeta*, 10 September 1992; Helsinki Watch, *Human Rights in Turkmenistan* (Washington, July 1993); *Moskovskie novosti*, 23–30 July 1995.

55 On the early development of these movements see J. Critchlow, *Nationalism in Uzbekistan* (Boulder, 1991); W. Fierman, 'The Communist Party, "Erk" and the changing Uzbek political environment', *Central Asian Survey*, 10:3, 1991, 55–72.

56 See Amnesty International, *Uzbekistan: Clampdown on Dissent – An Update* (London, September 1993); Y. Tokgozoglu, 'Uzbek government continues to stifle dissent', in Radio Free Europe/Radio Liberty, *Research Report*, 2:39, 1 October 1993, 10–15; US State Department *Uzbekistan: Human Rights Practices* (Washington, 1996).

57 *Open Media Research Institute*, 200, 13 October 1995.

58 *Nezavisimaya gazeta*, 5 February 1995; around the same time the government held secret talks with members of the opposition though the content of these remains unclear. *Segodnya*, 25 January 1995.

59 *Open Media Research Institute*, 79, 22 April 1996.

60 Much of the information used here is gleaned from the pages of the *Nezavisimaya gazeta* and *Kazakhstanskaya pravda*; for more detail on Kazakh political parties see M. Haghayeghi, *Islam and Politics in Central Asia* (London, 1995), pp. 103–5, 111–16, 127–9, and Olcott, 'Kazakhstan: A republic of minorities', pp. 326–7.

61 *Nezavisimaya gazeta*, 18 October 1995; *Kazakhstanskaya pravda*, 27 October 1995, 12 December 1995, 13 December 1995 and 20 December 1995.

62 Information on many of these groups is scattered around the pages of *Slovo kyrgyzstana*; on early developments see *Samodeyatel'nye obshchestvennye organizatsii*, pp. 84–102 and E. Huskey, 'Kyrgyzstan: the politics of demographic and economic frustration', in Bremmer and Taras, *Nations and Politics*, pp. 398–418.

63 See interviews with CPK leaders in *Slovo kyrgyzstana*, 13 February 1993, 1 May 1993 and 9 June 1993.

64   Information on some of these groups can be found in *Slovo kyrgzystana*, 13 April 1994, 31 May 1994 and 13 December 1994.

65   The SDK has been described by some critics as the new party of power, led as it is by a prominent businessman, a parliamentary speaker and a deputy prime minister. *Res publika*, 11–17 June 1996.

66   N. Lubin, *Central Asians Take Stock: Reform, Corruption and Identity* (Washington, 1994), p. 4.

67   These polls can be found in *Slovo kyrgyzstana*, 19 February 1994, 29 June 1994 and 24 September 1994.

68   *Kazakhstanskaya pravda*, 30 September 1995.

69   *Res publika*, 16 January 1996; another opposition figure suggested the use of the party list system as a means of overcoming the influence of tribalism. *Slovo kyrgyzstana*, 14–15 June 1996.

70   *Turkmenskaya iskra*, 17 January 1994.

71   I have detailed these shortcomings in more depth in 'Pseudo-elections and political development'.

72   For example, in the Kyrgyz parliament elected in February 1995 some 84 per cent of deputies were Kyrgyz, as opposed to around 55 per cent of the population, and 5 out of 104 were women. *Slovo kyrgyzstana*, 4 March 1995.

73   See the discussion of the relationship between strong presidencies and parliaments rooted in regional patronage networks in M. Shugart and J. Carey, *Presidents and Assemblies – Constitutional Design and Electoral Dynamics* (Cambridge, 1992), pp. 167–205.

74   *Nezavisimaya gazeta*, 21 April 1992.

75   *Nezavisimaya gazeta*, 18 October 1994.

76   See *Kazakhstanskaya pravda*, 10 March 1995, 14 March 1995 and 16 March 1995.

77   *Kazakhstanskaya pravda*, 18 March 1995.

78   *Segodnya*, 4 May 1995.

79   The results and final text of the constitution were published in *Kazakhstanskaya pravda*, 5 September 1995 and 8 September 1995 respectively.

80   *Open Media Research Institute*, 114, 12 June 1996.

81   *Slovo kyrgyzstana*, 10 December 1994.

82   *Slovo kyrgyzstana*, 13 January 1995.

83   *Slovo kyrgyzstana*, 31 December 1995.

84   *Slovo kyrgyzstana*, 9–10 January 1996 and 30–31 January 1996.

85   See a series of highly critical articles on the constitutional changes in *Res publika*, 16 January 1996, 24 January 1996 and 6 February 1996. Evidence of a growing impatience with radical opponents was made increasingly evident at the beginning of 1997 when T. Turgunaliev was sentenced to 10 years on a trumped-up criminal charge.

On his arrest see *Res publika*, 24–30 December 1996, and on his sentence see *Open Media Research Institute*, 7, 9 January 1997.

86 *Slovo kyrgyzstana*, 30–31 January 1996.
87 *BBC Summary of World Broadcasts*, 13 March 1996.
88 See the arguments put forward in J. Linz and A. Valenzuela, eds, *The Failure of Presidential Democracy, Volume 1, Comparative Perspectives* (Baltimore,1994), which is addressed in particular to the failures of presidential democracy in systems opting for a democratic transition, something which might at a pinch be applied to Kyrgyzstan.
89 S. Huntington, 'Democracy's third wave', in L. Diamond and M. Plattner, eds, *The Global Resurgence of Democracy* (Baltimore and London, 1993), pp. 17–18.

5

Laying the economic basis for independence

Perhaps the most fundamental problem facing the new states of Central Asia was that of establishing a viable economic order that would enable them to break away from past dependence on a single great power and meet the pressing needs of their populations. This in turn involved rethinking the very structures of inherited economic systems and searching for new international partners to provide additional support for economic reconstruction. In practice this was to prove a difficult process, in part, as Alastair McAuley has pointed out, because the political elites had little experience of independent economic policy-making, especially with regard to the all-important area of international economic relations. They also took over an economic structure that was distorted by regional specialisation and excessive trade dependence upon the other successor states, and countries in which popular expectations of both welfare provision and the benefits of market reform were inflated.[1] How they have attempted to deal with these problems is the subject of this chapter, which starts with a brief review of the legacy of the past. The bulk of the chapter provides an overview of some of the key aspects of economic development in the first half of the 1990s, touching upon the varying approaches chosen by four of the region's states (Tajikistan is largely excluded); the degree of commitment to market economics evident in policies regarding price liberalisation, privatisation, land ownership and the creation of national currencies; and the attempt of at least three of these states to develop the huge natural resources that they possess, often in an uneasy partnership with foreign investors. International economic connections are touched on in various places, though more will be said about these in Chapter 8, and we end with a review of the results of economic reform as of mid-1996.

The Soviet legacy

A century of rule from St Petersburg and Moscow had placed Central Asia in a highly unequal relationship with the centre. As it served primarily as a supplier of raw materials, both agricultural and mineral, the region had become ever more dependent upon other Soviet states for manufactured goods, whilst the growing emphasis on cotton production during the post-war years dramatically reduced the region's ability to feed itself. Such a broad generalisation, however, should not blind us to the fact that economically the region was not a single unit. For example, whilst cotton dominated the southern parts of Central Asia, it played a relatively minor role in Kazakhstan and Kyrgyzstan where 40 per cent of the region's population lived. Kazakhstan was also less dominated by agriculture than the rest, with only 15 per cent of the labour force being in this sector as against 45 per cent in Uzbekistan. In addition, the Kazakh economy was characterised by a north–south split, with the northern oblasts dominated by the industrial sector, which was closely tied into the southern Siberian economy and manned largely by Slavic and European personnel.[2]

For all these variations, the basic position of the region as dependent upon the centre remained. Three of the republics were forced into an over-reliance on cotton which damaged their long-term development and in turn made them dependent upon the centre for the supply of basic goods. For example, on the eve of independence Turkmenistan had to import some 45 per cent of its milk and dairy products, 65 per cent of its grain, 70 per cent of its potatoes, 100 per cent of its sugar, and an estimated 70 per cent of consumption goods from other Soviet states.[3] Even in the sphere of cotton it was evident by the 1980s that over-specialisation – with Uzbekistan devoting nearly 70 per cent of its sown area to cotton – was counter-productive as yields fell and the disastrous environmental consequences of mono-culture became increasingly clear.[4] All of these problems were further aggravated by substantial trade deficits in industrial products, which could not hope to be covered by surpluses in the agricultural sector, by proportionally lower levels of central investment in the region (excluding Kazakhstan), and by the common Soviet problems of antiquated stock and inefficient public services.

This was not entirely a one-sided relationship. With 95 per cent of Central Asian cotton being processed outside the region and Uzbekistan supplying 70 per cent of Russia's cotton needs, the Russian textile industry remained highly sensitive to the producers following independence. Moreover, in certain sectors these Central Asian republics made a major contribution to Soviet production, notably Uzbekistan with its substantial gold reserves, and Kazakhstan which produced over a quarter of Soviet grain during the last five-year plan.[5] Against this, central planners pointed out that Moscow supported the region with an expensive raft of subsidies – though it might be argued that these would have been unnecessary had economic development taken a more balanced form. The figures are contested, but in 1990 it seems that the centre accounted for around a quarter of the Uzbek budget,[6] whilst a later IMF report suggested that in 1991 the amount of republican budgets covered by transfers from the centre ranged from 22 per cent in Turkmenistan to 44 per cent in Tajikistan.[7] Such dependency inevitably raised questions as to how the Central Asian economies might cope with the challenge of independence.

Further difficulties for future development stemmed from demographic and environmental problems. As Patniak has pointed out, such modernisation and industrialisation as had taken place in the region had been based largely upon imported Slavic and European labour, and had generally failed to provide jobs for an ever-expanding and youthful population. In consequence the dynamic rural sector of the population faced a future of over-crowded collective farms with limited work opportunities, declining incomes and a limited social infrastructure of welfare, health and education.[8] Though there was some evidence to suggest that population growth was beginning to slow down and be subject to a certain degree of 'modernisation',[9] there remained on the eve of independence a huge reserve of youthful labour, large numbers of whom were effectively unemployed in a region facing short-term economic decline if not collapse.[10]

At the heart of the environmental problem lay the question of water, symbolised above all by the 30-year shrinkage of the Aral Sea and yet again inseparable from the cotton mono-culture imposed by Moscow. 90 per cent of the Aral's waters originally came from two rivers, the Amudarya and Syrdarya, yet by the late 1970s virtually none of this water was reaching the sea, having been drained off to provide the irrigation essential for cotton production. Such water as did flow was polluted by the over-use of chemical fertilisers and pesticides, the latter used at concentrations perhaps seven times that of generally accepted world standards.[11] All of this created additional dilemmas for the Central Asian states, particularly Uzbekistan, which could not diversify its economy so as to reduce its water usage overnight, and which now had to operate with no expectation of aid or support from a Russian centre whose policies had in many cases forced it into an excessive use of this precious commodity.[12] In such circumstances it was perhaps not surprising that the immediate post-independence period was to witness the resurrection of age-old regional disputes over water as the boundaries of the new states failed to coincide with the division of water resources created by Moscow on the basis of a single economic space.

With the break-up of the USSR most of these problems were further exacerbated by the reduction and removal of subsidies, and the new need to buy many products at world prices. This situation was made worse still by a number of other factors, including the collapse of inter-republican trade and the inexperience of policy-makers in the economic sphere. Whilst all the region's leaders were to speak of the need for market reform, few had any real understanding of what this entailed and most recoiled from the potential consequences of radical change. In particular they were aware that even in the best of economic circumstances, which these were not,[13] marketisation would create further problems for their long-suffering populations. Amongst these problems would be a fall in incomes and a drop in employment possibilities, and the increasing inability of the state to ensure welfare benefits or maintain the 'cradle to grave' promises of the past. In this situation elites remained cautious of pursuing policies that might threaten not just social harmony but their own positions.

Reform in theory and in practice

Approaches to economic reform

An examination of the political evolution of the Central Asian states since independence reveals the overwhelming importance of political leadership, and nowhere is this clearer than in the sphere of economic reform. Put simply, the preferences of the dominant politician have determined the economic choices of these states, though this is not to say that there are no constraints on their actions or that their objectives have been achieved. For example, in January 1992 all felt the necessity of following the example of Russia in introducing price liberalisation, but in all four cases this was only partial and in Uzbekistan amendment to the policy followed student riots on the streets of Tashkent, during the same month.[14]

In Kyrgyzstan, Askar Akaev very quickly made clear his commitment to market reform, arguing that given his country's limited economic potential the only hope for improving the well-being of his people was integration into the international market. By adopting the radical proposals put forward by institutions such as the International Monetary Fund (IMF) and by creating a favourable environment for foreign investors he hoped to attract the investment necessary for the modernisation of his country. To this end in early 1992 he accepted an austerity programme developed in conjunction with the IMF and moved some way in the direction of a 'shock therapy' approach with the liberalisation of prices and proposals for extensive privatisation.[15] This in turn brought in several tranches of IMF stabilisation funding, though in practice reform was to make little headway during this early period. Kyrgyzstan, with international support, was also to lead the way in introducing its own currency, an initially problematic process but one that would enable the country to escape the high inflation that came when the rouble zone collapsed at the end of 1993.

Other states have been more cautious, with only Kazakhstan making extensive use of market rhetoric. Thus whilst Nazarbaev has stressed the importance of developing the private sector, he has argued that for the foreseeable future Kazakhstan can only hope to evolve a semi-market economy. In part this stems from a fear of the consequences, for in an interview in early 1993 the Kazakh president suggested that revolutionary destruction of the old system when there was nothing ready to replace it would be irresponsible.[16] At the same time it reflects a belief that successful economic development in the much-admired 'Asian tigers' came from a combination of openness to the world market and strong state control over the reform process. Indeed, Nazarbaev has argued that if such prescriptions are followed, the long-term prospects of Kazakhstan may be even better than those of countries such as South Korea, because many of these lacked the natural resources with which Kazakhstan is so richly endowed.[17]

In Kazakhstan and Kyrgyzstan the official message is that the market is the goal but that some adaptation has to be made to social need and the lack of experience of life in the global economy. This measured approach has nonetheless engendered criticism, notably from trade union organisations and the reborn communist parties. In Kyrgyzstan the chairman of the republican *Znanie* (Knowledge) society early on expressed scepticism about the mad dash to free market economics, stressing instead the need to maintain a 'regulated market' based upon close links with the former Soviet republics.[18] More forcefully, in mid-1993 communist party leader Zh. Amanbaev argued that the slavish following of Western models was in danger of throwing the baby out with the bath water, pointing to the fact that in the late 1980s Kyrgyz collective and state farms were generally more profitable than their counterparts in Turkey and Iran, whilst the large size of Soviet farms had enabled the country to develop large cattle stocks.[19] In Kazakhstan the Coordinating Council of Kazakh Trade Unions was critical of its government's anti-crisis programme which had left many workers unpaid for several months in mid-1993 and which they claimed benefited only mafia and clan structures closely tied to the old nomenklatura.[20] Yet though the two governments occasionally moved in the direction of their critics, for example, by increasing welfare provision or providing subsidies to keep ailing industries going, both refused to change the basic formal direction of economic reform.

In the authoritarian states of Uzbekistan and Turkmenistan, the state's position was very different, with references to the market tempered by an emphasis on the key role of the state in evolving economic change. According to official statistics, this appeared to be working in Uzbekistan despite the absence of substantial reform. Claiming a growth of production in 1994, the Uzbek ambassador to Moscow explained his country's success in terms of the priority given to economics over politics and the leading role of the state in controlling reform.[21] Like his Kazakh counterpart, Islam Karimov looked to the successful Asian economies as an example, though stressing that his country would not be bound by any single model and would not be forced into measures that harmed the welfare of the population.[22] For this reason Uzbekistan did not accept IMF help until much later than its neighbours and even then did not always comply with the tight financial constraints that accompany such funding.

Greater scepticism could still be found in the attitude of Turkmenistan's President Niyazov, though he was not averse to the virtues of the free market when it came to selling his country's energy resources abroad. In February 1992 the Turkmen leader rejected the idea that market reform must mean uncontrolled price rises, the privatisation of everything, and a passive acceptance of the likely disastrous social consequences for the population. Pointing out that Western capitalism had evolved over two centuries, he stressed a gradualism which would allow privatisation by stages.[23] As the head of the state planning commission put it, 'the market is necessary for us, but we must get there via a plan'.[24] To this end a three-year stabilisation plan and a ten-year development plan were drawn up which sought to ensure that the move towards market economics was in accordance with the needs of the population and based upon the exploitation of the country's natural resources. To meet the needs of the population, Turkmenistan provided free utilities and promised free bread for those below a certain income level. In practice both plans and promises remained largely on paper, undermined by unrealistic expectations of an immediate natural gas boom that took no account of the problems that were likely to arise in the development and transportation of this asset. With genuine economic reform barely initiated and economic decision-making largely turning on the whims of the presidential coterie, Turkmenistan's economic situation remains difficult and its population is facing increasing material hardship.

The situation in Turkmenistan and other countries of Central Asia was further complicated by the introduction of their own currencies in 1993, although this may have given some impetus to processes of reform and in Kyrgyzstan served to reduce inflationary pressures. In the aftermath of Soviet collapse all five states continued to use the rouble but with no coordinated monetary control. With each state pursuing its own policies of credit expansion as it sought to prop up ailing industries, one country's policies often had dangerous inflationary effects upon all.[25] Whilst most felt the need to remain within the rouble zone, in May 1993 Kyrgyzstan, without seriously consulting its neighbours but with financial support from the IMF, introduced its own currency, the som. In part this represented an attempt to escape the high inflation rates then prevalent within the CIS, and to mop up the roubles in circulation which could be used to pay off a substantial debt to Russia. It was also hoped to further Kyrgyzstan's attractiveness to outside investors by bringing international liquidity. Many parliamentary deputies in Kyrgyzstan expressed concern that this was a premature step and rightly predicted that it might cause tensions with neighbouring states.[26] Within days both Uzbekistan and Kazakhstan came close to breaking off relations with Kyrgyzstan, with Uzbekistan cutting energy supplies to Kyrgyzstan and demanding that travellers from Kyrgyzstan pay in dollars. Problems also arose as contractors and enterprises in other successor states refused to accept payment in som and then stopped delivery of some goods.[27]

The other states proved reluctant to follow suit but Russian policy was soon to force them to. In July 1993 the Russian Central Bank withdrew from circulation all notes printed between 1961 and 1992, and in consequence the Central Asian states became a dumping ground for old roubles with the inevitable inflationary pressures. Russia in turn put pressure upon these states either to create their own currencies or to subordinate their monetary policy to Moscow. Kazakhstan, for example, was reportedly told to maintain large gold and currency reserves in Moscow if it wished to remain part of the rouble zone.[28] In consequence Turkmenistan issued its own currency (the manat) on 1 November 1993, with Uzbekistan and Kazakhstan coordinating the introduction of theirs (the sumcoupon and the tenge) on 15 November.[29] Only Tajikistan did not immediately introduce its own currency, in large part because its war-torn economy was effectively integrated into that of Russia. In May 1995, however, when it became increasingly difficult to function with the limited quantity of roubles supplied by Moscow, Dushanbe introduced the Tajik rouble. By the end of 1995 the stability of these currencies varied considerably, with only the Kyrgyz som appearing to enjoy some success, whereas most of the other currencies depreciated considerably during their first two years in operation, most notably the Turkmen manat which had been devalued four times by the end of 1995 and continued to collapse during 1996.[30]

Privatisation and land reform

Central to the rhetoric of marketisation have been proposals for extensive privatisation of sections of the hitherto state-dominated economies. Elements of this evolved even before the collapse of the USSR, affecting in particular small businesses in the trade, catering and retail sector, and in the first months of independence state assets quietly slipped into private hands, usually those of the old nomenklatura who were able to utilise their existing control over state enterprise to engage in extensive asset-stripping. As might be expected, Kazakhstan and Kyrgyzstan have been at the forefront in this area, Kyrgyzstan claiming that after five years of independence over half of GDP was produced by the non-state sector, and by the mid-1990s Uzbekistan was also claiming considerable progress in this field.

In Kazakhstan the government launched an ambitious pro-gramme of privatisation in 1992 but this met with little success, and in late 1993 a more gradual and better-thought-out policy was announced. Under the new scheme every citizen was to be issued with coupons or vouchers enabling them to buy shares in one of 140 investment funds which in turn used the coupons to purchase companies. These vouchers cannot be sold, though they can be transferred to relatives, and they give their owners no control over the enterprise in which their investment fund is involved.[31] The results of all this have been mixed. By the end of 1993 over half of Kazakhstan's housing stock appears to have been privatised and in early 1994 Nazarbaev suggested that around 44 per cent of small businesses had left the state sector, though the original 1992 plan had envisaged that this would be 100 per cent by that time.[32] Subsequent plans to privatise larger enterprises appear to have faltered, with only a small number of these being in the private sector by the end of 1995.

In Uzbekistan the state put forward a complex privatisation plan based upon the initial privatisation of most smaller enterprises, to be followed in the second half of the 1990s by an attempt to tackle the larger units. Yet in practice the state, or various ministries dominated by those close to President Karimov, have retained tight control over the privatisation process. In early 1994 the Uzbek ambassador in Moscow claimed that nearly all small and around 30 per cent of larger enterprises had been privatised, leaving nearly 40 per cent of production in non-state hands, but this figure is difficult to verify.[33] Moreover, other sources have suggested that the more ambitious privatisation process launched in 1994 largely resulted in the transfer of successful enterprises to those in the president's circle.[34] Here, as in other republics, there are frequent complaints about officials and bureaucracies unsympathetic to the development of an entrepreneurial spirit, and complaints regarding ongoing governmental intervention which makes the life of private firms extremely difficult.[35]

Across the region privatisation has generated considerable debate, and not just because of the success of the nomenklatura in buying up assets on the cheap. Concern was also expressed that this process might only benefit specific nationalities. In both Kazakhstan and Kyrgyzstan one finds claims that the last group likely to benefit from the turn to the market were the indigenous nationalities, for they either lacked the traditions of more settled peoples or had been disadvantaged by the specialisation promoted by the Soviet state, as in Kazakhstan where Slavs and Europeans dominated the richer, industrial north and were said to be in a better position to take advantage of privatisation. Such arguments have been reflected in debates over the ways in which privatisation should develop. Should anyone be allowed to buy? Should ownership be restricted to citizens, the dominant nationality group, or those who have lived in the republics for certain periods of time? In Kazakhstan some nationalists sought to restrict ownership to Kazakh nationals, and eventually the authorities met them halfway in requiring a five-year residency qualification. In Kyrgyzstan, the privatisation law introduced in 1992 did allow foreign ownership, but excluded natural resources from private ownership and specifically prohibited the creation of monopolies.[36] Once the processes were set in train further issues were raised by would-be purchasers, domestic and foreign, who complained about complex purchasing and registration procedures, and inadequate legal and regulatory structures.[37]

Whilst the principle of private enterprise in the retail and industrial sector appears to have been broadly accepted, its application in the agricultural sphere proved more controversial. Prior to the collapse of the USSR land reform had been discussed in a number of republics, and in early 1991 the Kyrgyz parliament had approved a Land Code, though one that was quickly vetoed by President Akaev because of its reference to the land belonging to the Kyrgyz nation alone.[38] In general, however, the public remained wary, an attitude which reflects both traditional and Soviet suspicions of private ownership of land. Whilst urban-based intellectuals in Kazakhstan tended to idealise private farming, perhaps drawing false assumptions from the success of Soviet-era private plots, those who would have to run them remained sceptical, with one poll in 1992 showing that only 5 per cent of Kazakh peasants favoured private landownership.[39]

Various types of argument were used by those opposed to private farming. Some feared that opening up a market in land in which property went to the highest bidder would allow in foreign interests and recreate a dependency from which the republic was seeking to escape. A more subtle and nationalistic version of this that emerged in Kyrgyzstan claimed that especially in the south of the republic private land ownership and farming would benefit the substantial Uzbek population, with their tradition of settled agriculture, rather than the indigenous Kyrgyz population.[40] Others argued that such changes did not fit well with national traditions. Hence during the constitutional debate that took place in early 1992 one Turkmen collective farm leader, a not entirely disinterested observer, suggested that the constitution should explicitly forbid the buying and selling of land on the grounds that this was part of the natural wealth of the country and thus belonged to all citizens.[41]

All of the Central Asian constitutions adopted in 1992–93 excluded the ownership or buying and selling of land, but this did not prevent the development of some degree of land reform. In early 1993 a modest programme was introduced in Turkmenistan which involved the allocation to each family of up to 50 hectares, with the possibility of leasing a further 500 hectares if they undertook to use this additional land to meet state orders. Under this proposal, participating individuals or groups would be given interest-free credit for five years, would be exempt from taxes, and would be given access to machinery possessed by units akin to the old Soviet machine tractor stations. Within the first few months some 11,000 people were said to have taken up this option, with an example being set by President Niyazov who proposed to sow a local variety of wheat in his patch just outside Ashgabat. At the end of two years those involved had to show that it was being used for agricultural purposes, and half of their produce had to be sold to the state at fixed prices. Throughout it was emphasised that this was not the same as private landownership and that, whilst property could be inherited, it could not be bought or sold.[42] Three years after its introduction, however, very few people had taken up the offer of private ownership and large state or collective farms continued to dominate agriculture.

Similar schemes essentially involving the leasing principle, whereby families or groups were given the usage of land for lengthy periods, were developed in other republics, though the details varied. In Kyrgyzstan arrangements introduced in early 1994 provided for 49-year leases, later extended to 99 years, with leases exchangeable and saleable, but with no mention of the land as privately owned.[43] Kazakhstan by 1995 edged even closer to the principle, with the creation of 100-year leases, the right of inheritance and the right to build houses and enterprises on the leased territory.[44] In both countries this issue was the subject of renewed discussion during reassessment of earlier constitutional settlements. Whilst both communists and nationalists remained suspicious, the presidents of Kyrgyzstan and Kazakhstan began to push for an open commitment to the principle. In late December 1994 in Kyrgyzstan President Akaev suggested that without private ownership agriculture could not hope to flourish and argued that the principle was essential to a genuinely free society.[45] Over the next two years the issue continued to be subject to heated debate, but in late November 1996 Akaev signed a decree allowing private ownership of land from the beginning of 1997.[46] In Kazakhstan the new constitution adopted in Kazakhstan in August 1995 appeared to allow private property in all areas except those of natural resources (Article 6).[47] In practice, however, the proper definition and protection of property rights and regulation of the land market is still not fully defined, despite a presidential decree 'on land' issued at the end of the year and a parliamentary law on land passed in February 1996.[48] Though such developments may appear to herald substantial changes in Central Asian agricultural practice, private ownership is all too easily sold to the region's population as a panacea for their woes and it remains to be seen how well it might perform in practice, especially given the constraints imposed by law, reluctant agricultural bureaucracies and public attitudes.

Playing to one's strengths

For all the Soviet successor states a central plank in moving away
from dependency upon the old centre has been the attempt to
develop those specialisms and resources which can be sold in the
international market. Only on this basis did they believe it would be
possible to accrue sufficient capital to develop their own economies
so as better to provide for the needs of their populations. In pursuit
of this end they have relied upon three broad types of resources:
energy, mineral and agricultural, though to these one might add the
potential offered by some parts of the industrial sector and the considerable supply of cheap labour that could be utilised in the region.

The energy sector is clearly the field that Turkmenistan, Kazakhstan and, to a lesser extent, Uzbekistan hope to make use of. Of
these, Turkmenistan possesses considerable potential for evolving a
profitable trade based primarily on its reserves of natural gas, said
to be the third largest in the world. In addition this small republic
sits on considerable oil reserves, sufficient at least to meet its own
needs.[49] Once independence was achieved it was decided to sell gas
at world market prices, even to the former Soviet countries,
although in the short term most countries were offered transitional
arrangements. Russia almost immediately agreed to pay close to
world prices, but in the following years Turkmenistan found itself
in a series of conflicts with Ukraine and the Caucasian states over
payments and arrears, tensions which led it to hold back supplies on
various occasions.[50] Yet for all the potential and the ability to attract
foreign investors to help in the development of these sectors, Turkmenistan has faced considerable difficulties in reaping the fruits of
its assets. Existing facilities for the extraction and processing of oil
and gas remain antiquated and will take time to restructure, whilst
for the foreseeable future Turkmenistan remains dependent upon
Russian pipelines to export its products. Alternative pipelines to
Europe exist via Iran and Turkey, but raising international finance
for these has been made difficult by Washington's resolute discouragement of economic ties with Iran and by mid-1996 it appeared to
be getting nowhere.

For Kazakhstan oil was the potential bedrock of its development,
and in 1992–93 it negotiated a major deal with the US company
Chevron to develop the Tengiz oil fields in the west of the country.
Under this deal it was proposed to give the joint US-Kazakh com-

pany the right to develop the field over a 40-year period, during which time production would rise from 65,000–700,000 barrels a day. Of the proceeds the state would take around 80 per cent.[51] A further project to develop gas fields in Karachaganak involving British–Italian–Kazakh cooperation was evolved on similar terms. However, it soon became apparent that these deals were problematic, above all because however much Kazakhstan was able to produce it still had to transport its products through Russia which in turn began to demand a cut of the action. In 1994 for example, Russia demanded upwards of 20 per cent of the Chevron revenues and 15 per cent of the British–Italian deal, and in pursuit of its goal temporarily cut off most of Kazakhstan's oil flow. This in turn delayed the opening of the new Tengiz fields and then to production cutbacks as only about a fifth of the oil produced could be shipped out. This led to Chevron cutting back its investment in the region. Further complications were added by negotiations over the construction of an additional pipeline to the Black Sea through southern Russia, with Turkey suggesting that the Bosphorus could not take the tanker traffic this would entail, and by successive financing arrangements for the project falling though until a deal was finally reached in the spring of 1996.[52]

For the other three countries the situation is more complex, as they are unlikely to be able to use their energy resources as foundations for economic redevelopment. As the Bukhara and Fergana oil fields came onstream in 1995 Uzbekistan was able to reduce its oil imports from Russia by 75 per cent, and self-sufficiency in the oil and gas sector should be realised before the end of the century. In contrast Tajikistan and Kyrgyzstan are highly dependent upon Russia and their neighbours for energy supplies, and on occasions both have found themselves in conflict situations resulting from their inability to keep up payments for energy supplies. Against this it should be noted that both have huge potential in the hydro-electric sphere with their mountainous terrains supplying large quantities of that most precious of commodities, water. Indeed, Kyrgyzstan currently exports electricity to Uzbekistan, Kazakhstan and China and is looking to expand its relationship with the latter. Yet even here relations with Russia remain paramount, and in March 1996 a deal was done giving Moscow a 49 per cent stake in the Kyrgyz state power company, thus ensuring guaranteed exports for Bishkek and cheap electricity for the Russian Federation.[53]

The second source of potential well-being lies in the exploitation of the region's mineral and metal resources, though the potential of each state varies considerably. Uzbekistan, Kazakhstan and Kyrgyzstan each have considerable gold mining potential, the first possessing around a quarter of CIS gold reserves and currently developing its mining infrastructure with European support and through joint ventures with US companies. Kyrgyzstan, despite various political scandals regarding the awarding of contracts for the exploitation of the Kumtor field, reckoned to be the seventh largest in the world, hopes to raise its annual production from 3 to 20 tons by 2000.[54] Most of these republics possess a variety of other mineral resources including silver, copper, lead, zinc, uranium, mercury and tin. Kazakhstan in particular is richly blessed in such assets and on the basis of these has developed strengths in ferrous metals and steel production. As in other areas, however, problems stem from dependence upon Russian markets and the need to modernise often primitive technologies and plants, all of which requires considerable capital investment.

Thirdly, Central Asian states are hoping to make use of their traditional specialisations in the agricultural sphere, including the hitherto vilified cotton mono-culture. Although the chief producers, Uzbekistan and Turkmenistan, have sought to reduce the amount of land devoted to cotton, with Uzbekistan reducing its harvest targets from around 5 million tons in the late 1980s to 4 million by the mid-1990s, cotton remains a highly marketable product. Thanks to regional specialisation, Russia and some other CIS states remain dependent upon Central Asian cotton, and their textile industries have pressurised governments to maintain links with the region. There is also an awareness of the possibility of acquiring hard currency through overseas sales, with Uzbek state and collective farms allowed to sell up to 40 per cent of their produce abroad since 1995. Turkmenistan has only reduced production slightly and is seeking to develop its own processing facilities, but is at the same time expecting CIS countries to pay more realistic prices. Thus in 1992 Russia took around 700,000 tons and paid about 70 per cent of world prices.[55] For all this, it remains questionable whether these levels of production can be kept up, given the ongoing water problems and the unabating reduction of the Aral Sea. For this reason the heavily cotton-dependent republics are seeking to diversify their output, in particular by turning more attention to grain production so as to reduce their food dependency upon other CIS states.[56]

More controversially, since the Afghan war drugs have become a major source of income for some in the region which became a transit point as well as a major growing area in the early 1990s. Thanks to the Tajik civil war, the indefensibility of many of the region's borders, the strength of clan and tribal links, and the weakness of the security services, Central Asia in general and southern Kyrgyzstan in particular has become a major player in the drugs trade, with the seizure of opium in Kyrgyzstan alone rising from 5 kg in 1992 to 627 kg in 1995.[57] Opium is transported from Afghanistan, through the Pamir mountains to Kyrgyzstan, with the southern Osh region also becoming a major growing area. For a while there was even discussion in parliament of the state exploiting this crop, but outside pressure and a certain moral revulsion has kept it illegal. Though 1994–95 saw various inter-regional and international agreements on dealing with the trade, in practice it has proved hard to combat such trade in a region where poverty and unemployment are endemic. As one Uzbek policeman put it, to curb the traffic we would have to cut the road between Osh and the Pamirs, and behind every militia man put another to keep an eye on him.[58]

The international dimension

Whilst the region has considerable potential in certain areas, the development of many of these will take time and their benefits may not be felt until well into the next century. Moreover, the energy and industrial sectors require considerable investment if they are to be made successful, and it was perhaps not surprising that during the initial euphoria over independence excessive hopes were placed on the attractiveness of the region for outside investors. This optimism lasted for only a short time because Central Asian leaders, lacking the experience of dealing with financial institutions and foreign businesspeople, found relationships with the various pillars of the global economy hard to maintain. In Chapter 8 more will be said about relations between Central Asia and specific regions, so in this section we offer just a few pointers to the type of relationships emerging in the region.

Broadly speaking, the Central Asian states have been the recipients of three types of economic support. The first, direct investment by foreign companies, is variable, but in the energy sector, at least, foreign companies are lining up to get a slice of the action, despite the many obstacles hindering successful deal completion. Other areas that have attracted large outside firms have included mineral exploitation and the assembling of cars and lorries, with Uzbekistan able to use its supply of cheap labour to attract firms such as Daewo and Mercedes Benz. Secondly, financial support has been forthcoming from individual countries, with the visits of foreign heads of state usually being accompanied by the announcement of further credit, cheap loans and investment in specific sectors of the economy. However, at the same time it has become apparent that the hoped-for investment from the 'Muslim world' will not be as extensive as perhaps was once expected. Meanwhile, the West, with the exception of Germany which is sensitive to the needs of co-ethnics in Kazakhstan and Kyrgyzstan, tends to be more interested in helping the western regions of the former USSR. For this reason an increasingly important player in Central Asia has been China which now accounts for nearly half of Kazakh imports in the consumer goods sector and is a major player in Kyrgyzstan where it has a free economic zone in the Naryn oblast.[59]

Finally, the international financial institutions have offered considerable support. The World Bank and the IMF have played a key role in providing stabilisation and restructuring funds from the very beginning of Kyrgyzstan's reforms, as well as in backing the creation of new currencies both here and in Kazakhstan. Other bodies playing a similar role in providing stabilisation and development aid have included the World Bank, the European Bank for Reconstruction and Development, and the Asian Development Bank.[60] In the pursuit of economic support the Central Asian states have taken a highly pragmatic line, refusing to be bound by ideological constraints. Hence their projection of themselves as part of the 'Muslim world' has not prevented the involvement of Israel as a significant actor in the restructuring of irrigation networks. Equally, Turkmenistan has refused to be deterred from close links with its neighbour Iran by Washington's publicly expressed unease. Constraints remain, however, with states finding that foreign aid often comes with ties and that those refusing to conform may find themselves being denied the hoped-for funding. Hence Turkmenistan, by failing to undertake serious reform, and Uzbekistan, as a result of its human rights record, have faced some difficulties in their dealings with the Western world, though Uzbekistan's problems appear to be easing by mid-1996, thanks in part to its willingness to follow Washington's line in its relations with Iran. Consequences for failing to conform to international standards were evident in the grant-making policies of United States Agency for International Development (USAID) which tended to link aid to democratisation, with the result, according to one report, that Kyrgyzstan had by the end of 1994 received around $16 per capita as against $2.5 for Kazakhstan and $1 for Uzbekistan.[61]

Overall the states of Central Asia have enjoyed some success in attracting foreign money, with Kyrgyzstan reported to have received nearly $500 million in investment, over $700 million in credit and $150 million in technical aid during the first five years of independence.[62] Even more successful has been Kazakhstan, with the UN Economic Commission for Europe reporting that in 1989–94 it had been promised $46 billion in foreign investment, more than any other former communist state.[63]

For all this, the states of Central Asia are still extremely dependent upon their relationship with Russia and other successor states and interdependence remains an economic reality. Foreign investment is slow in coming. Hence the region remains highly dependent upon the successor states both for certain categories of goods and for markets for its own. Though a two-way relationship, evident for example in Russia's continued need for Kazakh grain to feed its own population,[64] the relationship generally tends to favour the former metropolitan centre. Thus Kyrgyzstan sent some 60 per cent of its exports to the 'elder brother' and Uzbekistan in the first years of independence was in effect forced to barter its cotton for Russian oil – which accounted for 75 per cent of Uzbek needs – a deal far more advantageous to Moscow than Tashkent.[65] Whilst each of these states has sought to diversify its production and reduce its dependence – Uzbekistan by producing its own oil and by reducing the export of fruit and vegetables to Moscow – this is going to be a long process.

The impact of economic changes

From the perspective of the ordinary Central Asian citizen, such changes as have taken place are generally seen as being for the worse. Successive polls report that most people believe their economic prospects to have worsened considerably since 1991 and want to see the state retain some degree of control over prices.[66] Such responses were hardly surprising, given the dramatic economic problems that emerged or worsened during the first years of independence. All states witnessed rapid rises in inflation, reaching nearly 2,000 per cent in Kazakhstan, and around 1,200 per cent in Kyrgyzstan in the peak year of 1993. Though by 1995 both of these states along with Uzbekistan had brought inflation down to under 100 per cent (31 per cent in Kyrgyzstan), the impact of inflationary trends upon public confidence had been devastating.[67]

Alongside these pressures a series of other problems have emerged, notably the collapse of output in all sectors of the economy. For example, in Kazakhstan the fall in GDP from 1989–90 was around 50 per cent, with a fall of 25 per cent being recorded in 1994 on the previous year.[68] Similar levels of decline have been reported in Kyrgyzstan, with industrial production falling by around 60 per cent in the 1989–94 period and the country's traditionally important herds of sheep and goats being reduced by around as much as two-thirds as economic hardship made it impossible for herders to feed their flocks.[69] The same situation existed in Turkmenistan, with one source reporting that the number of cattle fell by around 75 per cent in 1993 alone.[70] Of all the Central Asian states, only Uzbekistan has consistently reported relatively small declines in production and, in 1993, claimed that production had actually risen by 4 per cent.[71]

The situation has been exacerbated by a number of other factors. First, there has been a growth in corruption and economic crime, which has seen potentially profitable state assets being bled dry by those with the right nomenklatura and clan connections. Then there have been massive budget deficits, which although in part stemming from the sudden loss of central subsidies and from massive borrowing, are also a product of failures in government revenue collection. Originating in inadequate regulatory and legal structures, this problem was made worse by the ability and willingness of many firms to avoid taxation, with Kyrgyzstan reporting that the state was able to collect taxes on only about one-third of goods legally produced in the country in 1993.[72] Such developments had knock-on effects as impoverished governments were unable to pay workers in the state sectors for months on end, leading to unemployment in some sectors and the emergence of large numbers of poverty-struck families which were able to survive only on the charity of families and friends.

Problems of this sort are likely to persist for some time as the Central Asian states struggle to rebuild their economies. Though there have been some signs of a slowing of decline and even of some stabilisation since late 1995, each of these states faces problems. Turkmenistan and Kazakhstan may possess enormous resources, but in each case it will be some time before these come onstream, especially in the former where the government seems to have little sense of economic reality and where sporadic bread riots would seem to indicate public dissatisfaction with the economic situation. In the case of Kazakhstan the prospects may be more hopeful, given its record in attracting foreign investment, its apparent stability, its commitment to good relations with Russian, and the ostensible move towards economic reintegration. Kyrgyzstan, the would-be Switzerland of the East, enjoys the sympathies of the Western world but has limited resources with which to attract external investment and though successfully bringing down inflation, only began to halt ongoing economic decline in late 1996. Tajikistan has been bankrupted by a civil war which in 1992 alone made over 800,000 homeless, destroyed or disrupted 80 per cent of industrial production and led to the exit of 90 per cent of Russian speakers, many skilled professionals necessary for economic reconstruction.[73] Finally there is Uzbekistan, a country with mixed prospects and where reform along the lines favoured by Western financial institutions has been slow to take off. With energy independence on the horizon, agricultural diversification taking place, an apparently stable currency and a substantial labour force available to would-be investors, Uzbekistan would appear to have some prospect of long-term economic prosperity should political stability be maintained.[74]

Whilst some of these states have considerable potential, in the short term the prospects of economic security let alone prosperity for the masses seem limited. Living standards continue to plummet and societal divisions rooted in very obvious inequalities may yet provoke unrest. Against this one should note that, for all the pessimistic predictions of the early 1990s, levels of economic decline perhaps greater than that of the Great Depression have not led to serious public unrest or to the violent removal of the existing regimes. Where violence has taken place it has tended to centre around other issues, in particular those of identity, which are themselves not without economic dimensions, and to which we will turn in Chapter 6.

Notes

1 A. McAuley, 'The economies of Central Asia: The socialist legacy', in Y. Roi, ed., *Muslim Eurasia: Conflicting Legacies* (London, 1995), pp. 255–68.
2 S. Islam, 'Capitalism on the silk route', in M. Mandelbaum, ed., *Central Asia and the World* (New York, 1994), pp. 147–76.
3 International Monetary Fund, *Economic Review – Turkmenistan* (Washington, 1992), p. 2.
4 Yu. Alexandrov, 'Central Asia – A specific case of economic underdevelopment', in V. Naumkin, ed., *State, Religion and Society in Central Asia* (Reading, 1993), pp. 106–23.
5 C. A. Werner, 'A preliminary assessment of attitudes towards the privatisation of agriculture in contemporary Kazakhstan', *Central Asian Survey*, 13:2, 1994, 296.
6 C. Cavanaugh, 'Uzbekistan's long road to the market', Radio Free Europe/Radio Liberty, *Research Report*, 1:29, 17 July 1992, 33–8.
7 S. Marnie and E. Whitlock, 'Central Asia and economic integration', in Radio Free Europe/Radio Liberty, *Research Report*, 2:14, 2 April 1993, 34.
8 A. Patniak, 'Agriculture and rural out-migration in Central Asia, 1960–91', *Europe–Asia Studies*, 47:1, 1995, 147–69.
9 M. Tolts, 'Modernisation of demographic behaviour in the Muslim republics of the USSR', in Roi, *Muslim Eurasia*, pp. 231–53.
10 Cavanaugh suggests that on the eve of independence unemployment in Uzbekistan alone was between 600,000 and 2 million. 'Uzbekistan's long road', 33.
11 *Nezavisimaya gazeta*, 23 November 1994.
12 For a general discussion see M. Glantz, A. Rubinstein and I. Zonin, 'Tragedy in the Aral Sea basin: Looking back to plan ahead', in H. Malik, ed., *Central Asia: Its Strategic Importance and Future Prospects* (New York, 1994), pp. 159–94.
13 In Kazakhstan national income in 1991 was about 10 per cent down on 1990, whilst inflation had reached the then staggering figure of 184 per cent. *Kazakhstanskaya pravda*, 29 January 1992.
14 *Pravda*, 17 and 20 January 1992.
15 *Izvestiya*, 8 July 1992.
16 *Izvestiya*, 26 January 1993.
17 N. Nazarbaev, *Without Right or Left* (London, 1992), p. 81.

18   *Slovo kyrgyzstana*, 10 January 1992.
19   *Slovo kyrgyzstana*, 1 May 1993.
20   *Nezavisimaya gazeta*, 27 July 1993.
21   *Segodnya*, 8 February 1994.
22   Cavanaugh, 'Uzbekistan's long road', 34.
23   *Turkmenskaya iskra*, 24 February 1992.
24   *Turkmenskaya iskra*, 9 June 1992.
25   Much of this section is based upon L. Maillet, 'New states initiate new currencies', *Transition*, 9 June 1995, 44–49 and 56.
26   *Slovo kyrgyzstana*, 5 May 1993.
27   See E. Huskey, 'Kyrgyzstan leaves the rouble zone', in Radio Free Europe/Radio Liberty, *Research Report*, 2:35, 3 September 1993, 38–43.
28   On developing tensions in Russian–Kazakh economic relations see *Izvestiya*, 3 November 1993 and *Nezavisimaya gazeta* of the same date.
29   *Nezavisimaya gazeta*, 16 November 1993; *The Economist*, 20 November 1993.
30   *Economist Intelligence Unit, Country Profile, 1995–96, Central Asia* (London, 1996), pp. 83–4.
31   See *BBC Summary of World Broadcasts*, 5 November 1993; *The Economist*, 30 April 1994.
32   *Economist Intelligence Unit, Country Report, 1st Quarter 1994* (London, 1994), p. 48.
33   *Segodnya*, 8 February 1994 and 5 May 1994.
34   *Economist Intelligence Unit, Country Profile, 1995–96*, p. 112.
35   Even in Turkmenistan, early 1992 witnessed complaints to this effect from businesspeople concerned about high tax regimes and the unwillingness of the authorities to provide help in finding start-up capital. *Izvestiya*, 27 November 1992.
36   For an extensive discussion of early developments in these two republics see B. Brown and J. Tedstrom, 'Kazakhstan and Kyrgyzstan: Central Asia's leaders', in Radio Free Europe/Radio Liberty, *Research Report*, 1:17, 24 January 1992, 58–66. Public attitudes to privatisation varied considerably. An opinion poll carried out in Kazakhstan in late 1992 suggested that 85 per cent viewed it favourably, though of those now working in private enterprises only 27.7 per cent believed themselves to be masters in their own house. Moreover, whilst few wanted to return to state ownership, many felt that privatisation had only benefited those with money and connections. *Kazakhstanskaya pravda*, 27 November 1992.
37   See the appeal of Kyrgyz businessmen to this effect in *Slovo kyrgyzstana*, 14 January 1994.

38 Brown and Testrom, 'Kazakhstan and Kyrgyzstan: Central Asia's leaders', 62.

39 Werner, 'A preliminary assessment of attitudes towards the privatisation of agriculture', 295–303; *Izvestiya*, 10 November 1992.

40 For a general discussion of this issue see G. Gleason, 'Central Asian land reform and the ethnic factor', Radio Free Europe/Radio Liberty, *Research Report* 2:3, 15 January 1993, 28–33.

41 *Turkmenskaya iskra*, 9 April 1992; more recently in Kyrgyzstan the argument has been made that by tradition land belongs to all the people and that therefore whilst private usage should be guaranteed, actual ownership should always remain in the hands of the people as a whole. K. Isaev and Zh. Bokontueva, 'Vozmozhen li plyuralizm form sobstvennosti na zemlyu', *Res publika*, 20 February 1996.

42 *Izvestiya*, 4 February 1993, 19 February 1993 and 10 April 1993.

43 *Slovo kyrgyzstana*, 23 February 1994.

44 *Nezavisimaya gazeta*, 24 April 1995.

45 *Slovo kyrgyzstana*, 7 December 1994.

46 *Open Media Research Institute*, 233, 4 December 1996.

47 *Kazakhstanskaya pravda*, 8 September 1995.

48 *Izvestiya*, 4 January 1996; *Labyrinth*, 3:2, 1996, 3.

49 *Izvestiya*, 27 May 1993.

50 See *Izvestiya*, 2, 3 and 6 February 1992 and 28 September 1992; *Turkmenskaya iskra*, 7 March 1992.

51 *Izvestiya*, 8 April 1993; on the environmental consequences of oil development see Z. Wolfson, 'Oil fever in Kazakhstan: Environmental angle', *Environmental Policy Review*, 8:1, 1994, 6–13.

52 M. B. Olcott, *Central Asia's New States: Independence, Foreign Policy and Regional Security* (Washington, 1995), pp. 77–81; on the conflict over the Caspian Pipeline Consortium and the eventual seeming resolution of the issue see *Economist Intelligence Unit Country Report, 2nd Quarter 1996* (London, 1996), pp. 26–9.

53 *Monitor*, 22 March 1996.

54 *Segodnya*, 25 May 1995.

55 *Turkmenskaya iskra*, 20 May 1992, 9 June 1992 and 31 July 1992.

56 On some of the problems of agricultural development see P. Craumer, *Rural Agricultural Development in Uzbekistan* (London, 1995).

57 *Res publika*, 2 April 1996.

58 *Moskovskie novosti*, 12 September 1993; *Transition*, 28 April 1995.

59 See Munro, 'Central Asia and China', pp. 230–3.

60 *Segodnya*, 25 May 1995; Radio Free Europe/Radio Liberty, *Research Report Supplement* 1994/28, p. 7; Olcott, *Central Asia's New States*, pp. 64, 90 and 132–3.

61 *Slovo kyrgyzstana*, 24 May 1995.

62 *Res publika*, 5 June 1996.

63 *Economic Intelligence Unit, Country Profile*, 1995–96, p. 13.

64 *Nezavisimaya gazeta*, 7 February 1995.

65 *BBC Summary of World Broadcasts*, SU/1795, G/1–2, 16 September 1993 and SU/W0276, A/5, 9 April 1993; *Nezavisimaya gazeta*, 3 November 1994.

66 See the surveys quoted in N. Lubin, *Central Asians Take Stock: Reform, Corruption and Identity* (Washington, 1994), p. 6.

67 The figures used here are taken from a variety of sources including various pages of the *Economist Intelligence Unit, Country Profile, 1995–96, Segodnya*, 3 November 1995, *Kazakhstanskaya pravda*, 7 December 1995, *Open Media Research Institute*, 19, 26 January 1996; it should be noted that all economic statistics from the region are questionable, especially those from Turkmenistan and Uzbekistan, and that even the estimates of bodies such as the International Monetary Fund and the European Bank for Reconstruction and Development often clash.

68 *Economist Intelligence Unit, Country Profile, 1995–96*, p. 13.

69 *Res publika*, 18 June 1996.

70 *Slovo kyrgyzstana*, 25 May 1994, *Economist Intelligence Unit, Country Profile 1995–96*, p. 90; *Res publika*, 16 January 1996.

71 *Segodnya*, 8 February 1994.

72 Olcott, *Central Asia's New States*, p. 101.

73 *Izvestiya*, 23 January 1993.

74 The more optimistic argument concerning Uzbekistan's prospects can be found in F. S. Starr, 'Making Eurasia stable', *Foreign Affairs*, January–February 1996, 80–92.

6

The search for identity: nation-building and the Islamic factor

During the first months of independence numerous outside commentators, all too often relying on impressionistic evidence rather than any solid knowledge of the region, suggested that the defining characteristic of Central Asia was its Islamic heritage and expressed fears that the region would unite with the wider Muslim world, increasingly seen as the new post-Cold War 'enemy'. Press articles discussed the possible rise of 'fundamentalism' on Russia's southern flank. Conversely, some Islamic activists in the Middle East and elsewhere saw Central Asia as a potential growth area for religious influence. These fears and hopes were seemingly reinforced by early reports of the rise of Muslim militias in the Fergana valley and, more significantly, by events in Tajikistan during 1992 where for a brief moment an Islamic-dominated opposition removed the old communist regime (see Chapter 7). Yet in reality the picture was more complex, for although culturally and historically these states belong with the Muslim world, any commitment to creating Islamic orders was limited to small groups of activists in Central Asia. For the Soviet-educated and largely secular elites, an appeal to Islamic symbols and traditions might be seen to be a useful political tool with which to reinforce their legitimacy, but they had no intention of allowing Islam any substantive political role.

Islam remained an important part of the region's social and cultural life and one that in many respects served to complicate the programme of nation-building embarked upon by these states after 1991. In particular, the growth in the public space offered to religion was one of the factors that served to alienate the substantial Russian-speaking population of the region, a group whose skills were likely to be needed in the short term but who felt threatened by their loss of status in the new Central Asia. This in turn was part of a much wider problem facing these states as they sought to make a reality of their independence. Because many of the region's peoples' identities and loyalties remained staunchly local and communal, despite 70 years of Muscovite attempts to forge national and supra-national loyalties. Though the Soviet state had created embryonic nation-states, the boundaries within which these were situated often sat loosely with the ethnic distribution of the population. This situation had been further complicated by voluntary and forced migration to the region during the Stalin years and after. All of this created a complex ethnic situation, with a potential for strife that had been revealed in the bloody communal violence that had swept the region in 1989–90. For the new rulers of Central Asia the challenge was to create a sense of belonging or common citizenship open to all residents of their territories whilst seeking to restore the traditions, culture and sense of identity of the titular nationality.

Nationalising the nation

The five new states that came into being in late 1991 had no previous experience of independent nationhood, and it remained unclear as to whether 70 years of Soviet-shaped nation-building had succeeded in engendering a sense of loyalty to the nation as such. Prior to 1917 the predominantly rural population's prime loyalty belonged with family and local communities, though some may have had a vague sense of being 'Muslim'. In the early 1920s the Soviet authorities created a series of embryonic states based upon ethno-linguistic criteria, but in the early period this seems to have done little to overcome traditional identities.[1] The situation was further complicated by the fact that Stalin sought to combine states created on an ethnic basis with some degree of economic rationality. In consequence many of these states were created on the basis of highly artificial boundaries. For example, Bukhara and Samarkand were included in Uzbekistan, despite that fact that at the time nearly 75 per cent of their population defined themselves as Tajik.[2] Other problematic areas included: the Fergana valley, the vast majority of whose population is Uzbek, but which came to be divided between three states – Uzbekistan, Tajikistan and Kyrgyzstan; parts of the Chimkent oblast in southern Kazakhstan where 90 per cent of that republic's Uzbeks were concentrated; and a whole variety of less substantial potential conflicts between the various states over territory, water and mineral rights, as well as tensions with the Caucasian minorities who had been deported to Central Asia by Stalin during the war years.[3]

Despite this, the last 70 years have witnessed a gradual, if halting, process of nation-building, with the definition of boundaries, the creation of administrative structures and the growth of literacy in the titular languages all helping to give people a sense of common belonging. Though the 'national communists' who set some of these processes in motion were·wiped out during the 1930s, the post-Stalin years witnessed, in somewhat distorted form, a return to their dream of republics controlled by native personnel who took into account the cultural particularities of their region. From the 1950s the percentages of native cadres in each republic's administration grew considerably, as did the general number of educated people amongst the wider population. Perhaps more significantly, one begins to witness during the Brezhnev years a growing nationalisation of the population of these republics. For example, Uzbeks made up 62.1 per cent of their republic in 1959, but 71.4 per cent thirty years later, whilst in Kazakhstan the number rose from 30 per cent to 39.7 per cent. In part these increases stemmed from natural increase, but from the late 1970s onwards this trend was exacerbated by out-migration, with around 300,000 Russians leaving in the 1980s.[4] Alongside this has gone the more recent trend towards strengthening the position of the titular nationalities in the urban areas. From the time of the Russian conquest these had tended to be dominated by Slavs, Tatars and other ethnic groups, and none of the Central Asian capital cities had majorities from the titular nationality in the immediate post-war years. Gradually, however, this has begun to change. In Uzbekistan the 1959 census revealed only 37.2 per cent of the urban population to be Uzbek, but by 1989 this had risen to 53.7 per cent, whilst the comparable figures for Kyrgyzstan were 13.2 per cent and 29.9 per cent.[5] These developments, alongside the lax control exercised over the region during the Brezhnev years, served to create anxieties amongst minorities, especially Slavs and Europeans, and these were only heightened by the bloody outbreaks of communal violence that took place in 1989–90. More importantly, perhaps, they served as the basis for a 'renationalisation' of the nation that was to be cautiously promoted from the late

1980s and given greater scope within the context of independent statehood in the 1990s.

From the end of 1991 representatives of the titular nationality were able, for the first time in the twentieth century, to take over the reins of government free of Moscow's tutelage. The consequences of this were felt in a number of spheres. In 1989–90 all five republics had passed language laws which established Uzbek, Kazakh, Kyrgyz, Tajik and Turkmen respectively as the state languages. From about the same period there began a process whereby numerous towns, streets and shops had been renamed, a process that accelerated in the first flush of independence. This in turn led to complaints that even in towns with large Russian-speaking populations it was impossible to find signs in Russian. In practice each state for a variety of financial and practical reasons – including the fact that many amongst the elites functioned better in Russian than in their own languages – has delayed full implementation of the languages laws.[6]

Together with the language changes have come slow but steady shifts towards the nationalisation of the political elite, with key Slavic officials in government, administration and economic management increasingly being replaced by representatives of the titular nationality. Such processes were not formally acknowledged in the region, despite the requirement of the Turkmen constitution that the president be an ethnic Turkmen rather than simply a citizen who met certain residence requirements and knew the state language as was demanded elsewhere in the region.[7] Nonetheless, the trend to the 'nativisation' of cadres was evident throughout Central Asia, even in Kazakhstan where Russians and other ethnic groups made up 57 per cent of the population. In 1994, for example, all six of the president's state counsellors were Kazakh, as were six of seven deputy prime ministers, and five of every six members of the presidential apparat, the education and the security ministries. Even in the northern oblasts where the vast majority of the population were Slavs such staffing patterns were reportedly common.[8] Evidence of ethnic engineering was also apparent in parliamentary elections, with all five republics producing legislatures in which the titular nationality was considerably over-represented, as in Kyrgyzstan where the elections of February 1995 produced a parliament that was nearly 75 per cent Kyrgyz at a time when they made up about 56 per cent of the population.[9]

Though such policies have been contested by representatives of minority groups, they are in the long term likely to be reinforced by demographic trends. On the one hand the higher birth rates of the region's traditional nationalities will speed up the trend of the post-Stalin years which saw their representation in the population increase. Conversely, and as we shall discuss later, the dynamism of the titular nationalities along with the post-independence changes in the position of Slavs and Europeans has dramatically increased the rate of out-migration on the part of the latter. In some cases this process has been further speeded up by the state's encouragement of immigration by co-ethnics currently living outside the borders of the state. This is most evident in Kazakhstan where the government initially offered considerable financial inducements to Kazakhs living in other Commonwealth of Independent States (CIS) states, Mongolia, China and elsewhere, to settle in the republic, especially in the northern areas currently dominated by Slavs. Though the expense and impact upon local Russian sensitivities had led to a curtailment of this policy by the mid-1990s, it indicated the desire of a republic dominated by an ethnic minority to further the nationalisation of its territory as a means of strengthening its prospects for survival as an independent state.[10]

Despite demographic improvements in the position of titular nationalities, the leaders of Central Asia still face many problems in seeking to create a sense of commitment to the nation-state. Leaving aside the position of the Russian-speaking community, fundamental problems stem from the continued strength of sub-national identities, which in Tajikistan have threatened the very existence of a unified state, as well as from the artificial boundaries created by the Soviet state in the 1920s. The latter has created potential tensions both within and between the states, with V. Kolossov of the Russian Academy of Sciences providing a very conservative estimate of 34 possible bones of contention between the region's states in 1991.[11]

As already noted, the national demarcation engineered by Stalin left representatives of each national group stranded in states dominated by others, and these have sometimes been seen as potential fifth columns by the host state and useful levers of influence by the 'parent' state. Whilst all the states have denied any irredentist inclinations, this has not stopped ethnic minorities from suggesting border changes, as did Uzbeks in the Osh region of Kyrgyzstan who in 1992 called for a referendum on whether to join Uzbekistan.[12]

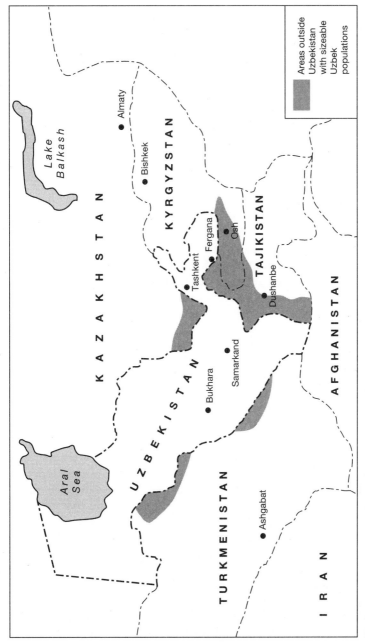

Map 2 Areas outside Uzbekistan with sizeable Uzbek populations

Perhaps more problematic have been Tajik–Uzbek relations, with the national demarcation leaving substantial minorities in each other's territory. In 1989 Tajiks in the town of Samarkand formed the organisation *Samarkand* to counter what it saw as the 'Uzbekisation' of the republic's Tajiks. Rejecting official claims that there were only 600,000 Tajiks in Uzbekistan, a figure that stemmed from a decades-old policy of persuading Tajiks to designate themselves as Uzbeks on their passports, *Samarkand* suggested that there were in fact 3.5 million. During 1991 this organisation enjoyed some success in persuading several thousand Tajiks to re-register themselves as such, but despite their public emphasis on more rights within Uzbekistan not union with Tajikistan, independence has led to increasing state pressures on Tajik activists, who have been repressed or forced into silence.[13] Whilst repression has been the experience of the most ardent activists, the Uzbek authorities have not been blind to the need to conciliate this sizeable proportion of its population. Officially there is no discouragement for those who wish to change their passport designation, the number of Tajik language classes available in schools has been increased, and in 1992 promises were made to increase the amount of television broadcasting in this language.[14]

Alongside tensions between the major nationalities of the region, there has also been a certain amount of hatred levelled at other minorities, evident both in the Fergana riots of 1989 which were directed against Mesketian Turks, and in the often tense relations between Kazakhs and Caucasian settlers during the early 1990s.[15]

Whilst such tensions create problems for the new states as they seek to find a balance between the often-conflicting claims of inclusiveness and nation-building, the continued persistence of sub-national loyalties within each ethnic community also poses certain difficulties. In Chapter 4 we discussed the continued importance of regional and tribal links in the politics of each state, and it is clear that in many parts of the region these override or run parallel to national identities. Though these rarely rise to the surface, such loyalties can create problems in developing a sense of national unity, as in Kazakhstan where the policy of giving key positions to members of the Greater Horde – real or perceived[16] – has aroused resentment in other Kazakh communities. On occasion this has resulted in the emergence of cross-ethnic alliances, as in the town of Pavlodar where attempts to impose a member of the dominant group as head of the local television station met protests from both Russians and Lesser Horde Kazakhs, each favouring the existing Russian candidate.[17]

What is less clear is the relative political salience of clan, regional and ethnic loyalties, though developments in Tajikistan indicate that sub-national divisions can have a devastating effect on political life. Such survey material as is available provides little evidence to suggest a strong sense of national identity. Lubin, for example, noted that when asked to which community it was most important to belong most Uzbeks and Kazakhs selected family or local community, with only 13 per cent in Uzbekistan and 4 per cent in Kazakhstan suggesting that the most important people were those 'of my nationality'. Nonetheless, over 90 per cent would prefer their children to marry someone of the same nationality,[18] whilst Novak reported that around 20 per cent of Uzbeks believe that Uzbekistan should be for the Uzbeks alone.[19] As suggested by Alexander Bennigsen, it seems to remain the case that most Central Asians have multiple identities in which communal, regional, national and religious loyalties co-exist.[20] In these circumstances it remains to be seen whether the leaders of Central Asia are capable of creating a sense of national unity which precludes the emergence of conflict within the state based upon these other inclinations, as well as whether this can be done in such a way as not to deny other nationalities a feeling of belonging.

Holding on to one's significant others

Central Asia's leaders have placed considerable emphasis on the need to preserve ethnic harmony within their republics, but special attention has often been devoted to conciliating the Slavic and European sections of the population. In part this stems from a recognition that these minorities, which tend to dominate the urban areas, possess many of the professional and technical skills which the new states require for the further development of their economy, the maintenance of social welfare structures and military establishments. For example, in Tajikistan on the eve of independence, Russians made up 7 per cent of the population but 21 per cent of specialists with a higher or specialised education, whilst the corresponding figures in Uzbekistan were 8.3 per cent to 17 per cent.[21] Though in the longer term representatives of the titular nationalities will be able to fill such positions, the almost total Slavic dominance of certain sectors could not be reversed overnight.

A second important factor is the sheer size of the Russian-speaking population. In 1989 there were nearly 12 million Russian speakers in Central Asia, with 9.5 million ethnic Russians, and of these around two-thirds had been born in the region. In three of the republics they made up less than 10 per cent of the population, but in Kyrgyzstan and Kazakhstan they made up a much larger proportion (21.5 per cent and 37.8 per cent respectively) and thus could not be ignored.[22] Finally these communities remained important players in the emerging relations between Russia and the successor states. Though virtually ignored during the first six months of independence, from late 1992 the fate and treatment of Russians in the 'near abroad' became a major issue in Russian politics. For Kazakhstan this was to be an especially sensitive issue, as Russian nationalists made frequent reference to its northern territories, with their predominantly Slavic population, as 'naturally' part of Russia.

The rhetoric of Central Asian leaders during the early months of independence was clearly aimed at reassuring the Slavic population that they were still wanted. To this end they have eschewed the narrow citizenship laws typical of the Baltic states and effectively offered membership of the community to all those resident at the time of independence – though some later introduced limited residency requirements for those wishing to buy privatised enterprises. Introducing the draft constitution in mid-1992, President Nazarbaev of Kazakhstan stressed that only if everyone worked together could independence be made a reality and he attacked nationalist groups such as *Alash* and *Jeltoqsan*, as well as the Union of Siberian Cossacks, for promoting national exclusivity.[23] In similar vein, Kyrgyzstan's President Akaev early on defined his nationality policy in terms of a simultaneous revival of Kyrgyz culture and sense of national identity with the realisation of the specific national interests of all ethnic groups.[24]

Yet in many areas rhetoric and reality clashed as the pressures of nation-building and reconciling minorities did not sit easily together. Nursultan Nazarbaev could speak of the need to create a multi-ethnic society, yet Article 1 of the 1993 constitution spoke about the republic as 'a state system determined by the Kazakh nation'. Simultaneously, as Neil Melvin has pointed out, the proclaimed commitment to equal rights for all citizens was undermined by a policy of 'nativisation' which sought to encourage the return of Kazakhs scattered across Asia, increasingly guaranteed top jobs for ethnic Kazakhs (or members of the Greater Horde) and saw the ever-expanding use of the Kazakh language in the media and administration.[25]

Of all the states it would appear to be Kyrgyzstan that has made the greatest efforts to encourage minorities, especially Germans and Slavs, to stay within the republic. Early in 1992 Akaev signed a decree setting up two German National Cultural Regions within the republic, with residents of these areas permitted dual citizenship (Kyrgyz and German) and the population given rights to decide certain socio-economic issues. Though some Kyrgyz nationalists opposed this development as an abrogation of sovereignty, proponents pointed out that the national regions remained subordinate to Bishkek politically and that the concession on dual citizenship should be treated as a special case.[26] A similar concern to conciliate the Russian population was evident in the decision to create a Slavonic University in Bishkek in 1992. This brought forth howls of protest, but was nonetheless opened in 1993.[27]

Conflicting pressures on the political leaderships could also be seen in the revitalisation of the language issue during Central Asian constitutional debates in 1992 and 1993. Questions seemingly resolved by the state language laws adopted in 1989–90 came to the fore once more, with many arguing for a change in the status of Russian, based upon the fact that very few Slavs knew the state language at the time of independence – those Russians fluent in the state language varied from 0.9 per cent in Kazakhstan to 4.5 per cent in Uzbekistan.[28] In Kyrgyzstan one contributor to the debate suggested that Russian speakers should not be discriminated against because the old Soviet system did not encourage them to learn the language. Along with other writers he complained about the inadequacy of facilities for learning Kyrgyz, pointing out that acquiring any real facility in a second language would take years and probably be impossible for the older generation.[29] Similar arguments were later taken up in Kazakh parliamentary debates where deputy N. Gert suggested that given the inadequacy of language-learning facilities it would be highly discriminatory to propose the removal of non-Kazakhs from key administrative posts within the relatively short time scale envisaged by the original laws.[30]

Others focused on the realities of the language situation in most of these republics, as in Kazakhstan where nearly half of Kazakhs under 40 found Russian easier to use.[31] Another variant of the realism argument pointed to the region's continued links with the CIS countries in which Russian would remain a natural medium of communication. Alongside this approach was the claim that for any of those involved in cultural or technical exchange, or for those seeking scientific education, all the major texts and scholarly publications that were not in European languages were likely to be in Russian.[32] Others appealed to international experience, with Switzerland a commonly used example. In Turkmenistan F. Kost wrote to the republican paper pointing out that many states worked quite well with two or more state languages, and he mentioned particularly Canada and Belgium.[33] Above all, however, it was the wider implication of failing to give Russian greater due that proved decisive for many writers. In particular there was the argument raised by 71 Russians in Kyrgyzstan who suggested that only by having two state languages was there any hope of staunching the mass outflow of Russian speakers from this and other Central Asian republics.[34]

Such arguments, though given considerable prominence in the Russian language press, were not left unanswered. Many pointed to the disastrous effect on the native languages of 70 years of Soviet rule which had left many young people without the means to recover their cultural and national identity. For opponents of change the analogy with the situation in Switzerland was inappropriate as this was a confederation with three distinctive cultural communities whose languages had deep historical roots and who had not been nearly wiped out by an assimilationist, imperial power.[35] The suggestion that Russian should operate as the language of 'inter-ethnic communication' was firmly rejected in Kazakhstan where one writer argued that the idea of the state telling people how to speak with each other was absurd. For example, did it make any sense for a Kazakh to speak with a Uighur in Russian when their own languages were much closer?[36]

These debates over language in turn reflected a wider concern amongst non-titular nationality groups that the new constitutions gave greater rights to one nation than the others. In Kyrgyzstan, veteran K. Tashiev expressed unease about the constitutional commitment to a 'national renaissance' and wondered what this would entail.[37] This disquiet was reflected in opinion polls undertaken in Kazakhstan which showed that 23.2 per cent of those questioned felt that the 1992 constitutional draft favoured one national group, whilst 27.7 per cent thought it failed to guarantee adequately the rights of citizens regardless of nationality.[38]

Such issues were impossible to solve in a way that satisfied everyone. If republican leaders were seen to make too many concessions to the Russian-speaking groups they endangered their nationalist legitimacy, but if they failed to satisfy the Russian-speaking groups they were in danger of losing tens of thousands of skilled citizens and complicating their relationship with a major state which still met many of their economic needs. Worse still, as Eugene Huskey has pointed out in relation to Kyrgyzstan, the language issue became a political football as rival sections of the titular elite struggled for position within their republics.[39] At the end of the day few concessions were made to the concerns of Russian speakers, though in Kazakhstan deputies did manage to insert a phrase describing Russian as the 'language of inter-ethnic communication'.[40] In neighbouring Kyrgyzstan, however, this phrasing was rejected by deputies on the grounds that it was simply meaningless in legal terms and that constitutions could only speak of state languages. Nonetheless Article 5 as adopted stressed the equal functioning of Russian and all other languages, and prohibited any discrimination on the grounds of not knowing the state language.[41]

Whatever the rhetoric and the good intentions of Central Asian leaders, developments such as these did little to reassure the Russian-speaking population that they had a future in the newly independent states. A study produced by the Moscow-based Gorbachev Foundation in 1993 suggested that for Russians in the near-abroad various factors were contributing towards the 'social discomfort of Russians'. These included:

- growing evidence of ethno-centric domination often leading to *de facto* limits on the rights of Russians and other minorities;
- state language laws which gave inadequate transition periods and made few arrangements for learning that language;
- discrimination in work, housing and education;
- the trend towards Islamicisation of everyday life in a number of states;
- worsening personal relations with neighbours and members of the

local community in everyday life, evident, for example, in the dismissive tone adopted by shopkeepers and providers of services;
- military conflicts in some states leading to a sense of personal insecurity;
- limitations on minority rights in the fields of privatisation, land reform etc.[42]

To this one might add the feeling that in Central Asia representatives of the non-titular nationalities were being excluded from political life. These perceptions of inequality were hardly helped by the pressures on minority activists, people such as Boris Suprunyuk in northern Kazakhstan whose fiery agitation for Russian rights led to his arrest and temporary imprisonment.[43] In similar vein, a group of Russian reporters who made a television programme for Moscow TV in which they discussed the emigration of Russians from Kazakhstan found themselves accused of stirring up ethnic hatred and ostracised by officialdom.[44] At the same time, one could understand why the authorities in this republic in particular might see their Russian communities as a potential fifth column, especially when meetings of the latter were sometimes accompanied by calls for the re-creation of the Soviet Union.[45]

Though Central Asian leaders sometimes suggested that the primary reason for Russian unhappiness and an inclination to leave stemmed from the economic hardships associated with transition, most studies indicated a wide range of issues contributing towards these people's 'social discomfort'. Surveys carried out in Kyrgyzstan in late summer 1992 showed that amongst the main reasons that made Russians think about emigration were a perceived worsening of inter-ethnic relations (59.7 per cent), the adoption of laws effectively reducing the rights of Russians (29.4 per cent), problems associated with getting a good education for one's children (16.5 per cent), and the threat of physical violence (13.2 per cent), whilst economic factors such as fear of unemployment (7.6 per cent) and price rises (6.6 per cent) were generally deemed less important.[46] In such circumstances, Russians and other minorities faced a series of choices in the early 1990s. Should they simply leave Central Asia, recognising that population dynamics and the growing nativisation of these states denied them any long-term future; or should they stay and seek to adapt to their new status, whether through passive acceptance, pushing the leaders of these states to provide stronger guarantees of their future, or looking to the larger Russian state for protection and support?

For those who could emigrate, this seemed to offer a way out. Even before the collapse of the USSR the Slavic proportion of the region's population suffered as a result of high local birth rates and emigration, but from the late 1980s this process was speeded up in the face of ethnic conflict and the perception that once these states achieved independence Russian speakers would lose many of the privileges they had long taken for granted. Though statistics on emigration are often contradictory, confused by both political considerations – with each state having an interest in understating the total and Russian nationalists often keen to inflate it – and the vague categories used – it is often unclear, for example, whether totals given refer to all emigrants, Russian speakers or ethnic Russians – sufficient information is available to give an idea of general trends.

The most dramatic shifts took place in Tajikistan where civil strife led 80 per cent of the 380,000-strong Russian population to leave by mid-1993.[47] In Uzbekistan it seemed initially that political stability would encourage many to stay yet by the end of 1995 about half a million had left, including Jews and Tatars. Simultaneously many who remained opted to take out Russian citizenship as a precaution against future difficulties.[48] In Kyrgyzstan Russian out-migration was stimulated by a number of factors, including the bloody communal violence of 1990, the adoption of the state language law and the anti-Russian tone that often pervaded the 1991 celebrations of the 75th anniversary of the 1916 uprising in the steppes.[49] Of the 918,000 Russians living there in 1989 (making up 21 per cent of the population), around 170,000 had left by 1994, whilst of the 102,000 Germans about 40,000 left during the same period.[50] Although the Kyrgyz authorities could by late 1994 point to a declining rate of emigration as evidence of their success in convincing these people that they had a future, it may simply be that emigration was a far tougher option for the elderly or for those who lacked family connections or marketable skills that could ensure their well-being back in Russia. Kazakhstan saw over a third of the million Germans living in the republic in 1989 depart by 1995,[51] and well over a million Russian speakers of the nearly 8 million resident in 1989.[52] By early 1996 it was being reported that nearly 3 million Russian speakers had left Central Asia since the late 1980s, roughly a quarter of the Slavic population.[53]

Emigration raised particular concern in Kazakhstan and Kyrgyzstan, where the first to go were often skilled personnel necessary to the management of the industrial sector or those playing a key role in the education and welfare areas. For example, in 1993 alone, Kyrgyzstan witnessed the departure of 1,000 doctors,[54] whilst the following year saw the single oblast of Ust-Kamenogorsk in Kazakhstan lose 302 teachers and 55 doctors.[55] Nonetheless, many *émigrés* did not find it easy in the new Russia and in 1994 alone, some 70,000 returned to Kazakhstan, of whom about 30,000 were ethnic Russians.[56] Most of these had lived all their lives in Central Asia and found the Russia to which they moved an alien world. Customs, the pace of life and even simple things like the heavy drinking habits in the motherland disturbed them. They were also politically alienated from the new quasi-democratic Russia, tending to blame perestroika and democratisation for the collapse of the USSR and their subsequent woes.[57]

Many Russian speakers remained behind, some unable to emigrate and others still unsure as to whether they could carve out a viable future for themselves and their families elsewhere. In Kazakhstan and Kyrgyzstan, where some form of autonomous organisation remained possible, activists gathered together and agitated for greater rights and more guarantees for Russian speakers. In Kazakhstan, a number of organisations emerged, some highly provocative and inclined to actions that provoked the republican authorities. Within this category should be placed the Russian Community, whose leader Boris Suprunyuk was arrested and charged with promoting racial hatred in 1994, and various Cossack organisations, whose meetings have often been accompanied by calls for the reunification of the northern oblasts with Russia. *Lad*, which started life coordinating the activities of Russian cultural centres but became increasingly political, has adopted a more conciliatory tone, campaigning in particular for improving the status of the Russian language and dual citizenship.[58] Though representatives of the latter organisation were hindered in their efforts to contest the December 1995 parliamentary elections, Nazarbaev appeared to make a conciliatory gesture in inviting one of its leaders, Mikhail Golovkov, to serve as one of the seven presidentially-nominated senators.[59] Similar organisations appeared in Kyrgyzstan, with the most influential appearing to be *Soglasie*, created in 1994, whose objective was to persuade Russians that they had a future in the new state.[60]

Whilst Russian speakers sought ways to improve their position, government leaders strove to encourage them to stay. Addressing a round table discussion on 'Russians in Kyrgyzstan' in June 1994, President Akaev argued for the development of a new state ideology based upon the slogan 'Kyrgyzstan – Our Common Home'. What this would mean in practice might, he suggested, include the creation of nationality-based quotas for elections, giving greater rights to the Russian language, developing more Russian–Kyrgyz economic ventures, and perhaps even reconsidering the vexed question of dual citizenship.[61] That summer he issued a decree postponing the full implementation of the language law until 2005,[62] and then, addressing a constitutional convention in December, albeit one in which Slavs were severely under-represented, he went on to propose further changes to Article 5 of the constitution dealing with the state language. These would permit, in those areas where nationalities other than Kyrgyz predominated, the use of the dominant language in an official capacity. In addition Russian would be recognised as an official language in the spheres of industry and health care, in technical areas and in other areas 'where the achievements of progress were associated with the use of Russian'.[63] Though discussion petered out in 1995, in March 1996 the Kyrgyz parliament accepted in principle a proposal to give Russian the status of an official language, and this was approved by the Constitutional Court in June 1996.[64] In Kazakhstan the issue was not discussed to quite the same extent by the leadership, though some movement was evident in a decision of mid-1995 to postpone the full introduction of Kazakh in state administration until 2010.[65]

The final option for those unhappy with the new dispensation lay in appeals to the protection of Moscow. Initially disinterested in the fate of 'its' minorities, the Kremlin was made increasingly aware of the issue by the rise of nationalist and 'patriotic' forces in Russian politics. Although Foreign Minister Kozyrev preferred to deal with the issue through quiet diplomacy, after growing conservative criticism during 1993 and especially after the December parliamentary elections, he started to make bellicose statements about Russia's right to protect Russian speakers in the 'near abroad'.[66] Mounting pressure could be seen in a number of areas, starting with the relatively quiet pressure on the language issue during the constitutional debates of 1992–93. Only occasionally did these reach the public domain, as in March 1993 when the Russian ambassador in Kyrgyzstan delivered a letter to Akaev from Boris Yeltsin calling for Russian to be given a special status.[67] A second issue constantly under discussion in diplomatic meetings related to the question of dual citizenship, though apart from Turkmenistan and Tajikistan the Central Asian states were unwilling to compromise on this issue. As one Kazakh official put it, dual citizenship could all too easily lead to 'dual loyalty'.[68]

The other hope, expressed in particular by some Russian speakers in northern Kazakhstan, was that Moscow would seek ways to reincorporate part of the territory into southern Russia. Such discussions aroused considerable ire in Almaty, with the Kazakh Procurator-General seeking to ban the paper *Komsomol'skaya pravda* from the republic in May 1996 after it published Alexander Solzhenitsyn's call for the creation of a greater Russia incorporating these territories.[69] In practice, however, all but a few diehards recognised that such proposals were impracticable without the restoration of the Soviet Union.[70] For the moment those remaining have to make a choice as to whether or not they can live with the existing pressures, and perhaps have to take important decisions regarding their possible future under the next generation of Central Asian leaders who will not have received their political education in Soviet institutions and will probably lack the sensitivity of existing presidents to Russian concerns. Given this Russians who can probably will continue to leave, but a substantial minority will be forced to stay and make the best of their new-found and much-reduced status.

The role of Islam

One of the factors sometimes cited as contributing to their 'social discomfort' by Slavic and European residents of Central Asia was the growing role of Islam in public life. During the latter part of the Gorbachev period, the position of Islam had altered considerably. Though changing religious policies had been slow to affect Muslims, by 1989 the impact of the new dispensation was becoming apparent. Mosques began to be reopened, more personnel entered theological training institutes, leading Islamic figures were elected to parliamentary bodies and made appearances in the media, key religious feasts were turned into public holidays (except in Kazakhstan), and political elites took pains to be seen showing respect for Islam. At the same time it was made clear that religious institutions could neither aspire to an overt political role nor escape their duty to support state institutions. Thus in the spring of 1991 the mufti of Central Asia and Kazakhstan Muhammed Sadyk called on all Muslims to perform their military service, something he described as a sacred duty.[71]

With independence the largely secular elites of Central Asia faced a dilemma. On the one hand they needed to develop for themselves sufficient Islamic credentials to reinforce legitimacy but on the other they had no intention of allowing Islamic activism to challenge their own positions. In consequence, as Martha Olcott has pointed out, these regimes have come to recognise that in practice Islamic revival has taken two forms, one which they can live with and one which they have firmly rejected.[72] Insofar as Islamic revival has entailed a rediscovery of an ancient cultural heritage and a greater degree of participation in religious ritual, the authorities do not necessarily feel threatened, although one side-effect of allowing more scope to religious institutions may be to give religious leaders greater authority amongst the population. Moreover, the nature of this revival, the content of which has mainly to do with cultural and customary spheres of life, suggests that the people of the region have yet to acquire a politically salient Islamic identity. For example, surveys carried out in Uzbekistan and Kazakhstan in mid-1993 reported that only about half of respondents in the former and a quarter in the latter described themselves as practising believers (though the sample included Slavs as well as Muslims). The same survey revealed differences according to age – with only 39 per cent of those Uzbek respondents in their twenties calling themselves believers as against two-thirds of the over-sixties – and according to region – not surprisingly the Fergana valley recording higher levels of practice than Tashkent. More importantly, religious identities were consistently placed below loyalties to family or local community. The same survey showed that only 11 per cent of Muslim respondents in Uzbekistan and 2 per cent in Kazakhstan saw an Islamic state as desirable, whilst very few in Uzbekistan felt that the religious affiliation of the state leader was important.[73] Equally clear is that even amongst the more active Islamicist constituency a commitment to change, moral purity or social justice is not always matched by any real understanding of Islamic teaching or deep familiarity with the Koran.[74]

Nonetheless, wary of the potency of religion, the leaders of Central Asia have taken steps to ensure control over religious institutions and to prevent the politicisation of Islam. Each state has passed laws prohibiting political parties that are based upon religion and each has maintained some degree of state control over religion. In this they were aided by the break-up of the Soviet-created Muslim Administration of Central Asia and Kazakhstan in the early 1990s which led each republic's Muslim establishment to set up its own institutions. First to do so was Kazakhstan where, under Nazarbaev's patronage, Ratbek Nisanbaev became mufti of an independent board. Here, where the president stood out in refusing to describe himself as a Muslim, the mufti supported the official view that the creation of Islamic parties would endanger ethnic harmony in this multinational and multiethnic republic.[75] Consquently Kazakhstan has kept in place a Council for Religious Affairs attached to the republican Council of Ministers, whose responsibilities appear to include not just the guaranteeing of religious freedom, but also ensuring that religious institutions do not act beyond the parameters established by the state.[76]

In Kyrgyzstan President Akaev has proved more willing to utilise Islamic symbols, but is equally suspicious of religious activism. For this reason the previously-favoured mufti Sadyqan Kamalov was replaced in 1993, reportedly because of his close ties to Islamicists in Uzbekistan's Fergana valley.[77] During the summer of 1995 a presidential decree forbade the teaching of religion or atheism in public schools,[78] and in August 1995 a state body to monitor religious organisations was established, a move that may have stemmed from security service claims about the growth of 'fundamentalism' in the southern regions of the country. Yet this body soon appeared to be following the practices of its predecessors in seeking to ensure political control over religious bodies, in late 1996 organising a gathering of the republic's Muslims at which the incumbent mufti was replaced.[79] Turkmenistan's approach has in many respects followed Soviet practice and, despite the expansion in the number of mosques, religious activities and appointments remain under the control of the state. Yet simultaneously Niyazov has sought to bolster his Islamic credentials. Though the constitution speaks of the state as secular, the president has proposed the teaching of Islamic history in schools, permitted the decriminalisation of traditional marriage practices and allowed morning radio broadcasts to begin with a prayer, albeit one that emphasises loyalty to the leader as incumbent upon good Muslims.[80]

Of all the states of Central Asia it is perhaps Uzbekistan that has the strongest religious traditions, with the Bukhara region having played a vital role in the development of Islamic theology and Sufi mysticism, and the Fergana valley having provided the religious activists who occasionally challenged Russian rule from the late nineteenth century onwards. It was in Uzbekistan, along with Tajikistan, that the second form of religious revival identified by Olcott took place and this was far less warmly received by Uzbekistan President Islam Karimov. Despite the ravages of the Stalin years a few traditional Muslim teachers survived, spreading their message to individuals and small groups outside the confines of the official Islamic establishment. Of these the most significant seem to have been located in the Fergana valley, with Uzbek scholar Abdujabar Abduvakhitov ascribing particular importance to the role of Hakim Qari (born around 1898) in Margilan and his estranged pupil Rahmatulla (1950–1981). With a small number of colleagues the latter appears to have been especially influential, counting Uzbek mufti Muhammed Sadyk amongst his pupils. From the late 1970s many of these people were involved in spreading radical Islamic views through illegal Koranic schools and distributing literature throughout the Fergana valley. By the late 1980s some of these activists and their students were able to become imams of restored and reopened mosques, whilst others became involved in efforts to create Islamic political movements in Uzbekistan and elsewhere.[81] It may also be that activists from these circles had influence beyond the boundaries of Central Asia, for a 1989 report of the Russian Federation Council for Religious Affairs noted that at least one of the activists behind Islamic demonstrations of that year in the capital of Daghestan, Makhachkala, had trained under a leading 'fundamentalist' in the Andizhan region.[82]

During 1989–90 various attempts were made to create Islamic political organisations, of which the most significant was the Islamic Renaissance Party (IRP). In early June 1992 some 200 ulema and activists from around the USSR met in Astrakhan to set up the IRP and proclaimed their commitment to revitalising Islam within the context of the Soviet Union. Though a Central Asian branch of the party was established this was dominated by Tajik activists, rooted in the dense network of unofficial mosques and Koranic schools which had flourished in that republic during the late Soviet period.[83] In Uzbekistan the state consistently refused to register the IRP, claiming that its charter contradicted the law on freedom of conscience which prohibited religious involvement in political activity.[84] An equally hostile response was met by the Islamic Democratic Party of Turkestan based in Uzbekistan but seeking to unite all the Muslims of Central Asia in an independent state following Islamic law.[85] The denial of legal status could not in itself prevent the direct challenges to the Uzbek state's authority posed by developments in the Fergana valley from mid-1991 onwards. As the Soviet Union collapsed, various Muslim militias were formed to make good the deficencies of the authorities in combating what was seen as a rising tide of crime and immorality. In Namangan alone there were reported to be some 60 groups with 2,500 members meting out justice on the spot to alleged offenders who had little opportunity to defend themselves against false charges.[86] By the beginning of 1992 it appeared that Fergana was developing its own self-government independent of the state, and it was clear that religious leaders often enjoyed greater authority than their state counterparts. In March after a visit to the region and, according to some reports, following the discovery of oil there, Karimov ordered a clamp-down which led to the arrests of dozens of Islamic and other opposition activists in the region.[87]

Perhaps more importantly it alerted the authorities to the potential challenge that Islam might pose to their position, a threat reinforced by developments in Tajikistan. In consequence Karimov has sought to ensure that whilst religious institutions enjoy greater scope for their activities than hitherto this should not be read as giving them the right to interfere in the public sphere. At one level this stance has led to the creation of a committee for religious affairs attached to the government, which though headed by a mullah has in large part replicated past Soviet efforts to seek control over religious life.[88] The state has also become involved in religious appointments, with the vetting of those put forward for leading positions and the removal of offending clerics. First amongst these was mufti Muhammed Sadyk who was 'retired' in 1993, following allegations of financial irregularities, but in fact was probably sacked as a result of his calls for a greater Islamicisation of the republic and his ties with Islamic activists in the Fergana valley and Tajikistan.[89] Though seemingly subdued the problem would not go away, as Islamic leaders retained their influence in many communities and as some continued to spread the idea of Islamic rule, albeit a little more discreetly. In the face of this there were reports in 1994 that the state had begun to resume old Soviet practices, refusing to register new mosques and monitoring closely what was being said in sermons.[90] More outspoken clergy also came under pressure, with one popular Andizhan imam arrested at Tashkent airport and then disappearing,[91] whilst the popular Tashkent imam Obidkhon Nazarov was forcibly removed from his position in 1996 despite the protests of believers.[92]

Conclusion

On the eve of independence many commentators were writing of an 'Islamic threat' to Central Asia, though the evidence to back up such a claim was somewhat limited. Whilst the leaders of the region have been willing to use Islam to reinforce their own legitimacy at home and abroad, they have frequently made it clear that religion has no place in political life. Nor are they willing to develop a distinctly Islamic-leaning foreign policy. Economic decline, though real, has so far not produced the mass unrest that some predicted and which might have found in Islamic slogans a rallying cry or mobilising force. Extremism of all sorts has been discouraged, though regional leaders have not been insensitive to religious concerns. Thus Uzbekistan has reportedly banned religious proselytism, whilst in Kazakhstan protests from both the Russian Orthodox Church and the Muslim establishment led the republic's Council for Religious Affairs to discuss ways of limiting the multiplicity of religious sects that had tried to find a foothold in the country since 1991.[93] Yet such actions reflect less concern about religion *per se* than the overriding desire of regional leaders to preserve stability within their own states and the region as a whole. Such an imperative has also been at the heart of their nation-building efforts by means of which they have attempted, not always successfully, to find ways of giving all citizens a sense of belonging in the new state whilst simultaneously rebuilding a sense of national unity and pride amongst the titular nationality. For this reason regional leaders have been quick to discourage the activities of ethnic, regional or religious groups that might upset the stability of their states or threaten to create the Tajik-style scenario that will be discussed in Chapter 7.

Notes

1   See the comments in M. E. Subtelny, 'The symbiosis of Turk and
    Tajik', in B. Manz, ed., *Central Asia in Historical Perspective* (Boul-
    der, 1994), pp. 51–2.
2   *Nezavisimaya gazeta*, 25 December 1992.
3   G. Gleason, 'Uzbekistan: from statehood to nationhood?', in I.
    Bremmer and R. Taras, eds, *Nations and Politics in the Soviet Suc-
    cessor States* (Cambridge, 1993), pp. 350–1; R. Kaiser, 'Ethnic
    demography and interstate relations in Central Asia', in R. Szporluk,
    ed., *National Identity and Ethnicity in Russia and the New States of
    Eurasia* (New York, 1994), pp. 230–65.
4   Kaiser, 'Ethnic demography and interstate relations', pp. 234 and
    250.
5   Yu. Novak, 'Mezhetnicheskie otnosheniya v Uzbekistane', *Sotsio-
    logicheskie issledovaniya*, 1994:4, 41–52; on Kyrgyzstan see I.
    Kostyukova, 'The towns of Kyrgyzstan change their faces:
    Rural–urban migrants in Bishkek', *Central Asian Survey*, 13:3, 1994,
    425–34; Kaiser, 'Ethnic demography and interstate relations',
    p. 240.
6   See the discussion of this in W. Fierman, 'Independence and the
    declining priority of language law implementation in Uzbekistan', in
    Y. Roi, ed., *Muslim Eurasia – Conflicting Legacies* (London, 1995),
    pp. 205–30.
7   Many Russians and representatives of other groups argued that even
    the latter formulation was discriminatory given the tiny minority
    who knew the dominant language, something that stemmed from
    Soviet policies which did not encourage them to learn it rather than
    from any lack of commitment to the states in which many had lived
    all their lives. *Nezavisimaya gazeta*, 7 April 1995.
8   *Nezavisimaya gazeta*, 2 April 1994.
9   *Slovo kyrgyzstana*, 4 March 1995 and 28 March 1995.
10 I. Bremmer and C. Welt, 'The trouble with democracy in Kaza-
    khstan', *Central Asian Survey*, 15:2, 1996, 184.
11 V. Kolossov, *Ethno-Territorial Conflicts and Boundaries in the Former
    USSR* (Durham, 1992), pp. 49–50.
12 *BBC Summary of World Broadcasts*, SU/1387, B/7, 22 May 1993; see
    Karimov's rejection of irredentist claims in *Nezavisimaya gazeta*, 15
    May 1992.
13 See *Moskovskie novosti*, 22 March 1992; *Nezavisimaya gazeta*, 22
    December 1992; E. Naby, 'Ethnicity and Islam in Central Asia', *Cen-
    tral Asian Survey*, 12:2, 1993, 151–68.
14 *Nezavisimaya gazeta*, 25 December 1992; it is not entirely clear that

the latter has happened, with one observer noting very little Tajik broadcasting even on the local Samarkand channel. R. Foltz, 'The Tajiks of Uzbekistan', *Central Asian Survey*, 15:2, 1996, 313–16.

15 This affected both Chechens deported to the region during the war and Caucasians brought in to work in the energy sector. *Izvestiya*, 19 October 1992; *Nezavisimaya gazeta*, 29 April 1993.

16 The available evidence makes it hard to assess the extent to which Horde and tribal connections do play a role in appointments and Shirin Akiner has suggested that divisions based upon economic differences rather than those rooted in kinship networks are more significant in modern Kazakh politics. S. Akiner, *The Formation of Kazakh Identity: From Tribe to Nation State* (London, 1995), pp. 75–6.

17 N. Melvin, 'Russia and the ethno-politics of Kazakhstan', *World Today*, November 1993, 210.

18 N. Lubin, 'Islam and ethnic identity in Central Asia: The view from below', in Roi, *Muslim Eurasia*, pp. 62–5.

19 Novak, 'Mezhetnicheskie otnosheniya', 49–50.

20 A. Bennigsen, 'Several nations or one people? Ethnic consciousness amongst Soviet Central Asian Muslims', *Survey*, 24:3, 1979, 51–64.

21 R. Abdulatipov, 'Russian minorities – The political dimension', in V. Shlapentokh, ed., *The New Russian Diaspora: Russian Minorities in the Former Soviet Republics* (New York, 1994), p. 39.

22 More detailed statistical information can be found in N. Melvin, *Forging the New Russian Nation* (London, 1994), p. 3; Kaiser, 'Ethnic demography and interstate relations', pp. 234 and 255.

23 *Kazakhstanskaya pravda*, 2 June 1992.

24 *Slovo kyrgyzstana*, 7 January 1992.

25 N. Melvin, *Russians beyond Russia – The Politics of National Identity* (London, 1995), pp. 108–10.

26 *Slovo kyrgyzstana*, 7 January 1992 and 25 February 1992.

27 *Nezavisimaya gazeta*, 7 October 1992; Radio Free Europe/Radio Liberty, *Supplement*, 1993/37, p. 8.

28 Emil Pain, 'The disintegration of the empire and the fate of the "imperial minority"', in Shlapentokh, *The New Russian Diaspora*, p. 24.

29 *Slovo kyrgyzstana*, 10 February 1993; on 21 February 1995 the same paper reported that around 6 per cent of Russians knew Kyrgyz.

30 *Kazakhstanskaya pravda*, 12 December 1992.

31 *Kazakhstanskaya pravda*, 25 July 1992; according to a later report some 75 per cent of Kazakhs were fluent in Russian, but only 1 per cent of Russians knew Kazakh.

32 *Turkmenskaya iskra*, 6 April 1992; *Slovo kyrgyzstana*, 10 March 1993.

33 *Turkmenskaya iskra*, 3 April 1992.
34 *Slovo kyrgyzstana*, 12 March 1993.
35 *Kazakhstanskaya pravda*, 22 September 1992 and 10 October 1992.
36 *Kazakhstanskaya pravda*, 4 August 1992.
37 *Slovo kyrgzstana* 24 March 1993.
38 *Kazakhstanskaya pravda*, 29 August 1992.
39 Huskey notes the presence of three groups in the language debate: the internationalists, made up of conservative Kyrgyz communists and leaders of European communities who seek to block meaningful implementation of the language laws, indigenisers including the leaders of nationalist groups, some intellectuals and many southern Kyrgyz, and moderates including the president who tend to come from the north and have a long history of intermingling with the Slavic community that is so prominent here. E. Huskey, 'The politics of language in Kyrgyzstan', *Nationalities Papers*, 23:3, 1995, 549–72.
40 *Nezavisimaya gazeta*, 27 January 1993.
41 See Akaev's speech to the Supreme Soviet on 12 April 1993. *Slovo kyrgyzstana*, 14 April 1993.
42 *Nezavisimaya gazeta*, 7 September 1993.
43 *Segodnya*, 15 April 1994.
44 *Nezavisimaya gazeta*, 28 May 1993.
45 See *Moskovkskie novosti*, 20–27 November 1994 and *Nezavisimaya gazeta*, 3 December 1994.
46 A whole series of tables dealing with motivations for emigrating or staying can be found in I. A. Subbotina, 'Russkaya diaspora: chislennost', passelenie. Migratsii', in A. I. Ginzburg, ed., *Russkie v novom zarubezh'e: Kirgiziya* (Moscow, 1994), pp. 55–86.
47 *Nezavisimaya gazeta*, 29 April 1993.
48 *Segodnya*, 8 June 1994; *Open Media Research Institute*, 38, 22 February 1996.
49 A. D. Nazarov and S. I. Nikolaev, 'Russkie v kirgizii: est' li alternativa iskhoda', in Ginzburg, *Russkie v novom zarubezh'e*, pp. 15–36.
50 *Slovo kyrgyzstana*, 14 June 1994; *BBC Summary of World Broadcasts*, SU/2294, G/1, 4 May 1995.
51 *Kazakhstanskaya pravda*, 2 September 1995.
52 *Nezavisimaya gazeta*, 26 May 1994; *Open Media Research Institute*, 169, 30 August 1995.
53 *Segodnya*, 6 March 1996.
54 *Megapolis ekspress*, 3 August 1994.
55 *Kazakhstanskaya pravda*, 4 April 1995; migration also had the potential to increase ethnic polarisation, as in Kazakhstan where many Russian speakers went not to Russia but from the southern to the northern oblasts, thus accentuating the north–south divide in the

country. Melvin, *Russians Beyond Russia*, p. 118.

56 *Nezavisimaya gazeta*, 24 April 1995 and 26 May 1995.
57 *Nezavisimaya gazeta*, 2 June 1993.
58 The last few sentences draw heavily on Melvin, *Russians Beyond Russia*, pp. 112–16, and accounts in the Moscow press of the pressures facing Russian activists.
59 *Nezavisimaya gazeta*, 3 February 1996.
60 *Slovo kyrgyzstana*, 31 May 1994.
61 *Slovo kyrgyzstana*, 14 June 1994.
62 *BBC Summary of World Broadcasts*, SU/2097, G/2.
63 *Slovo kyrgyzstana*, 7 December 1994.
64 *Open Media Research Institute*, 52, 13 March 1996; *Slovo kyrgyzstana*, 20 June 1996.
65 *Open Media Research Institute*, 116, 15 June 1995.
66 More will be said about this in Chapter 8, but see Melvin, *Forging the New Russian Nation*, pp. 27–48 on the relationship between this issue and domestic politics in Russia.
67 *BBC Summary of World Broadcasts*, SU/1642, B/12, 20 March 1993.
68 *Nezavisimaya gazeta*, 26 May 1994.
69 *Open Media Research Institute*, 105, 30 May 1996.
70 See the comments of the chairman of the Dzhalal-Abad branch of the organisation 'Slavic Diaspora' to this effect in *Slovo kyrgyzstana*, 21 February 1995.
71 *Turkmenskaya iskra*, 29 April 1991.
72 M. B. Olcott, 'Islam and fundamentalism in independent Central Asia', in Roi, *Muslim Eurasia*, pp. 23 and 25.
73 Lubin, 'Islam and ethnic identity in Central Asia', pp. 53–70.
74 R. G. Landa, 'Islamskii fundamentalizm', *Voprosi istorii*, 1993:1, 38–40.
75 On Islam in Kazakhstan see *Nezavisimaya gazeta*, 2 July 1992; R. Altoma, 'The influence of Islam in post-Soviet Kazakhstan', in Manz, *Central Asia in Historical Perspective*, pp. 164–81.
76 *Kazakhstanskaya pravda*, 21 July 1995.
77 Olcott, 'Islam and fundamentalism', p. 28.
78 *BBC Summary of World Broadcasts*, SU/2425, 4 October 1995.
79 *Open Media Research Institute*, 133, 11 July 1995; *Res publika*, 3–9 December 1996; *Open Media Research Institute*, 2, 3 January 1997.
80 See *Turkmenskaya iskra*, 8 June 1992 and 27 October 1992; *Segodnya*, 5 February 1994 and 1 June 1994.
81 A. Abduvakhitov, 'Islamic revivalism in Uzbekistan', in D. Eickelman, ed., *Russia's Muslim Frontiers* (Bloomington, 1993), pp. 79–87; Olcott, 'Islam and fundamentalism', pp. 35–7.
82 This document can be found in the State Archive of the Yaroslavl

region, f. 1033, Op. 1, d. 106, a copy of which is in the possession of Keston Institute in Oxford.

83 A brief account of the early development of the IRP can be found in J. Anderson, *Religion, State and Politics in the Soviet Union and the Successor States* (Cambridge, 1994), pp. 201–2.

84 *Pravda vostoka*, 1 February 1991.

85 M. Atkin, 'Islamic assertiveness and the waning of the old Soviet order', *Nationalities Papers*, 20:1, 1992, 64.

86 *Izvestiya*, 5 December 1991.

87 *Nezavisimaya gazeta*, 21 March 1992.

88 *Nezavisimaya gazeta*, 3 April 1992.

89 On various attempts, abortive and then successful, to remove the mufti, see *Nezavisimaya gazeta*, 16 January 1992 and Radio Free Europe/Radio Liberty, *Supplement*, 1993/20, p. 6.

90 *Nezavisimaya gazeta*, 6 January 1994.

91 *Open Media Research Institute*, 231, 29 November 1995.

92 *Nezavisimaya gazeta*, 6 March 1996 and 29 May 1996.

93 See *Kazakhstanskaya pravda*, 13 June 1995, 17 June 1995 and 21 July 1995; during the debate over a new constitution in July 1995 one letter-writer suggested a total prohibition of the activities of foreign-based religious organisations. *Kazakhstanskaya pravda*, 22 July 1995; though not going this far, in December President Nazarbaev called for a close watch to be kept on religious sects that might endanger society. *Kazakhstanskaya pravda*, 16 December 1995.

7

Islam, ethnicity and regional conflict: the case of Tajikistan

Situated on the southern fringes of the USSR, Tajikistan was the poorest of the Soviet republics and one whose close subordination to Moscow disguised tensions beneath the surface. Not until 1921 did the Red Army establish formal control over this region, but in some parts resistance lingered on into the late 1920s. As a result of the national demarcation Tajikistan was designated an autonomous republic within Uzbekistan and only in 1929 was it given union republican status, at which time it acquired parts of the Fergana valley to which the Uzbek state had aspired. Even then, it was far from clear that residents of this artificial state had any clear sense of national belonging, for, with the exception of a few intellectuals aware of their Persian heritage, most residents of this predominantly rural country identified themselves in terms of family, communal and regional ties. This weak sense of national identity may have been compounded by the fact that as late as 1979 Tajiks still made up only 59 per cent of the population, whilst Uzbeks, located largely in the northern and western regions, comprised nearly a quarter. One consequence of this was that many, including former party First Secretary R. Nabiev, came from mixed Uzbek–Tajik parentage and, though forced to choose a nationality by the Soviet passport system, often had little clear sense of ethnic identity.

It was in this state that bloody conflict erupted in 1992, a struggle that was atypical in independent Central Asia but warned regional leaders of what might happen should they prove unable to contain ethnic, regional and religious differences. This chapter starts with a brief description of the events of 1992–93 before discussing the various factors – regional, religious and economic – underlying the struggles of rival factions. In the last section we look

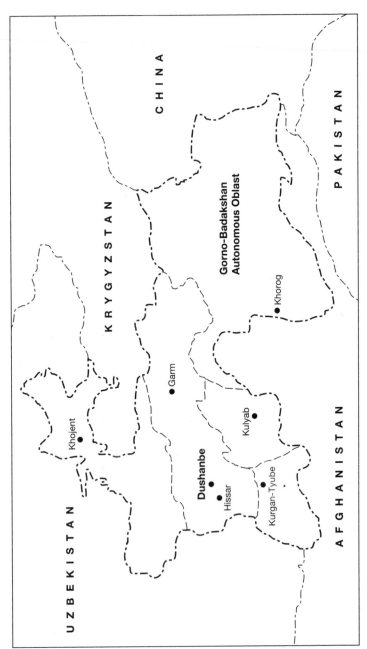

Map 3   Tajikistan

at the ways at which the struggle has spilled over into the international arena and at attempts, domestic and international, to prevent Tajikistan from breaking up along the lines seen in neighbouring Afghanistan.

The emergence of the Tajik conflict[1]

The potential for conflict in Tajikistan had first become apparent in February 1990 when demonstrations and riots in the capital Dushanbe left over 20 dead and many more injured. The spark for these events had been rumours that thousands of Armenian refugees from the Nagorno–Karabakh conflict were to be given housing in the republic at a time when many Tajiks were effectively homeless. These rumours seem to have been spread by elements within the party elite seeking to stage a palace coup. To this end they played on the real grievances of people in a republic where poverty and unemployment were growing and where the leadership seemed incapable of responding. The details remain unclear, but it appears that elements within the party elite led by Gosplan Chairman B. Karimov sought to use these events to overthrow First Secretary Kh. Makhkamov. In the event the republic's leaders declared a state of emergency, brought in Ministry of Interior troops and responded harshly to mass unrest.

After the event official explanations pinned the blame on a variety of groups, including the elite plotters, who were promptly expelled from the party, Islamic 'fundamentalists' and the informal organisation *Rastokhez* (Rebirth). *Rastokhez* was established in 1989 as an organisation concerned with the safeguarding and development of Tajik culture and language, and was primarily an organisation of the urban intelligentsia in the capital. During the February events some of its leading members joined with the leader of Tajik's Muslims in calling for calm, and sought to adopt a mediating role between the party leadership and the crowds of demonstrators. Other members, however, called for the resignation of Makhkamov and seemed to have linked up with the malcontents amongst the elite. Yet whilst elite groups played their own games, the potential political force of Islamic activists was made apparent during these events as in some rural areas local mullahs played a role in mobilising young men and directing them to the capital.[2]

For the authorities the events of 1990 served as an excuse for the restoration of 'order' in the republic, something they believed to have been undermined by Gorbachev's misguided policies. Yet the events of 1990 contributed towards a greater polarisation in Tajik society, and led to a growth in opposition-minded organisation. Alongside *Rastokhez* there emerged the Democratic Party of Tajikistan (DPT) led by Shodmon Yusupov, and *Lali Badakhshon* (Ruby of Badakhshon) which sought greater autonomy for the Pamiri people of the Gorno–Badakhshan region in the east of Tajikistan. More importantly, perhaps, the banned Islamic Renaissance Party (IRP) began to attract ever more members, largely in the rural communities of the south and of the centre of the republic.

During the August coup in Moscow the republican leadership supported the leaders of the Emergency Committee, but when their bid for power failed Makhkamov was forced to resign as party chief and on 9 September Tajikistan's Supreme Soviet declared the country's independence. For a brief while developments followed those in other republics, as Acting Head of State K. Aslonov oversaw the nationalisation of party property and the prohibition of its activities, whilst the mayor of Dushanbe took the symbolic step of removing the statue of Lenin from the town centre. Yet in this last outpost of conservatism the old order remained strong, and the communist-controlled Supreme Soviet quickly ended the ban on the party, removed Aslonov from power, and put in his place Rakhmon Nabiev, a former First Secretary of the republican communist party.[3] This rejoinder provoked fresh demonstrations in the capital during September as thousands protested at what they saw as the restoration of communist power. Some of the crowd called for the election of kazi Abkhar Turadzhonzoda as president, but he suggested that his role was that of spiritual leader. Gorbachev also sought to mediate, sending to the republic St Petersburg mayor Anatoli Sobchak in an unsuccessful effort to find a compromise.[4] A presidential election eventually held in November was a two-horse race, with Nabiev taking 57 per cent of the vote against the opposition candidate and film-maker Davlat Khudonazarov's 30 per cent. With substantial evidence of electoral irregularities and little control over ballot-counting, the latter declared the elections unfair, claiming that his total was around 37 per cent of the vote.[5]

Though the opposition continued to protest the election and demand the resignation of the government, the republic remained relatively quiet over the winter. Nabiev issued sharp attacks on what he called the 'politics by ultimatum' of the opposition,[6] yet simultaneously made concessions to society by proclaiming key religious festivals as state holidays at the end of January 1992.[7] From March 1992, however, thousands of demonstrators began to gather in Dushanbe and elsewhere, in part provoked by the arrest of the former mayor of Dushanbe – charged with corruption but in reality harassed for sanctioning the removal of Lenin's statue – and the sacking of Interior Minister M. Navzhuvanov, one of the few Badakhshanis in key posts, who whilst heading the Interior Ministry had refused to impose a state of emergency in September 1991.[8] The demonstrators, with increasing support from the kazi, successfully called for the resignation of parliamentary Speaker Sarafali Kendzhaev who was replaced by A. Iskanderov, an establishment figure who was inclined to search for a *modus vivendi* between government and opposition. Yet Nabiev soon flung Kendzhaev's resignation back in the opposition's face by making him head of the security services.[9]

At the height of this period there were over 100,000 demonstrators, including those supporting the opposition, and those in counter-demonstrations organised by the government and then by Dushanbe citizens who simply wanted their streets back. Large numbers were brought in from outside, with the IRP organising the arrival of many villagers from the east of the capital, whilst the government rallies were largely manned by people from the southern Kulyab region. As tensions rose, Nabiev sought to impose a state of emergency, restored Kendzhaev as parliamentary speaker, and then started arming groups of his own supporters. Almost inevitably violence followed, with clashes on 5 May leaving a number of dead and raising the temperature still further. The following days witnessed more fighting, and on 11 May Nabiev agreed to the creation of a coalition government in which a third of posts could go to the opposition. In consequence the latter gained control of the media and one of the IRP's leaders, Davlat Usman, was appointed a deputy prime minister.

These developments only served to exacerbate the conflict and reveal the extent of the polarisation within Tajik society. Almost immediately the regional soviets in Nabiev's home region of Khojent and the southern Kulyab region announced that they would not accept the decisions of the new government and would only obey presidential decrees. This announcement also heralded a new and more bloody stage of the conflict. In the southern regions of the country there emerged a series of armed militias, often run by former criminals such as Sanjak Safarov and owing but nominal allegiance to formal political institutions or forces. Safarov's Kulyabi group committed itself to the old regime and the overthrow of Islamic and democratic forces, and in this capacity started to act as judge and executioner in the regions it controlled. Alleged oppositionists were attacked and killed, and the administration of the Kurgan-Tyube region, in which the Democratic Party of Tajikistan had a strong voice, was overthrown. In these two southern oblasts violence became the normal means of settling political conflicts as rival groups fought amongst themselves, but with the Kulyab militias increasingly taking control of the region. At some personal risk Davlat Khudonazarov sought to mediate in the region and to prevent the violence, but to little avail. [10]

The consequences of these developments were two-fold. In the first place, they created a growing refugee problem as those fearful of militia retribution fled, either to Afghanistan or to neighbouring Central Asian states. Secondly, it aroused a hitherto-slumbering Commonwealth of Independent States (CIS) into action. Though Tajikistan's neighbours had already expressed concern that events might spill over their borders, the summer of 1992 witnessed Russia waking up to the problem. In early September President Yeltsin joined his Uzbek, Kazakh and Kyrgyz counterparts in calling on all sides to cease hostilities and to seek a compromise. [11] Such concerns were exacerbated by fears that both sides were being armed, the militias by elements within the Russian 201st Motorised Division and the opposition by Afghan mujihadeen.

In Dushanbe tensions culminated in further demonstrations, the enforced resignation of Nabiev in September 1992 and his replacement by Iskanderov as acting president. Some attempt was made to placate the northern and traditionally dominant region of Khojent by appointing one of Nabiev's more conciliatory local colleagues, A. Abduladzhanov, as prime minister, but in effect the opposition had now taken control of the government at the centre. Elsewhere it had little hope of enforcing its authority or resisting the onslaughts of the various militias. In late October armed groups led by Kendzhaev briefly took control of parts of Dushanbe, whilst in the north a rump Tajik Supreme Soviet rejected the decisions of Dushanbe and elected a former Kulyabi collective farm chairman, Imomali Rakhmonov, as parliamentary speaker and acting head of state. Within six weeks the armed militias that made up the so-called National Front of Tajikistan had retaken the capital and forced opposition leaders to flee. Many supporters of the opposition were less fortunate, with militia members rounding up alleged and real oppositionists, often defined in terms of the place of birth, and shooting them.[12]

By early 1993 it seemed that the old regime, albeit now dominated by the southern Kulyabis rather than by the traditional Khojent elites, was back in control. Yet the problems they faced were enormous. One year of conflict had destroyed around 800,000 homes, disrupted or destroyed the bulk of industry in the south of the republic, created bitter resentments within society, and created at least 200,000 refugees. To this should be added the fact that since 1989 some 300,000 of 380,000 Russian speakers had left, many of them people with skills the republic sorely needed.[13] Moreover, the government's writ did not run throughout the country and until at least the middle of 1993 armed units of the opposition were functioning within 30 kilometres of the capital, though these were eventually to be flushed out with the help, according to opposition sources, of the Uzbek airforce.[14] Though the regime in Dushanbe was formally to ban the four main opposition parties and ensure the selection of a 'less political' mufti,[15] it was to fail in reconciling society. Indeed, the large-scale abuse of human rights involving arrests, disappearances, torture and summary execution[16] further embittered many and radicalised supporters of the opposition. Now based in Afghanistan, they were to build up their armed units and in the following years were on occasion able to launch strikes deep into Tajik territory.

Alongside continued opposition sniping there were increasing signs of strain within the victorious coalition. The spring of 1993 had witnessed the removal of Safarov from the scene following a shoot-out between rival militia leaders, but armed groups remained strong and effectively controlled much of the south. Recruited largely in the Kulyab region and Kendzhaev's Hissar district to the west of Dushanbe, tensions emerged as the latter felt itself shortchanged in the division of posts in the new administration. More importantly, divisions stemmed from the fact that it was the Kulyabis who had 'restored order' and who now expected to dominate the new regime, rather than the traditionally pre-eminent elites of Khojent whose relatively prosperous region continued to hold the key to economic recovery. Hence the coalition remained fragile, with divisions personified in the mutual loathing of Parliamentary Speaker Rakhmonov and Prime Minister Abduladzhanov. When the latter 'resigned' in December 1993, Rakhmonov sought to preserve some sort of regional balance by appointing another northerner in his place, but the difficulties between the two regions remained.[17] There were also tensions in other areas, with the eastern Gorno–Badakhshan region seeking to maintain some form of autonomy from the capital, whilst remaining equally wary of the Sunni-Muslim-dominated opposition. Finally, there was the problem of restoring the shattered economy which in the short term led Tajikistan to seek integration into the Russian economy upon which it was so dependent and effectively gave Moscow control over the republic's financial and monetary policy.

Explaining the conflict

Attempts to explain the Tajik conflict have focused on a variety of factors, including the unreadiness of the republic for independence, the psychological impact of the mujihaddin victory in Afghanistan, ideological conflict between communism and Islam, the struggle of modernity and tradition, exploitation by outside actors, and the machinations of drug traders and other criminal elements. Each of these has undoubtedly played a part and are indeed often interrelated, but the underlying roots of the conflict should probably be seen in terms of the Soviet inheritance. Moscow's policies in the region, perhaps unwittingly, promoted and exacerbated the potential for tensions rooted in religious, ethnic and regional differences.

On the surface the initial phases of the conflict appeared largely ideological as a coalition of religious, nationalist and democratic forces sought to remove the forces of the status quo as represented by the communist party. The latter, having initially supported the August coup, used its position in parliament and the bureaucracy to keep the opposition at bay in the dying months of 1991. Yet this was essentially a rearguard action, concerned less with preserving Marxist-Leninist ideology against a new philosophy than with protecting positions and influence built up over decades. In particular this was an action in which the elites of the northern province of Khojent (previously Leninabad) sought to preserve their dominance within Tajikistan. Such people were not immune to change and, as elsewhere in the former USSR, elites quickly learned to diversify their power bases by taking a key role in the new business class and within the newly privatised enterprises of the north. They were, however, reluctant to accommodate themselves to the more radical challenges posed by the various opposition groups which would have dramatically reduced their hold on power. For this reason the Tajik Communist Party during 1992 sought to portray itself as the representative of secular modernity seeing off the forces of tradition represented above all by the Islamicist or 'fundamentalist' threat.

In practice, the opposition during the early stages of the conflict was much more variegated than suggested by the old regime, being essentially a loose alliance of groups opposed to the existing order. These included the Democratic Party of Tajikistan and *Rastokhez*, both made up largely of secular intellectuals – with strong support for the former in Gorno–Badakhshan and the latter in Dushanbe – who professed respect for Islam as the religion of the Tajiks, but who stressed the need to create a non-religious and liberal state. Also involved was *Lali Badakhshon*, representing the Ismaili community of the Pamirs, people traditionally wary of the Sunni activists associated with Islamicist movements. Nonetheless, it was the latter groups which enjoyed the greatest potential for mass mobilisation, something that was perhaps inevitable given the predominantly rural nature of Tajik society and the way in which Islam had served as a bulwark against Soviet policies designed to destroy traditional practices and ideas.

Over 70 years the Soviet state had attacked Islam in its efforts to bring about what it saw as the modernisation of Central Asia in general and Tajikistan in particular. Mosques had been closed, mullahs and imams persecuted, and the teaching of religion to the younger generation strictly forbidden. At the same time it had recognised that complete eradication of religion was a long-term process and had allowed it to function within the context of a controlled religious establishment and in less than 20 legally recognised mosques in Tajikistan. More problematic was dealing with 'everyday Islam', with the near-universally-practised rites of circumcision and burial. With the maintenance of traditional structures, in the context of the mahallah, village or collective farm based upon close-knit kinship groups, it was virtually impossible for the state to eradicate such customs. Indeed, by 1987 one propagandist was suggesting that as circumcision remained virtually universal, why should this not be recognised, with the transferral of the practice taking place from the mullah to the state in the shape of medical institutions?[18] Moreover, it was not only rites of passage that the state had to contend with, for despite the closure of most mosques, *de facto* prayer houses functioned in virtually every population settlement where prayers were led and rites carried out by unofficial mullahs such as Said Abdullo Nuri, who was imprisoned in 1986 but to be found heading the exiled United Tajik Opposition in the mid-1990s. Such people were also involved in the spread of religious literature and the creation of Koranic schools to which the republican press devoted so much attention from the late 1970s onwards. These were the activists who were variously to be described as 'fundamentalists' or 'Wahhabis' by the state's ideological apparatus and occasionally to be denounced by the state-sponsored Islamic establishment, though it seems that in many cases official and unofficial imams and mullahs worked closely together.[19]

Whilst the extent of any religious revival has been the subject of debate,[20] it was within the context of a society where religious traditions remained strong that the IRP was born, although it appears that underground Muslim organisations with political overtones had first emerged in the late 1970s. When the IRP was created in mid-1990, the Central Asian grouping, dominated by Tajiks, proved to be the strongest, although in Tajikistan it met with blanket hostility from the authorities who denied it registration. Conscious of the negative image of Islam in the wider world, one of the party's leaders, lawyer Davlat Usman, emphasised the IRP's aims as primarily religious, concerned to defend the interests of believers and regenerate the faith of people whose religious heritage had been fundamentally weakened by state atheism. Any interest in creating an Islamic state or pursuit of a Iranian model of development was firmly denied,[21] as it was to be in subsequent interviews with IRP leaders. Not all took the same view, with Said Nuri telling Arthur Bonner that politics and religion were the same and stressing his hope that the people would choose to be governed by the Shariat.[22] In similar vein, some activists involved in the demonstrations of 1992 called for the immediate creation of an Islamic state. Their leaders, however, recognised that such an objective publicly stated would be counter-productive. Indeed, kazi Abkhar Turadzhonzoda initially remained sceptical, calling on his clergy to remain strictly neutral in political matters.[23] Yet by early 1991 he too had begun to take a more radical stance, speaking out publicly on the need to defend the rights of Muslims and seeking to persuade parliament to make religious holidays public ones and turn Friday into the day of rest.[24] By the end of the year, Turadzhonzoda, who came from the Garm district where the IRP was strong, was working increasingly closely with the Islamic and nationalist opposition, whilst at the same time seeking to keep the temperature down and to ensure peaceful solutions to disagreements.

At some levels the Islamicists appear to have been much stronger than other groups, being not limited to a geographically defined base like *Lali Badakhshon* or to the relatively small urban intellectual bases of the DPT and *Rastokhez*. Moreover, they had a ready-made organisational network in the shape of the mosques to be found in every village which could serve as mobilising agencies when manpower was needed for demonstrations. They also had greater access to the growing army of unemployed males, disillusioned with socialism and scornful of the cautious approaches of their elders. At the same time their potential should not be overstated. Islamicist strength was largely confined to certain parts of the country and their long-term ideological goals were supported by only a minority of the population. Opinion polls carried out in 1991–92 suggested that whilst most wanted Islam to be given greater space in society, only 5–7 per cent of the population as a whole viewed the idea of an Islamic state favourably.[25] In such circumstances it was hardly surprising to find Abkhar Turadzhonzoda suggesting that in general the people were so ignorant of real Islam that establishing a political order based upon it was something that would not even be able to be discussed for decades.[26]

Whilst the ideological differences were strong, especially in the early stages of the conflict, they were reinforced by a series of ethnic and regional cleavages. The creation of Tajikistan as a union republic in 1929 had involved the location of substantial Uzbek populations within Leninabad and the western parts of the country, with the 1989 census revealing that in both Leninabad and Khatlon (briefly merged from Kurgan-Tyube and Kulyab, to be merged again following the victory of the Kulyabis) regions, Uzbeks made up nearly a third of the population. This in turn created further problems in the early 1990s when some Uzbeks in Leninabad, adjacent to the Fergana valley region of Uzbekistan and enjoying better economic relations and communications with Uzbekistan than the rest of Tajikistan, as well as those in the Hissar region, on occasion flirted with the idea of reuniting with their larger neighbour. During the civil war that broke out at the end of 1992 the Uzbeks were to side firmly with conservative forces, as was the state of Uzbekistan, though by the middle of the decade they were to become increasingly antagonistic to a regime which they felt had let them down and at the beginning of 1996 Uzbek-led army units were to stage a brief revolt against the government of Tajikistan.

More important, however, in explaining the conflict was the lack of a true sense of national identity within Tajikistan, a country in which kinship and shared occupations created loyalties that were essentially local rather than national or ideological.[27] In the words of one proverb: 'the Pamiris dance, the Kulyabis defend, Dushanbe produces, and Khojent trades and rules'.[28] These distinctions were in effect reinforced by the Soviet state, despite its proclaimed commitment to destroying traditional ties. Nowhere was this more apparent than in its maintenance of the traditional dominance of Leninabad–Khojent within the country. Before the revolution this northern region served as the trade centre of eastern Bukhara and under Soviet rule this position was strengthened in a number of ways. First, the region came to dominate the political system with all first secretaries from 1943 until the collapse of the USSR hailing from the north, and other senior posts being overwhelmingly taken by candidates from the region. This changed slightly in the early 1970s after a northerner who was sent to head the Kulyab party organisation found himself in the morgue within days of taking up the appointment. After this some Kulyabis were appointed to leading positions, although not the very top posts, and a few Pamiris were appointed to second-ranking positions within the party and state apparatus. In general, however, rule remained with the north.[29]

This northern dominance was also evident in the economic sphere, with Leninabad, along with the Hissar valley to the west of Dushanbe, receiving the bulk of central investment, providing the site of most of the republic's industry and producing up to 65 per cent of its GNP. This situation was further reinforced during the civil war and after, because little of the armed conflict took place in the north, most of the region's industry remained intact, and its managerial class developed close links with emerging private enterprises in neighbouring states and Russia.[30] In contrast other regions struggled, the poorest being the Gorno–Badakhshan Autonomous Oblast in the east, which contained 45 per cent of Tajik territory but only about 2 per cent of the population, mostly dependent upon subsistence farming. In the southern regions cotton predominated, with some production of fruit and vegetables, but these remained overwhelmingly poor areas of the country, vulnerable to bad harvests and natural disasters.

In the south the situation was further complicated by a series of resettlements that took place between the 1930s and early 1960s. These brought peoples from mountainous areas just south of Leninabad, from the Garm region and even from part of neighbouring Kulyab to be resettled in the Kurgan-Tyube oblast. The prime motive was to provide labour for the intensive cultivation of cotton that was encouraged by the Soviet state, but the social consequences were often disastrous and fed into the conflicts of 1992 and after. These communities were transplanted with little thought of the need to provide a social infrastructure and in the process some died. In general they failed to integrate with their predominantly Uzbek neighbours and, though each found themselves uprooted from traditional familial, clan and occupational connections, they tended to cling together in order to maintain some form of common identity. As a result each community failed to mix, animosities developed and, during 1992, rival groups which were particularly alienated from the system provided fertile recruiting ground for both Islamic movements and armed militias. Subsequently, many of the first bloody clashes that took place in Kurgan-Tyube during that year involved clashes between settlers and long-term residents.[31]

These regional distinctions were apparent throughout the 1990s. The events of February 1990 in part represented an attempt by Garmis and Pamiris to stage a palace coup after which they lost what limited representation they had. Then in 1992 regional and ideological cleavages often overlapped, with the opposition leaders generally coming from the disadvantaged regions and enjoying their greatest level of support in them. Thus the surveys that were quoted earlier which revealed limited national support for the creation of an Islamic republic, revealed responses of 18.6 per cent and 14.7 per cent in Kurgan-Tyube and Dushanbe respectively, that is, in areas where opposition support was generally stronger, whilst the notion was almost totally rejected in Khojent, Kulyab and Hissar.[32] Equally, in more recent clashes between government and opposition forces it is in the traditional strongholds of the Islamicists that anti-government forces have enjoyed greatest success, areas such as Garm and Tavildar, the latter being strategically located on the main highway between Dushanbe and the southern Pamir region.[33]

Overall the Tajik conflict is one to which ideological, religious, ethnic and regional differences have all contributed, and at the same time many of the hostilities between the various groups have been exacerbated by the bloody events of the last six years. The regime, largely dominated by the Kulyab region, cannot enforce its will on much of the territory and lacks real control over many of the armed groups purporting to act in its name. Meanwhile the opposition has become radicalised, with the armed struggle serving to increase the role of the Islamicist groups. As in Afghanistan, violence has developed its own logic, as individual opposition groups branch out into the drug trade, initially seen as a means of raising money for weapons but increasingly becoming an end in itself for some. In such circumstances where vested interests in continuation are developing and both sides find it hard to make substantive compromises, finding a negotiated settlement to the conflict has proved to be extremely difficult.

Resolving the conflict: domestic and international aspects

From very early on, Tajikistan's immediate neighbours, in particular Uzbekistan's President Karimov, facing his own Islamicist troubles in the Fergana valley, expressed considerable concern at developments within Tajikistan. During the summer of 1992 Karimov joined together with other Central Asian heads of state in pressuring Russia to take a more active position, and in September he appealed to the United Nations (UN) for assistance, pointing to the spread of arms from Afghanistan as a factor likely to further destabilise the situation. In October 1992 the CIS took the decision to create a peace-keeping force, based upon the Russian 201st Motorised Division already based in the republic but with the addition of an Uzbek battalion. These were joined in 1993 by more troops from Russia, and by battalions from Kazakhstan and Kyrgyzstan sent to man the southern borders of the republic. Such forces were treated with considerable suspicion by opposition forces following reports that Russian troops had taken part in the conflict on the side of the pro-government militias, that individual commanders had supplied arms to them, and that Russian units had stood by and watched atrocities being carried out. Such doubts were reinforced after Uzbek airforce planes bombed opposition positions in the Romit gorge during the spring of 1993.[34]

For Tajikistan's neighbours and Russia, the fear of contagion was paramount, with some commentators pointing to the likelihood of an Afghan-style conflict embroiling the region and eventually reaching Russia's southern borders. In practice the policies adopted by Dushanbe's backers served to increase the possibility, because the bloody civil war created tens of thousands of refugees, now radicalised and deeply embittered, many of whom fled to Afghanistan where they were to receive military training in camps run by fellow Tajik Shah Akhmed Massoud as well as in those run by his rival Gulbadin Hekmatayar. There was also an overlapping of the Tajik and the ongoing Afghan conflict, with the refugees finding themselves dependent upon different camps of mujihadeen. Those who found themselves on the territory of the Uzbek General Abdul Rashid Dostum in the Mazar-i Sharif area were prevented from staging armed incursions back into Tajikistan, a development reflecting the Afghan general's close ties with the Tashkent government and President Karimov.[35] Elsewhere, however, military training was made available and in consequence an armed force of some 3,000–5,000, organised in separate bands, began to emerge. Since mid-1993 such groups have waged a persistent guerilla war against the Tajik regime, both within the country and in repeated incursions across the southern borders. In turn, following a Tajik–Russian agreement of May 1993 allowing Russian commanders to become involved in combat duties, Russian aircraft and gunships have made frequent retaliatory attacks on refugee camps and alleged guerilla bases.

The problem facing the CIS in general and Russia in particular was how to balance the peace-keeping role with the apparent desire to prop up a Tajik government made up of conservative forces with which it had little in common. Justification was found in terms of the threat of 'Islamic fundamentalism', which was the line taken from the beginning by President Karimov when he sought to persuade Russia to adopt his hard-line approach. Even Andrei Kozyrev, Russia's liberal foreign minister, took up this argument in an article which appeared in August 1993 entitled 'What does Russia want in Tajikistan?' In this article he spoke of Russia's shared historical links with Tajikistan and the need to stop the spread of tribal and religious extremism throughout the region. For this reason, Russia and its neighbours had to get involved in guaranteeing the security of Tajikistan's southern borders and preserving peace in the region. At the same time, Kozyrev recognised that ultimately this was a Tajik problem and one that required an internal settlement.[36] Whilst seeking a regional solution, there were also some efforts to involve the UN whose Secretary-General had in April 1993 appointed a special envoy to help with efforts at resolving the conflict. Whilst Russia formally welcomed this development, it expressed the desire to keep control over peace-keeping efforts and at the end of 1993 was to request unsuccessfully that the CIS force in Tajikistan be given a UN mandate.[37]

From mid-1993 onwards Russia put increasing pressure on the Tajik regime to seek discussions and reconciliation with the opposition. Kozyrev and other diplomats carried out a constant round of shuttle diplomacy in Central Asia and Afghanistan, seeking to bring the two sides together. The problem facing would-be peace-makers remained the intransigent attitude of the Dushanbe regime which felt that it was the legitimate power and therefore could not be expected to make any concessions of substance. Nonetheless, under Russian pressure Dushanbe eventually agreed to send a delegation to UN-sponsored talks in Moscow during April 1994. On the government side the delegation was headed by Minister of Labour Shukur Zukhurov (following the March assassination of the deputy prime minister who had been scheduled to lead the group), whilst the opposition side included Turadzhonzoda and IRP Chairman Muhammedsharif Himmatzoda of Said Abdullo Nuri's Movement of Islamic Opposition, members of the Coordinating Centre of Democratic Forces of Tajikistan based in Moscow, the Democratic Party, *Rastokhez*, and groups representing the refugees. Observing the talks were observers from Russia, Kazakhstan, Uzbekistan, Afghanistan, Iran and Pakistan. The issues discussed included the question of demilitarising the conflict – with the opposition side wanting the replacement of the commanders of the 201st division by officers who had no connection with Tajikistan and thus no interest in a continuation of the conflict[38] – the return of refugees, and a reconsideration of the constitutional structure that would permit the unhindered participation of opposition forces. Though little of substance was agreed, it was decided to hold a further round of talks in the near future.[39]

A second round of negotiations was held in Tehran during June 1994, where the government delegation focused on the need for a ceasefire and on the return of refugees, whilst the opposition led by journalist Otakhan Latif stressed the need to release political prisoners, end the prohibition on political parties and allow the opposition access to the media as a precondition for a ceasefire.[40] The communique issued at the end of the meeting stressed the commitment of both sides to a negotiated settlement, despite continued fighting on the ground, and in September a temporary ceasefire was formally signed. A third round of talks opened in late October 1994 in Islamabad, but finding a genuine meeting of minds proved as problematic as ever. Nonetheless it was agreed to prolong the ceasefire agreed at Tehran for a further three months to 6 February 1995, to exchange prisoners (though the numbers remained contested), and to seek further negotiations.[41]

Whilst these talks were going on, shifts were also evident on the domestic front, as the Dushanbe government sought to legitimise its position through the introduction of a new constitution, followed by presidential and parliamentary elections. In April 1994 a draft constitution was published which proposed to reconstitute the presidency. Though the press remained tightly muzzled, it was clear that not all were happy with the new document. The few remaining Russian speakers were critical of the failure to include Russian as a state language or to allow for dual citizenship, whilst intellectuals in Gorno-Badakhshan argued for the creation of a federal state in which their republic would become an autonomous republic.[42] Some also pointed to the fact that people were being asked to vote on the same day in a constitutional referendum which established a presidential republic and simultaneously to choose that president. The opposition, totally excluded from discussion or running a candidate, called for a boycott, arguing that this would not be a genuinely free election, but in the event two candidates ran, Parliamentary Speaker Imomali Rakhmonov and former Prime Minister Addumalik Abduladzhanov. According to official reports an unlikely 90 per cent turnout led to the confirmation of the constitution and the victory of Rakhmonov with 60 per cent of the vote – though his rival's supporters suggested widespread falsification in an election which international observers had boycotted, claiming that it could not be genuinely free.[43]

Parliamentary elections held on 26 February 1995 were accompanied by further charges of violations and abuses, starting with the exclusion of genuine opposition groups from participation and the harassment of loyal opposition parties such as Abduladzhanov's Popular Unity Party which eventually called for a boycott of the elections as unfair. In the event two ballots produced a parliament of 181 deputies, most of them drawn from the state and economic apparatus, with nearly a quarter comprising commanders of the pro-government militias. Following the elections Rakhmonov sought to ensure some degree of regional balance in the appointment of deputy parliamentary speakers, but this could not hide the fact of continuing Kulyabi dominance. More importantly, it was far from clear that the election had in fact contributed to the legitimation of the regime for the excluded opposition refused to be bound by its results or cease their attacks on the government. Only one major opposition figure appeared to have been won over by these domestic events, and that was Shodmon Yusupov, chairman of the Democratic Party, who in early 1995 following a meeting with Rakhmonov praised the presidential elections as a model of democracy and attacked the opposition as dominated by extremism. But Yusupov represented only one faction within the party, for at an extraordinary DPT Congress held in Alma Ata the previous December he had been deposed as party chairman.[44]

None of these developments could hide the ongoing problems in finding a peaceful solution to the conflict. There were persistent violations of the southern border and an increasing number of incursions deep into Tajik territory. Moreover, there were signs that Dushanbe's supporters in Tashkent and Moscow were losing patience with the intransigence of the Tajik government, whilst in Kazakhstan there was a growing public view that the country should withdraw its peace-keepers from the southern borders of Tajikistan where Kazakh troops were dying for a cause that was not their own.[45] Further complications stemmed from proposals to hold the fourth round of talks in Moscow. Previous ceasefires had not been binding on Russian troops and opposition spokesmen expressed unease at the Russian bombardment of refugee camps.[46] In February

1995 the opposition leader Said Abdullo Nuri put forward a programme for peace, including the scrapping of all political trials, the
disarming of all groups, the return of refugees, a strict limitation on
the role of Russian and CIS forces, and the creation of an interim
council representing all interests in the country. At the same time he
warned that if there was no progress the opposition had the capacity to wage armed struggle indefinitely.[47] Awareness of the potential
longevity of the conflict may have been one of the factors that
turned Uzbekistan's Islam Karimov from strong backer to stern
critic of the Dushanbe government. Behind closed doors at the
Alma Ata summit of the CIS in February, he launched a bitter attack
on Imomali Rakhmonov for his failure to negotiate seriously with
the opposition, and two months later he met with the previously
execrated opposition leaders in Tashkent.[48] This pressure increased
in subsequent months, with relations between the former allies
reaching the level of insult by May as Rakhmonov alleged that
Uzbek mercenaries were now fighting with the opposition.[49]

Talks began again in Moscow during April 1995 but were broken
off immediately following Andrei Kozyrev's statement that Russia
would take all necessary military means to prevent incursions across
the Afghan border. Despite this, in May there took place the first
meeting between Rakhmonov and opposition leader Said Abdullo
Nuri in Kabul. Here the latter reiterated his demand for an interim
government made up of neutral personalities and called for CIS
peace-keepers to be supplemented by those from Pakistan and
Turkey. At this meeting he also suggested that Rakhmonov might be
allowed to stay on as president for a further two years during which
time he would share power with an interim Council of National
Accord.[50] Subsequent meetings led to an agreement to a fifth round
of talks scheduled to begin in Ashgabat in December, but as before
these were accompanied by an almost immediate opposition walk-
out in protest at Russian bombardment of resistance positions in the
Garm region.

By this stage it was hard to see how progress could be made, as
each side adopted increasingly intransigent positions, in the opposition case encouraged by a number of military victories within the
country during the winter of 1995–96. By January 1996 Russia
seemed to have changed its position again, with Deputy Foreign
Minister Albert Chernyshev claiming that now it was the opposition's advance of 'unacceptable positions' amounting to a call for

the removal of the government which undermined any real possibility of a negotiated settlement.[51] Within Tajikistan violence once again seemed on the increase, as was made evident by the murder of the mufti and his family in January, repeated opposition successes against government troops in the Tavildar region, and then the revolt of a number of Tajik government forces led by ethnic Uzbeks. The purported objective of the force led by M. Khudoberdiev was the removal of certain government ministers, a demand which was met by Rakhmonov as a means of halting the revolt. Though some claimed that Tashkent was behind these developments, with the aim of seeking to undermine the Rakhmonov administration or forcing it to recognise its fragility and the need for a political settlement, Uzbekistan's interests would seem to dictate that it avoid measures that add to the instability of the region.[52]

At the time of writing (January 1997) the possibility of finding a peaceful solution seemed as far away as ever, as renewed peace talks faltered yet again and increasing tensions suggested that Tajikistan could break up along the lines seen in Afghanistan. The regime effectively controls only part of the country, and remains distrusted by ostensible allies in the northern province, some of whom openly discuss the possibility of joining Uzbekistan. In the north, disquiet was evident in demonstrations that took place in Khojent, Ura-Tyube and other northern towns in May 1996 which led to the removal of numerous Kulyabi law enforcement officials.[53] To the south many Kulyabis are unhappy that their dominance in government seems to have brought so little benefit to their region, whilst the opposition continues to pose major problems. Though it cannot win the war so long as Russia remains committed to a role, it is hard to see how it can be defeated by military means. Yet should Russia withdraw and Tajikistan collapse, the prospects of a wider conflict in the region are considerable, as other powers including China and Pakistan may play a role in seeking to prevent the emergence of a political vacuum. For the people of Tajikistan, especially those in the southern regions, the future looks bleak, as persistent warfare continues to prevent economic recovery and there is little possibility of exploiting even the limited resources that the country posseses.[54] Ultimately a solution would appear to depend upon both the willingness of the major domestic players to compromise and the mediation of outside powers, but the unlikelihood currently of the former would appear to undermine the possibilities of arbitration by the latter. And as events in Afghanistan have shown, with no internal will to achieve reconciliation, outside intervention would seem to be of little use.[55]

Notes

1   On early developments in 1992 see S. Morozova and M. Lashch, *Tadzhikistan: vesna i leto 1992* (Moscow, 1992); a useful overview of developments in Tajikistan can be found in B. Rubin, 'Tajikistan: From Soviet republic to Russian–Uzbek protectorate', in M. Mandelbaum, ed., *Central Asia and the World* (New York, 1994), pp. 207–24.

2   On these events see B. Brown, 'Unrest in Tajikistan', Radio Free Europe/Radio Liberty, *Report on the USSR*, 23 February 1990, pp. 28–31; *BBC Summary of World Broadcasts*, SU/0705, B/6–7, 6 March 1990; A. Niyazi, 'The year of tumult: Tajikistan after February 1990' in V. Naumkin, ed., *State, Religion and Society in Central Asia* (Reading, 1993), pp. 264–89.

3   *Izvestiya*, 23 September 1991.

4   *Izvestiya*, 3 October 1991.

5   *Izvestiya*, 26 November 1991.

6   *Narodnaya gazeta* (formerly *Kommunist Tadzhikistana*), 28 January 1992.

7   *Narodnaya gazeta*, 30 January 1992.

8   *Moskovskie novosti*, 22 March 1993.

9   See *Moskovskie novosti*, 19 April 1992 and *Izvestiya*, 23 April 1992; and the later profile of Iskanderov in *Nezavisimaya gazeta*, 24 February 1994.

10   On these conflicts in the south see *Izvestiya*, 20 June 1992 and 23 July 1992; *Nezavisimaya gazeta*, 10 June 1992 and 4 July 1992.

11   *Nezavisimaya gazeta*, 5 September 1992.

12   *Nezavisimaya gazeta*, 16 December 1992 and 18 December 1992.

13   *Nezavimaya gazeta*, 23 December 1992 and 27 May 1993; *Izvestiya*, 3 April 1993.

14   *Nezavisimaya gazeta*, 23 February 1993.

15   *Moskovskie novosti*, 21 February 1993.

16   *Nezavisimaya gazeta*, 21 April 1993; Amnesty International, *Tadzhikistan* (London, 1993).

17   *Nezavisimaya gazeta*, 21 December 1993.

18   Bess Brown, 'Religion in Tajikistan: A tough nut for the ideologists', in Radio Liberty, 7/1988, 28 December 1987, which is quoting an article in *Nauka i religiya*, 1987/10.

19 M. Atkin, 'Islam as faith, politics and bogeyman in Tajikistan', in M. Bourdeaux, ed., *The Politics of Religion in Russia and the New States of Eurasia* (New York, 1995), pp. 247–72.

20 The extent to which there has been an Islamic 'revival' in Central Asia has been the subject of considerable debate. See the letters to the editor 'on Soviet Islam' in *Problems of Communism*, 36:3, 1987, at 87; M. Atkin, *The Subtlest Battle: Islam in Soviet Tajikistan* (Philadelphia, 1989); and A. Hetmanek's extremely critical review of the latter in *Central Asian Survey*, 9:3, 1990, 99–111.

21 *Komsomolets Tadzhikistana*, 21 November 1990.

22 A. Bonner, 'Islam and the state in Central Asia: A comparative essay', *Central Asian Monitor*, 1995, No. 6, pp. 32–3.

23 *Keston News Service*, 362, 8 November 1990, pp. 6–7.

24 *Komsomol'skaya pravda*, 23 March 1991.

25 See M. A. Olimov, 'Ob ethnopoliticheskoi i konfessional'noi situatsii v Tadzhikistane i veroyatnosti mezhetnicheskikh konfliktov', *Vostok*, 1994/2, 88; G. Kosach, 'Tajikistan: Political parties in an inchoate national space', in Y. Roi, ed., *Muslim Eurasia – Conflicting Legacies* (London, 1995), pp. 134–6.

26 *Rossiiskaya gazeta*, 27 August 1993.

27 L. Chvyr, 'Central Asia's Tajiks: Self-identification and ethnic identity', in Naumkin, *State, Religion and Society*, pp. 245–61.

28 Quoted by perceptive journalist Igor Rotar in *Nezavisimaya gazeta*, 30 September 1992.

29 On the cadres issue see *Nezavisimaya gazeta*, 30 September 1992 and 3 March 1993; K. Martin, 'Tajikistan: Civil war without end', in Radio Free Europe/Radio Liberty, *Research Report*, 2:32, 20 August 1993, 18–29.

30 See *Nezavisimaya gazeta*, 30 September 1992 and 2 September 1994; Bess Brown, 'Whither Tajikistan', in Radio Free Europe/Radio Liberty, *Research Report*, 1:24, 12 June 1994.

31 V. I. Bushkov and D. V. Mikul'sky, *Tadzhikskoe obshchestvo na rubezhe tysyacheletii – etnopoliticheskaya situatsiya v nachale 1990x godov* (Moscow, 1992), especially pp. 8–15 and 33–8.

32 Kosach, 'Tajikistan: Political parties', p. 135.

33 B. Pannier, 'Tajikistan – weathering another storm of violence', *Transition*, 2:5, 8 March 1996, 36–8.

34 *Nezavisimaya gazeta*, 23 February 1993.

35 Rubin, 'Tajikistan: From Soviet republic to Russian–Uzbek protectorate', pp. 17–18.

36 *Izvestiya*, 4 August 1993.

37 I. B. Neumann and Sergei Solodovnik, 'The case of Tajikistan', in L. Johnson and C. Archer, eds, *Peacekeeping and the Role of Russia in*

Eurasia (Boulder and Oxford, 1996), pp. 83–101.

38 In early 1994 some had argued that Russia in general and the military in particular had no desire to see an end to the conflict as their presence in Tajikistan could no longer be justified. Igor Rotar pointed to the silence of the Russian embassy when seven baptists and an Orthodox deacon were murdered by armed groups close to the regime. *Nezavisimaya gazeta*, 13 March 1994.

37 *Nezavisimaya gazeta,* 8 April 1994; *Segodnya*, 14 April 1994.

40 *Nezavisimaya gazeta*, 21 June 1994, 23 June 1994 and 29 June 1994.

41 *Nezavisimaya gazeta*, 2 November 1994.

42 *Nezavisimaya gazeta*, 11 June 1994 and 23 June 1994; *Segodnya,* 21 July 1994.

43 *Moskovksie novosti*, 13 November 1994; *Nezavisimaya gazeta*, 9 November 1994.

44 *Nezavisimaya gazeta,* 23 February 1995 and 25 March 1995.

45 *Nezavisimaya gazeta*, 14 September 1994.

46 *Nezavisimaya gazeta*, 18 January 1995.

47 *BBC Summary of World Broadcasts*, SU/2233, G/3–4, 21 February 1995.

48 *Moskovskie novosti*, 12–19 February 1995; *Nezavisimaya gazeta*, 5 April 1995.

49 *Segodnya*, 30 May 1995.

50 *Open Media Research Institute*, 97, 19 May 1995; *BBC Summary of World Broadcasts*, SU/2314, G/2, 27 May 1995.

51 *BBC Summary of World Broadcasts*, 31 January 1996.

52 *Nezavisimaya gazeta*, 30 January 1996 and 6 February 1996.

53 *Nezavisimaya gazeta*, 16 May 1996. The continuing difficulty of finding common ground between government and opposition was evident at a further round of talks held in Moscow during December 1996, and subsequent developments as the two sides failed to agree on the make-up of a proposed National Reconciliation Council. *Nezavisimaya gazeta*, 11, 17, 19 and 24 December 1996.

54 By the end of 1995 there were a reported 400,000 on the verge of hunger and the cotton harvest was roughly equivalent to that of 1953. *Nezavisimaya gazeta*, 15 May 1996.

55 B. Rubin, 'The failure of an internationally sponsored interim government in Afghanistan', in Y. Shain and J. Linz, eds, *Between States: Interim Governments and Democratic Transitions* (Cambridge, 1995), pp. 211–36.

8

The international politics of Central Asia

In seeking to make a reality of their independence, the Central Asian states initially assigned a key role to the development of new ties in the international arena. Of special concern here was escaping from Russian political, economic and military hegemony through the cultivation of new partners who would support the reconstruction of their countries. During the early stages of this process there was, as Olcott has pointed put, a certain euphoria about the possibilities open to them:

> Foreigners would help generate the capital that economic development required, through the purchase of energy and other valuable raw materials, through international funding (in part through joint ventures) of Soviet era plans for resource extraction as well as through the further expansion of these projects, and through the use of foreign aid, international credits, and joint ventures to reform agriculture and to modernise and expand the industrial base.[1]

Very soon, however, this approach became tempered by an awareness that the region, despite its potential wealth in mineral and energy resources, was not a priority area for much of the outside world and that the old connection to Moscow could not be broken overnight.

In the search for new partners the primary concern was economic, with regional leaders keen to restructure their economies so as to increase living standards and thus stave off the perceived threat of political unrest. Yet whilst they might, in Olcott's words, seek to play ethnic, religious or Asian cards in pursuit of this end,[2] Central Asian elites proved unwilling to be bound by such 'natural' ties or to become dependent upon any new 'big brothers'. To this end, early on they developed connections with both secular Turkey and 'religious' Iran, but rejected any hegemonic ambitions on the part of the former whilst not allowing links with the latter to preclude the evolution of good relations with Israel, whose experience in irrigation and agricultural reform were of particular interest to Central Asia.

For some outside observers, developments in the region during the early 1990s bore similarities to the 'great game' of the nineteenth century, with the contemporary key players being the forces of modernisation represented by Turkey and backed by the USA struggling for influence with 'fundamentalist Islam' represented by Iran. This, however, failed to take into account the relative economic weakness of these two states. More importantly, as Roland Dannreuther has suggested, the analogy was inexact insofar as it did not take into account Russia's continued domination of the region and the absence of a clear challenge to its position similar to that provided by Britain in the last century. In addition it failed to take into consideration the fact that these states were now independent actors with their own priorities and some capacity for choosing their own allies.[3]

For all this, in their understanding and handling of relations with the outside world the newly independent states have been hampered by their lack of experience in foreign relations. Under Moscow's rule diplomacy had been handled centrally and personnel in the Foreign Ministry and the majority of embassies had been largely Slavic. In the absence of staff and diplomatic missions the Central Asian states often had to rely on the good will and facilities of Russian embassies abroad to promote their interests, whilst sending potential diplomats to foreign institutes for specialist training.[4] Perhaps even more importantly, these states lacked any clear sense of their national or security interests beyond the simple need to survive as independent entities. Did they have explicit goals they wished to pursue in the international arena, what were the major security threats facing them, and what were the practical possibilities in developing economic and military connections that would bolster their independence rather than create a new dependency?

In this chapter we discuss various developments in the international politics of Central Asia, building on the considerable literature on the region's geopolitics that has emerged in recent years. In the first section we examine the attempt to create ties with the outside world, starting with the West of which so much was hoped in the early years of independence, and then looking at the evolution of relations with more 'natural' partners in the Islamic and Asian world. The second section focuses on halting efforts at evolving greater regional cooperation within Central Asia. We then turn to relations with Russia and suggest that for most of these states this 'auld alliance' is likely retain its significance for some time to come. A final conclusion seeks to draw together the main themes of the book, focusing in particular on the relationship between the domestic and international politics of Central Asia.

The search for new friends

In the West

Many within Central Asia initially saw the wealthy states of the West as potential benefactors, as countries that had encouraged, however ambiguously, the break-up of the USSR and that were capable of providing the levels of capital investment required for the regeneration of the region. At one level attention focused on private interests in these countries who would be attracted by the rich energy potential of the region. Simultaneously it was expected that Western states would lean on international financial institutions to provide support for a variety of tasks, ranging from economic stabilisation to cleaning up the environmental disasters left by the Soviet developmental model. In addition there was expressed the hope that the West would offer some security guarantees to states seeking to escape Russian hegemony. It was not just elites who looked in this direction, for surveys carried out in Kazakhstan and Uzbekistan during 1992 revealed that far more respondents looked to the West for support than to Russia, the Islamic world or China.[5]

In practice the West in general and the USA in particular has been far less interested in Central Asia than in other parts of the former USSR. Explaining this, Robert Cullen has suggested that developments in the region do not generally impact upon any vital US or Western national interests and that therefore it was always unlikely to receive major investments of time or money. Nonetheless, he isolated a number of concerns shared by the Western states and asked four questions:

- Will developments in the region add momentum to radical Islamic movements that might threaten Western interests?
- Will outside investors be given a fair chance to compete for contracts, whilst minimising Iranian involvement, to exploit energy resources which might in turn reduce Western dependence upon the Gulf?
- Might nuclear weapons or regionally-produced uranium fall into the hands of rogue governments or terrorists?
- Should the West accept the growing role in Central Asia of regional powers such as Turkey, Iran or Russia?[6]

To these factors Nancy Lubin has added American concerns with the challenges posed by drugs and organised crime which have been exacerbated by the Tajik conflict, as well as fears that social and economic problems in the region might precipitate major conflicts in the future.[7]

With regard to Cullen's first question, and despite events in Tajikistan, Western policy-makers have largely moved on from their earlier panic that a 'fundamentalist' upsurge was about to sweep the region. Nonetheless, Washington remains concerned about any possible spread of Iranian influence in the region and has sought to prevent US firms from investing in various Turkmen–Iranian schemes to build transport links and pipelines through Iran. To this end it has been able to play on regional rivalries, most recently pursuing better relations with Uzbekistan, traditionally condemned for its poor human rights record but in late 1995 garnering considerable US praise for its temporary backing of the trade embargo against Iran.[8] In the economic sphere Western investors have been given a fair crack of the whip in some sectors, despite ongoing bureaucratic obstacles to economic negotiations, but by the mid-1990s those working in the crucial energy sector were facing considerable problems as Russia sought to muscle in on various deals, using its control of pipelines to exert crucial leverage. On the security issue, Kazakhstan, the only nuclear state in the region, was of primary concern, and by early 1994 Washington was making it clear that to some extent aid was tied to success or otherwise in destroying the remaining nuclear arsenal and becoming a non-nuclear power. Towards the end of that year the USA undertook a secret operation to remove all weapons-grade uranium from Kazakhstan and by mid-1995 the last weapons had been destroyed or removed.[9]

For the USA, and to some extent other Western powers, a primary concern has been to link good relations to democratisation, and organisations such as United States Agency for International Development (USAID) have generally responded more readily to the needs of Kazakhstan and Kyrgyzstan than to the overtly authoritarian regimes in Turkmenistan and Uzbekistan. The latter two states have had to listen to lectures on human rights from visiting US officials though, as already noted, Uzbekistan's critical stance *vis-à-vis* Iran had led to a thaw in relations between Uzbekistan and the USA. Of the European states, and leaving aside the activities of private oil and gas companies, Germany has been the most involved, especially in seeking to provide economic incentives that might persuade ethnic Germans to remain in Kazakhstan and Kyrgyzstan. From the East considerable interest has also been exhibited by Japan, which has developed close relations with Kyrgyzstan and by 1996 was playing a key role in the modernisation of Bishkek's Manas airport.[10] For all this, Central Asia remains marginal to Western concerns, focused as they are on stability in Russia, and by the mid-1990s the leaders of the Central Asian states had developed a more realistic assessment of what was likely to be forthcoming from Western sources.

In the Muslim world

Much of the early commentary on the geopolitics of the region focused on what were perceived to be the 'natural' ethnic and religious affinities of Central Asia. Some noted the fact that the vast majority of the population of the region was Turkic and suggested that close relations with Turkey might ensue, whilst others, pointing to the Islamic and Persian heritage of the region, expressed the fear that Iran might come to exert an influence that would be presumed to be unhealthy.[11] This in turn tied in with discussions of a new 'great game' in which both the West, and to some extent Russia during the early 1990s, promoted Turkey as a regional player so as to hinder Iranian involvement.

For Turkey under President Ozal, the rediscovery of millions of Turkic brothers and sisters appeared to present new opportunities to a country whose identity and self-confidence was under threat. Though long tied into the Western alliance, attempts at greater integration with Europe had been halted in 1989 when the European

Community deferred consideration of Turkey's application to join. The appearance of five new Turkic states (including Azerbaijan) thus came at an opportune moment, offering the possibility of extending Ankara's influence. Much was made of shared linguistic roots and Turkish delegations hurried to the region offering credits, expertise and trade opportunities. Simultaneously Turkey played a key role in gaining international recognition of these states and on occasion representing their interests abroad.

For Soviet-educated Central Asian elites, Turkey's secular model of development was particularly attractive, though in practice the promise of 1991–92 has not been fulfilled. Though extensive ties have developed in the cultural sector, with Turkish support for the modernisation of communications networks and the provision of higher educational places for Central Asian businesspeople, diplomats and army officers, Ankara has been unable to supply the level of aid originally hoped for. On the one hand, Turkish businesspeople have been frustrated by the persistent problem of bureaucratic obstruction and the fact that all too often Central Asian companies can only pay for goods with other goods rather than with hard cash. Against this, Central Asian leaders have come to realise that in practice Turkey, despite providing over $1 billion in loans, credits and investment, has its own economic difficulties which preclude extensive involvement in the region. Moreover, Turkey has remained sensitive to Russian concerns over its actions in the region, and alive to the fact that for all the cultural affinities, its trade with Russia is around ten times that with Central Asia.[12] Problems have also arisen with the discovery that supposed 'natural' links between the two regions are less close than was thought, with Central Asians being far more Sovietised than had been assumed and with the linguistic ties between the region and Turkey being much less close. For the Central Asian states, additional concerns included an awareness of continued dependence upon Russian good will, for example, in getting natural resources out of the region, the distance from Turkey and a fear of simply replacing one 'big brother' with another, a particularly acute concern in the face of Ankara's often-insensitive talk of its role as guide to the newly independent states.[13]

With Iran relations are more complex.[14] Tehran's natural affinity is with Tajikistan, as the two states share a common language and a cultural tradition. However, the 'greater Tajikistan' which lay at the heart of this Persian common heritage no longer exists, its cultural centres of Samarkand and Bukhara now being located in Uzbekistan and having been considerably 'Turkified' over the last 70 years. Iran was the first state to establish an embassy in Dushanbe, on the renamed Tehran Street, and was active in funding mosque construction in this tiny republic during 1991–92. This reinforced the outside perception that Iran had a hand in the emergence of the Islamic movement, though in fact this was largely a domestic product. Despite these links, Iran's political, security and economic concerns have led it to pay relatively little attention to Tajikistan, which is geographically a peripheral state.

Of far greater interest, for both geographical and practical reasons, has been the evolution of Iran's relations with Turkmenistan and Kazakhstan. Each of these ties has its roots in mutual interests in the energy and transportation sector. Whilst direct aid has been precluded by the poor state of Iranian finances, Tehran has been responsive to Turkmen needs for alternative means of exporting its goods to those offered by Russia. To this end, major agreements have been signed on developing rail links between the two republics and building pipelines through which gas and oil can be exported to Europe. Whilst the latter projects are likely to take time and have been hampered by US restrictions on investment projects involving Iran, the much-delayed rail link was opened with great fanfare in May 1996 in the presence of many regional heads of state.[15] Yet, despite these close ties, there have been signs of tension between the two states, especially following Ashgabat's decision to grant the contract for the management of the Turkmenbashi oil refinery to an Israeli company.[16]

Iranian relations with Kazakhstan have also been rooted in energy concerns, and following a visit to Tehran by Nazarbaev in May 1996, it was agreed that Kazakh oil would be shipped to Iran for refining and later export.[17] Relations with Uzbekistan, however, have proved more difficult, with Islam Karimov being openly critical of his neighbour Niyazov for allowing 'fundamentalism' a foothold in the region,[18] and this despite the tight control over Islam exerted by the Turkmen authorities and Iran's general caution about promoting its ideological preferences in Central Asia.[19]

Whilst the relations of Turkey and Iran with Central Asia have attracted the most attention, other parts of the Islamic world have become involved in the region. Amongst the more active have been Saudi Arabia, Indonesia, some of the Gulf states and Pakistan, with the latter expressing considerable interest in developing close ties. In part this stems from Islamabad's search for allies in the face of its troubled relations with the USA since the collapse of communism. Yet here as elsewhere discussions have focused on economic issues, with Pakistan seeking energy supplies and cotton from its northern allies, in exchange for credits, goods and medicines.[20] Prior to the civil war especially close links were being developed with Tajikistan with projects for the provision of hydro-electric power by the latter being under discussion. More recently there have sprung up numerous joint ventures in both Uzbekistan and Kazakhstan.[21] There has also been talk of establishing a major rail connection from Central Asia to Karachi, but it is difficult to see how this could be developed so long as the civil war in Afghanistan continues to rage. Indeed, Tahir Amin has suggested that the potential for Pakistan to get involved in the region is severely limited, not simply because of the Afghan conflict, but also because of the general lack of financial resources available to Pakistan.[22] Equally Central Asian leaders have proved unwilling to develop any political links with Pakistan that might jeopardise the close economic ties with India built up during the Soviet era.

In general the region's states have sought to develop close connections with the wider Muslim world but always on their own terms. Whilst proclaiming a return to past traditions and ties with the Islamic community, they have refused to adopt the anti-Israeli positions favoured by some Islamic organisations and by the end of 1992 Israel had more joint ventures in the region than any other Middle Eastern state.[23] Throughout the driving force has been economics, evident in the attempt to draw some of the Gulf states into the exploitation of energy resources,[24] and the early accession to the Economic Cooperation Organisation (ECO) which joined them together with Iran, Turkey, Afghanistan and Pakistan. Even then early hopes have not always been fulfilled, with ECO failing to deliver on its earlier promise, in part because of the economic weakness of the three founder states but also because tensions within the organisation have ensured that most of the dealings between member states are carried out on a bilateral basis.[25] In the long term it is conceivable that two of these states, Uzbekistan and Turkmenistan, might be drawn more closely into the Middle Eastern or Islamic sphere of influence, but for the time being, especially given the ongoing importance of Russia in the region, this looks a distant possibility.[26]

In Asia

As Martha Brill Olcott has observed, Central Asian leaders have not been averse to utilising their 'Asianness' in the development of their international relations. Though this brings with it its own dangers – for many centuries the region has been subject to invasion and repression from the East – the apparent successes of many Asian economies has proved attractive. In particular it has been noted that these states, whether we are talking of communist China or the 'Asian tigers', have discovered developmental models which at least in the early stages combined tight political control with a key role for the state in the restructuring of their economies. At the same time it was hoped that a common sense of Asian identity might attract some of these states to aid the region's development, a hope that has been partially realised in Japan and South Korea's involvment in both investment and aid projects.

In practice, however, it is China which looks set to play a key role in Central Asia,[27] something not entirely surprising given the long border it shares with Kazakhstan and Kyrgyzstan and the close ethnic ties with the Xinjiang region in which lived around a million Kazakhs at the time of Soviet collapse as well as over 7 million Turkic-speaking Uighurs. For their part, Kazakhstan and Kyrgyzstan provided a home to around a quarter of a million Uighurs, often with family ties across the border. Since independence ties with China have deepened considerably, as leading political figures from both sides of the border have travelled extensively promoting trade and good relations, and during Li Peng's visit to Almaty in April 1994 the long-running border dispute was finally resolved. At the centre of these new relations have been economic concerns, with China becoming the largest trading partner of the region after Russia. Since the early 1990s Chinese traders have been busy in the region and according to some estimates by 1992 up to 50 per cent of Kazakh consumer goods were coming from China, in exchange for fertilisers, steel and ores. Indeed Munro reported that China's two-way trade with Kazakhstan exceeded Turkey's with all five Central Asian republics.[28] Beijing's involvement in Kyrgyzstan is if anything more extensive, with thousands of Chinese businesspeople being active in the republic, especially in the free trade zone created in the Nayrn oblast, and extensive discussion taking place concerning joint exploitation of the river systems they share.[29] More fanciful perhaps have been discussions with Turkmenistan regarding the possibility of building a gas pipeline through China to Japan.

Whilst developing these links both sides have been quick to assure Russia that they have no intention of threatening Moscow's interests in the region. During his April 1994 visit to Uzbekistan, Chinese premier Li Peng spoke of reopening the old silk route through the republic but stressed that Chinese involvement was not intended to counter the interests of any other party, i.e. Russia. This recognition of Russia's 'natural' interest in the region was also evident in discussions in Shanghai during April 1996 following which Russia, China and the Central Asian leaders sharing a border signed a confidence-building treaty involving the demilitarisation of these areas.[30]

For all the growth in trade, relations between Central Asia and China have not been unproblematic. On the economic front China has proved an attractive partner insofar as it is more willing to accept barter arrangements than most other countries, but there have been tensions with Kazakhstan which increasingly wishes to be paid for goods in convertible currencies. Central Asian leaders, especially those of Kazakhstan and Kyrgyzstan, have also been extremely unhappy with continued Chinese nuclear testing carried out at Lop Nor to the east of the Kazakh border.[31] On China's part, concerns have focused on the ethnic issue, with fears that Xinjiang's restive Muslims might link up with their fellows in the former Soviet Union. On various occasions Beijing has pressurised Central Asian leaders to curb the activity of Uighur separatists on their territory and, whilst they have generally been kept under tight rein within the region,[32] their organisations in Kazakhstan and Kyrgyzstan continue to agitate for the creation of a larger state based upon Xinjiang province.[33] For all these tensions, China looks set to become a major influence in the developing economic life of the region and one with the potential to intervene in other ways in the event of continued instability in the region or reduced Russian involvement.

Regional cooperation

Despite the search for new allies, there has been a growing recognition on the part of the Central Asia states that they have certain interests in common, not least to prevent the reassertion of Russian hegemony. As a result they have sought to evolve more meaningful regional cooperation. Even before the collapse of the USSR republican leaders held a series of talks to discuss common problems and responses to policies emanating from Moscow. Alongside these had gone meetings of opposition activists, sometimes calling for loose political association but in some cases propagating pan-Turkic ideas. Further impetus to collaboration came from the decision of the three Slavic heads of state on 8 December 1991 to form a commonwealth, a step they had taken without consulting other Soviet republics. In response Central Asian leaders gathered four days later in Ashkhabad and decided to seek membership of the Commonwealth of Independent States (CIS) on condition that they would be treated as equal members. On 21 December 1991 eleven states (excluding the Baltic states and Georgia) met in Alma Ata to formally announce the creation of the CIS.

At the Ashkhabad meeting Kazakhstan's Nursultan Nazarbaev had put forward a proposal for some form of Turkic or Central Asian union, based loosely on the European Community. Though this may have originated as a bargaining chip to persuade Russia to retain its ties with the region, it was an idea that was not to go away. During a further summit in Bishkek the following April the possibilities of economic cooperation were discussed again, though at this same meeting it became apparent that regional collaboration was not on everyone's minds. Turkmenistan, already inclined to reject collective deals within the CIS, proved unwilling to sign up to anything of substance, rejecting proposals for price-setting and the creation of a common investment fund. In addition there seems to have been a general fear that any closer union would be dominated by Uzbekistan.[34] Further statements of intent to cooperate in the economic field, in the resolution of the Tajik conflict and in protecting the Aral Sea were made at a summit in Tashkent in January 1993. Though the same meeting witnessed a symbolic name change from Middle to Central Asia (thus encompassing the previously excluded Kazakhstan), President Nazarbaev continued to make clear his view that the successor states would be best served by close relations within the CIS.[35]

Nonetheless events did appear to be pushing Central Asia towards closer cooperation, especially after Russia's decision in mid-1993 to push them out of the rouble zone. Within a year

Nazarbaev, a long-term proponent of integration – up until late 1991 within the USSR, and then within the CIS – put forward a proposal for what he called a Eurasian Union. This would have more teeth than the CIS but he strongly denied that it would mark the effective restoration of the USSR. Under his draft constitution for this body there would be created a common economic space and collective defence arrangements. Its primary aim would be the creation of a union of equal and independent states whose goal was a considerable degree of integration so as to preserve stability and ensure the conditions for socio-economic modernisation. Though the states would retain clearly defined rights, there would also be collective decision-making on a range of specified issues, with a qualified majority voting system along European Union lines introduced to ensure broad support. Though this plan garnered the support of some influential politicans in Russia, it failed to get off the ground and was treated with some scepticism by Uzbekistan and Turkmenistan.[36]

By late 1993 it was apparent that in most areas regional cooperation was a non-starter. True, Kazakhstan and Uzbekistan had taken similar positions in the United Nations, their presidents addressing the General Assembly and calling for special recognition of the region's needs. Both leaders called for steps to be taken to prevent further outbreaks of ethnic violence, and asked the United Nations to help with the environmental clean-up of the region.[37] Then in early 1994 Kazakhstan, Kyrgyzstan and Uzbekistan signed an agreement to create a common economic space by the end of the century. This would entail moving towards the free circulation of goods, services, labour and capital, and the development of coordination in customs, taxation and monetary policy. Subsequent agreements covered the creation of a Central Asian Bank for Cooperation and Development, common information policies, though it was not clear how these would work given the varying degrees of pluralism in the three republics, migration and military–technical cooperation. Together with these agreements went the creation of various inter-republican committees and councils of ministers.[38] It is still too early to see what this economic union might mean in practice. Whilst the members enjoy considerable potential in the energy and agricultural sector, they remain vastly unequal economically, with Kazakhstan producing about two-thirds of their output. Also unclear is whether the economic union created (on paper at least) in

March 1996, which brought together Russia, Belarus, Kazakhstan and Kyrgyzstan, will undermine cooperation between the latter two states and Uzbekistan.

For all these attempts at cooperation, any notion that a shared heritage and mutual interests might draw these states together must be balanced with some discussion of potential areas of conflict between them.[39] From the outset tensions were evident in Turkmenistan's preference for going it alone, with President Niyazov seeking to avoid commitment to any regional bloc or collective arrangement, arguing that only what he called 'positive neutrality' (a status recognised by the United Nations at the end of 1995) could make a reality of his republic's independence. Thus he tended to keep the CIS at arm's length, in May 1992 refusing to join the Commonwealth's collective security agreement and then rejecting the possibility of sending Turkmen troops to Tajikistan. All of this was based upon a perception that Turkmenistan had the economic potential to go it alone, and that collective arrangements or regional cooperation might tie its hands in seeking to exploit these to the full.

Cooperation was sometimes rendered problematic by the different political styles of the region's leaders, with countries such as Kazakhstan and Kyrgyzstan having to pay more attention to public opinion on issues such as sending their soldiers to defend Tajik borders. These states also expressed resentment at the activities of the Uzbek security services which appeared to act with considerable freedom in the area, for example seizing oppositionists on the streets of Bishkek and Almaty and shipping them back for trial with little reference to the states concerned. These political differences were sometimes reinforced by personal rivalries, with Kazakhstan's Nazarbaev and Uzbekistan's Karimov reportedly pursuing hegemonic goals within the regions, and both finding it hard to take Turkmenistan's Niyazov seriously. In addition Karimov has been highly critical of Turkmenistan's developing links with Iran, suggesting that developing close road and rail links might encourage the penetration of the region by radical Islam.[40] Further problems arose following the seeming victory of the Taliban in Afghanistan in the autumn of 1996 with Niyazov refusing to join CIS attacks on a movement which promised security guarantees for Turkmen efforts to create a pipeline through their country to Pakistan.[41]

Some of the old tensions date back centuries. For example, Tajikistan and Kyrgyzstan have plentiful supplies of water, on which both Uzbekistan and Turkmenistan depend. During the early 1990s difficulties have been apparent in this area, particularly concerning plans by the two former states to divert some of their water eastwards or southwards in deals with China and Pakistan. Turkmen–Uzbek relations have also been soured by the water issue, as Uzbekistan's use of shared rivers has a major impact on the amount of water available to Turkmenistan. Though the question was reportedly patched up at a much delayed meeting between the two presidents in January 1996, the continued centrality of water to the economic future of the region makes further conflict likely.

Relations between the states are also complicated by the ethnic distribution of the population which, as we discussed earlier, left sizeable minorities outside their nominal country though often in areas contiguous to it. Though each leader has rejected irredentist claims, the treatment of minorities always has the potential to become a bone of contention. All of these issues are reinforced by economic arguments that stem partly from the unequal distribution of economic resources and potential in the region. Problems have arisen over the introduction of new currencies, payments for goods, and the relative prices at which natural resources will be exchanged between neighbours – for example, in early 1995 Uzbekistan threatened to cut off gas supplies to southern Kazakhstan unless it met its debts.[42] Whilst most of these tensions have been resolved by diplomatic means, the smaller states remain vulnerable to pressure from their larger neighbours, with Uzbekistan and Kazakhstan possessing substantial armed forces that could in theory be used to impose their will in the region.[43] In such circumstances, regional cooperation cannot be seen as a panacea though it might be argued that it does provide further channels for ensuring that conflicts are resolved in a peaceful manner.

The continued importance of Russia

For all the new contacts with the outside world, by the mid-1990s the Central Asian states had become acutely aware that unravelling the political, economic and military interdependence with Russia built up over the previous century or more would take time. During the months following the collapse of the USSR the Kremlin largely turned its back on the region, preferring to focus on developing good relations with the West, and only in April 1992 did Foreign Minister Andrei Kozyrev visit Central Asia. But under the impact of developments in Tajikistan during that year, and under pressure from Uzbekistan's President Karimov, Russian interest was re-awakened. In particular concern began to be expressed that Russia's security might be threatened by the rise of ethnic conflict or religious 'extremism' in the south, and that Russia's own Muslims might be open to radicalisation.[44] The problem facing Moscow was how to intervene in the region without appearing to resurrect an imperialist past or becoming embroiled in an open-ended conflict as had happened in Afghanistan. As presidential adviser Andranik Migranyan was to warn in early 1994, intervention carried with it the danger of reinforcing the appeal of Islamicist movements because it entailed propping up regimes such as that in Dushanbe which had limited legitimacy and a record of human rights abuses.[45] Despite these cautions Russia was gradually pulled into the conflict. By the end of 1992 the 201st Motorised Division was forming the basis of CIS peace-keeping efforts in the republic, and responsibility for guarding the borders remained with Russian personnel. At the same time Kozyrev made repeated calls to the Dushanbe government to seek national reconciliation, if necessary by holding talks with the opposition. This was reinforced by President Yeltsin, addressing Central Asian leaders in the Kremlin in August 1993, when he suggested that whilst Russia would maintain its military presence, the conflict could never be resolved by outside powers or by force. Simultaneously he rejected the idea that this was primarily a Russian intervention, arguing that the security of CIS members in Central Asia was of concern to the CIS as a whole and that it was in its name that Russian and other troops were involved in the Tajik conflict.[46]

Further pressure for Russian involvement in the region stemmed for domestic political factors, as Russian nationalists and communists joined forces in calling for foreign policy to be oriented less to the West and more to Russia's own backyard.[47] Though the subsequent policy was far from coherent, Moscow began to develop a more assertive stance towards all of the successor states during 1993. Soon even Andrei Kozyrev was talking in more strident language of the need to defend Russian interests within the former Soviet Union and to elaborate what some described as the 'Monrovsky doctrine' in which the borders of the southern republics were to be treated as essentially those of Russia and to be defended accordingly. This policy shift emerging in the mid-1990s was evident in political, economic and military relations with Central Asia. The political aspect was touched on in an earlier chapter, where we pointed to the ways in which Moscow has used the issue of Russian speakers in the 'near abroad' to exert political leverage though, with the exception of Tajikistan and Turkmenistan, it made little progress on the question of dual citizenship, and saw only limited changes to the status of the Russian language in these republics.[48]

In the economic sphere, changing Russian attitudes were evident in two ways. On the one hand, Russia began to use its might, evident in the continuing control of pipelines, to gain a stake in the various deals for energy exploitation between Western companies and the Central Asian states. In consequence the Russian state oil company Lukoil acquired a 20 per cent share in the Kazakh–Chevron deal to explore the Tengiz oil field and then leant further on Kazakhstan to ensure that the proposed new pipeline went through Russian territory. Even when proposals to route such supply lines outwith Russian territory have been put forward, as in the Turkmen plan to ship gas through Afghanistan to Pakistan proposed in August 1996, Moscow was able to ensure a substantial stake for Gazprom, the Russian state gas company.[49]

On the other hand, there was growing Russian pressure for economic reintegration amongst the states of the former Soviet Union. Though interdependence is a two-way process, with Russia still needing Central Asian cotton and Kazakh grain, the relationship is clearly an unequal one. Most of these states remain indebted to Moscow and have often been forced to trade goods or even cede ownership in various enterprises in order to pay off these debts or acquire certain categories of goods. For example, at the beginning of 1996 Kyrgyzstan ceded majority Russian ownership in two major tobacco firms and part ownership in a number of other enterprises in exchange for debt reduction.[50] For their part the Central Asian states have reacted in varied fashion to the growing realisation of their ongoing dependence on Russia. Turkmenistan and to a lesser extent Uzbekistan have generally sought to avoid extensive reintegration, whereas Kazakhstan and Kyrgyzstan have taken the attitude that a considerable degree of economic integration is in their best interests. Both were willing to sign up to an economic union created with Russia and Belarus at the end of March 1996, though the creation of such an association may have had more to do with the forthcoming Russian presidential election than any substantive changes in economic relations between these states.[51]

The third issue, brought to the fore by both the Tajik conflict and the nuclear arms factor, was that of regional security.[52] As the USSR fell apart, considerable concern was expressed in the West that a single nuclear power was being replaced by four such powers, with special attention being focused on the idea of the creation of an Islamic nuclear power in Kazakhstan. With 104 intercontinental ballistic missiles and 40 nuclear bombers, this Asiatic republic looked a formidable power, although Moscow and Kazakhstan sought to reassure Washington that operational control remained with Russian leaders. To this end Nazarbaev rejected nationalist protests and promised to transform Kazakhstan into a non-nuclear state. In late 1993 he signed the Nuclear Non-Proliferation Treaty following which, and with US financial support, the removal or dismantling of weapons and bombers in Kazakhstan gathered pace, to be finally completed in mid-1995.[53]

Though each of these states sought to create their own armed structures during the early 1990s, and all but Tajikistan signed up to NATO's Partnership for Peace programme, each relied heavily on the continued loyalty of the Slavic personnel who dominated the officer corps.[54] More importantly, in the face of armed struggle in Tajikistan and incursions from Afghanistan the Central Asian states naturally looked to Russia as guarantor of their security, and this led to some attempts at reintegration of military policy. Early signs of this came at a CIS summit held in Tashkent during May 1992 when all but Turkmenistan adhered to a collective security agreement. Following this a number of bilateral deals were signed which effectively created a common defence space under broad Russian protection. Each differed slightly in emphasis. Deals with Turkmenistan, for example, included provision for a Turkmen national army under joint Russian–Turkmen control, though air defence and border guards remained under Russian command, whilst Uzbekistan signed agreements concerning joint provisioning and equipping of its relatively strong armed forces, though it rejected Russian control of its borders.[55] Leaving aside Tajikistan, the closest military ties have been those between Russia and Kazakhstan. Nazarbaev has recognised that only Moscow can provide the security guarantees necessary for his state and thus has encouraged the evolution of close links, including proposals for the unification of the two armed forces.[56] Despite this relations have not always been easy, as was evident in the tortuous negotiations over the Baikonur space centre in Kazakhstan, eventually resolved in the spring of 1994 with an agreement that Russia would lease the base for an initial twenty-year period, the cost to come in the first instance from Kazakhstan's debts to Russia.[57]

This trend towards growing Russian involvement in the successor states as a whole was reinforced in September 1995 when Yeltsin issued a decree entitled 'the establishment of the strategic course of the Russian federation with members states of the CIS'. In this document he effectively called for the subordination of the policies of these states to Russian interests, stressing in particular the need for proper guarantees of the rights of Russian minorities, greater economic integration, and the creation of a unified defence structure. Implicit in the document was the suggestion that Russia's borders should be equated with those of the old Soviet Union and that Russia reserved the right to intervene should it feel its security threatened.[58] For the Central Asian states this implied that from Moscow's perspective their sovereign status was to be subject to constraints, and suggested that despite independence their decision-making processes could not ignore the interests of their powerful northern neighbour.

Conclusion

Though Russia impinged upon Central Asian consciousness much earlier, it was not until the middle of the nineteenth century that the region began to perceive Russian actions as posing a major threat to its autonomy and independence. With the ending of St Petersburg's ambitions in the West following the Crimean War, its rulers turned eastwards and found in Turkestan scope both for colonial expansion and a new location for pursuing their rivalry with England. In the years that followed the region was to become a land of ongoing struggle, initially overt but, after the Bolshevik consolidation of power, covert until the end of the 1980s. During the initial phases this pitted traditional rulers against would-be conquerors, and then, in the light of failure here, against reformers and revolutionaries within their own societies. Yet from the end of the century the fate of Turkestan and the steppes was closely bound into that of the Russian empire, and when the latter fell both traditionalists and reformists within the region lacked the strength or solidarity capable of resisting the single-minded assaults of the Bolsheviks. From then until the Gorbachev years the struggle with central power took a more discreet form, as traditional networks were at first overwhelmed by the extent and brutality of the transformation pushed through by Stalin. Gradually the old society, not itself uninfluenced or unshaped by Soviet rule, fought back, subverting central goals in a variety of ways, from the maintenance of traditional customs, through the misreporting of economic results, to an increasing ability to control local cadre selection.

It was this society, found in state formations essentially created by Soviet rule, which suddenly had independence thrust upon it at the end of 1991. Though reluctant converts, the leaders of all the new states quickly sought to give meaning to their sovereign status through developing new international contacts and, perhaps more importantly, by attempting to create political orders and build nation-states out of countries in which other, sub-national loyalties remained strong. Underlying these goals was the awareness of the old Soviet-trained elites that true independence required a degree of autonomy in economic decision-making and that their continued legitimacy might well depend upon the economic well-being of their populations. To this end each leader has stressed the priority of economics over politics, with even would-be democrats such as Akaev and Nazarbaev explaining the growing expansion of presidential power in terms of the need to push meaningful economic reform through recalcitrant and conservative legislatures. At the same time each state has been active in seeking international economic partners, at first with perhaps excessive optimism as to the region's ability to attract investors, and then more with a measured awareness of the need for a more focused approach rooted in the particular strengths of each country.

Despite these efforts, since late 1993 Central Asian leaders have increasingly had to come to terms with a Kremlin in which the imperatives of domestic politics dictate a more assertive role in Russia's traditional 'back yard'. One response to this has been the pursuit of regional cooperation though in reality this has proved to be problematic and had been undermined by tensions between the

Central Asian states. In such circumstances each state has tended to evolve its own relationship with Moscow and develop its own strategies for coping with renewed Russian involvement. Some have little choice but to succumb, as in the case of Tajikistan whose current regime is completely dependent militarily and economically on Moscow.

For Kazakhstan and Kyrgyzstan close ties with Russia have been a matter of necessity. For Kyrgyzstan this is the only realistic option given its limited economic potential, dependence upon Russian goods and substantial Slavic and European population. Burgeoning economic relations with neighbouring China may change this by the beginning of the next century, but from Bishkek's viewpoint Moscow's dominance probably remains preferable to that of Beijing. Kazakhstan's stance reflects Nazarbaev's awareness of the fragility of a republic which is ethnically divided along broadly geographical lines. With long shared borders, its northern regions dominated by Russian speakers and to a considerable degree tied in with the economy of southern Siberia, Kazakhstan cannot afford to alienate its northern neighbour, especially when more nationalistically inclined Russian politicians frequently make noises about reclaiming these territories. Nazarbaev's response has been to pursue integrationist approaches to relations within the CIS, and to support various proposals for economic union. At the same time he has been unwilling to compromise on anything that might be seen as an infringement of Kazakh sovereignty, for example rejecting Russian criticisms following the arrest of local Cossacks who called for a redefinition of borders. Nonetheless, the problems cited above would seem to ensure that for some time to come Kazakhstan's foreign policy orientation will be towards Russia, with an inclination to depict Kazakhstan as some form of bridge between East and West.[59]

Turkmenistan and Uzbekistan have remained wary, though they cannot ignore Moscow. For all his bluster and persistent rejection of collective deals within the CIS, Turkmenistans's President Niyazov remains dependent upon Russia for the guarding of his borders and for the transportation of his country's natural gas. Uzbekistan's situation is more complex. On the one hand favouring close ties with Russia and Russia's continuing security presence in the region, President Karimov has been critical of pushing integration for its own sake. Instead he has frequently stressed that new agreements and institutions should only be created when situations arise that demand a joint response.[60] Relying on a rich potential resource base rooted in cotton, gold and some oil, Uzbekistan has sought to develop new links, and has to some extent recognised that it forms a natural part of an Islamic crescent. Here demography, language laws and appointment policies are reducing the role and number of Slavs and, in the absence of a common border, there is perhaps less need to placate Russia than there is in Kazakhstan to the north. Uzbekistan is all too aware that it remains dependent upon Russia for many basic consumer goods and that for the time being it needs Russian guarantees for its security and support on issues such as resolving the Tajik conflict. Thus, whilst culturally shifting towards what Henry Hale has called 'Islamic and Turkic' values, in part to undermine accusations by domestic opponents of selling out to Russia, it has sought to maintain civilised relations with the CIS states.[61] Nonetheless, Uzbekistan has refused to countenance subservience to Russian goals and in early 1996 Karimov expressed considerable hostility towards the new integrationist trends evident in the March economic union, warning that if the region passively accepted Moscow's current policy line it was likely to return to its old status of raw material supplier for the metropolitan centre.[62]

By late 1996 the prospects for Central Asia remained unclear, as the region found itself in a continuing transition with no clearly defined ends. The process of defining interests and needs remains incomplete, hampered to some degree by renewed Russian involvement in the region. Though this may have been partially diverted by events in Chechnya and continued uncertainties within the Russian elite created by the poor health of Boris Yeltsin, Moscow will clearly remain a key player in the region for the foreseeable future. In the light of this Central Asian elites have to come up with policies that make the most of this connection, that utilise it for their own ends whilst ensuring that they continue to enjoy the limited degree of independence and sovereignty that is open to any state in the modern world. In pursuit of this end they appear to depend to a considerable degree upon the current generation of leaders, men largely schooled in the Soviet era. For this reason the transition may well be prolonged, requiring at the very least a successful succession process which throws up new elites capable of bringing domestic stability, of holding their states together (something that looks increasingly unlikely in the case of Tajikistan), and able to deal with the great power aspirations of a resurgent Russia.

Notes

1 M. B. Olcott, *Central Asia's New States – Independence, Foreign Policy and Regional Security* (Washington, 1996), p. 5.

2 *Ibid.*, pp. 21–37.

3 R. Dannreuther, *Creating New States in Central Asia* (London, March 1994), p. 5.

4 J. Critchlow, 'The ethnic factor in Central Asian foreign policy', in R. Szporluk, ed., *National Identity and Ethnicity in Russia and the New States of Eurasia* (New York, 1994), pp. 266–8.

5 N. Lubin, *Central Asians Take Stock: Reform, Corruption and Identity* (Washington, 1994), pp. 20–1.

6 R. Cullen, 'Central Asia and the West', in M. Mandelbaum, ed., *Central Asia and the World* (New York, 1994), pp. 130–46.

7 N. Lubin, 'Central Asia: Issues and challenges for United States policy', in A. Banuazizi and M. Weiner, eds, *The New Geopolitics of Central Asia and its Borderlands* (Bloomington and Indianapolis, 1994), pp. 261–72.

8 S. Frederick Starr, 'Making Eurasia stable', *Foreign Affairs*, January–February 1996, 92; S. Hunter, 'Uzbekistan challenges for the leadership of Central Asia', *Middle East International*, 24 May 1996, 19–20.

9 See *International Herald Tribune*, 15 February 1994; *Financial Times*, 24 November 1994; *Open Media Research Institute*, 101, 25 May 1995.

10 During the first half of the 1990s Japan was one of the major investors in Kyrgyzstan, providing 14.5 per cent of its credits and 13.5 per cent of its technical aid. *Res publika*, 5 June 1996.

11 See the comments to this effect of Iranian Foreign Minister Ali Akbar Veliayati reported in *The Independent*, 3 March 1992.

12 Olcott, *Central Asia's New States*, p. 26.

13 This section relies heavily on S. Sayari, 'Turkey, The Caucasus and Central Asia', in Banuazizi and Weiner, *The New Geopolitics of Central Asia*, pp. 175–96; an unpublished paper on Turkey and Central Asia by Patricia Carley presented at the annual conference of the American Association for the Advancement of Slavic Studies, Philadelphia, November 1994; P. Robins, 'The Middle East and Central Asia', in P. Ferdinand, ed., *The New Central Asia and its Neighbours* (London, 1994), pp. 55–74; M. Aydin, 'Turkey and Central

Asia: Challenges of change', *Central Asian Survey*, 15:2, 1996, 157–77.

14 See M. Atkin, 'Tajikistan's relations with Iran and Afghanistan' and S. Sajjadpour, 'Iran, the Caucasus and Central Asia', in Banuazizi and Weiner, *The New Geopolitics*, pp. 91–117 and 197–215; and Robins, 'The Middle East and Central Asia', pp. 65–74.

15 *The Independent*, 14 May 1996.

16 *Economist Intelligence Unit, Country Profile, Turkmenistan, 2nd Quarter 1996*, p. 30.

17 *Open Media Research Institute*, 92, 13 May 1996.

18 See *Nezavisimaya gazeta*, 21 October 1993; *Segodya*, 1 July 1994.

19 According to most sources Iran has been much less active in promoting Islam, building mosques etc. than Saudi Arabia or Pakistan.

20 *Segodnya*, 20 August 1994.

21 A. Hyman, 'Central Asia's relations with Afghanistan and South Asia', in Ferdinand, *The New Central Asia and its Neighbours*, pp. 86–91.

22 T. Amin, 'Pakistan and the Central Asian States', in Banuazizi and Weiner, *The New Geopolitics*, pp. 216–31.

23 Robins, 'The Middle East and Central Asia', pp. 55–6.

24 *Middle East International*, 3 April 1992, at 16.

25 Atkin, 'Tajikistan's relations with Iran and Afghanistan', pp. 91–3.

26 D. Pipes, 'The event of our era: Former Soviet Muslim republics change the Middle East', in Mandelbaum, *Central Asia and the World*, p. 85.

27 See K. Martin, 'China and Central Asia: Between seduction and suspicion', Radio Free Europe/Radio Liberty, *Research Report*, 3:25, 24 June 1994, 26–36; R. Munro, 'Central Asia and China', in Mandelbaum, *Central Asia and the World*, pp. 225–38; P. Ferdinand, 'The new Central Asia and China', in Ferdinand, *The New Central Asia and its Neighbours*, pp. 95–107.

28 See Note 27 above.

29 Olcott, *Central Asia's New States*, pp. 109–10.

30 *BBC Summary of World Broadcasts*, SU/2598 G/1, 29 April 1996.

31 *Open Media Research Institute*, 113, 11 June 1996 on Kazakh reaction to the test carried out three days earlier.

32 Kyrgyzstan's Justice Ministry suspended the Uighur organisation *Ittipak* in the spring of 1996 for encouraging separatism. *Open Media Research Institute*, 70, 9 April 1996.

33 J. J. Rudelson, 'The Uighurs in the future of Central Asia', *Nationalities Papers*, 22:2, 1994, 291–308.

34 On the summit see *Izvestiya*, 23 April 1992; on some of the problems of regional cooperation see B. Brown, 'Regional cooperation in Cen-

tral Asia?', Radio Free Europe/Radio Liberty, *Research Report*, 2:5, 29 January 1993, 32–4.

35   *BBC Summary of World Broadcasts*, SU/1579, B/1, 6 January 1993; SU/1682, B/3–4, 7 May 1993. H. Dieter, 'Regional integration in Central Asia: Current economic position and prospects', *Central Asian Survey*, 15:3/4, 1996, 369–86.

36   *Nezavisimaya gazeta*, 8 June 1994.

37   See the reports of their speeches in *Kazakhstanskaya pravda*, 9 October 1992 and *Nezavisimaya gazeta*, 20 October 1993.

38   See *Slovo kyrgyzstana*, 12 July 1994; *Nezavisimaya gazeta*, 18 April 1995.

39   A critical view of the idea of a united Central Asia pursuing common goals can be found in M. B. Olcott, 'Ceremony and substance: The illusion of unity in Central Asia', in Mandelbaum, *Central Asia and the World*, pp. 17–46.

40   *Segodnya*, 1 July 1994.

41   *Open Media Research Institute*, 198, 11 October 1996.

42   *Segodnya*, 11 May 1995.

43   R. Woff, 'Independence and the Uzbek armed forces', *Jane's Intelligence Review*, December 1993, 567–71; R. Kangas, 'Taking the lead in Central Asian security', *Transition*, 2:9, 3 May 1996, 52–5.

44   See the analyses in *Nezavisimaya gazeta*, 29 May 1995; and M. Mesbahi, 'Russia, foreign policy and security in Central Asia and the Caucasus', *Central Asian Survey*, 12:2, 1993, 181–215.

45   *Nezavisimaya gazeta*, 18 January 1994.

46   *BBC Summary of World Broadcasts*, SU/1763, C1/1, 10 August 1993.

47   On the relationship between domestic and foreign policy see N. Melvin, *Forging the New Russian Nation* (London, 1994), pp. 27–48; I. Zviagelskaia, *The Russian Policy Debate on Central Asia* (London, 1995).

48   See Chapter 6.

49   *Open Media Research Institute*, 154, 9 August 1996.

50   *Open Media Research Institute*, 75, 16 April 1996.

51   *Nezavisimaya gazeta*, 29 March 1996.

52   An early discussion of some of these issues can be found in M. Shashenkov, *Security Issues of the Ex-Soviet Central Asian Republics* (London, 1992).

53   On developments till the end of 1994 see M. Webber, *The International Politics of Russia and the Successor States* (Manchester, 1996), pp. 140–63.

54   For example, in Kazakhstan only about 5 per cent of the officers were Kazakh at the time of independence. Robert V. Barylski, 'Kazakhstan: Military dimensions of state formation over Central Asia's civilisa-

tional fault lines', in C. Danopolous and D. Zirker, eds, *Civil–Military Relations in the Soviet and Yugoslav Successor States* (Boulder, 1996), p. 124.

55 M. B. Olcott, 'Sovereignty and the "near Abroad"', *Orbis*, Summer 1995, 357.

56 *The Guardian*, 21 January 1995.

57 See *Nezavisimaya gazeta*, 28 December 1993, 10 February 1994, 27 March 1994 and 3 April 1994.

58 See the discussion of this document in *Prism*, 6 October 1995.

59 See the interview with the Kazakh Foreign Minister T. Suleimenov, 'Some lines of Kazakh foreign policy today', *International Affairs*, 1994:3–4, 22–8.

60 *Nezavisimaya gazeta*, 21 June 1994.

61 Henry Hale, 'Islam, state building and Uzbekistan's foreign policy', in Banuazizi and Weiner, *The New Geopolitics of Central Asia*, p. 72.

62 'Uzbek president condemns CIS integration accords', *Transition*, 2:10, 17 May 1996, 63; *BBC Summary of World Broadcasts*, SU/2588, G/1, 17 April 1996.

Bibliography

Books and articles

Akiner, S. *The Formation of Kazakh Identity: From Tribe to Nation State* (London, 1995)

Akiner, S. ed., *Cultural Change and Continuity in Central Asia* (London, 1991)

Akiner, S. ed., *Political and Economic Trends in Central Asia* (London, 1994)

Alder, G. *British India's Northern Frontier, 1865–95* (London, 1963)

Allworth, E. *The Modern Uzbeks From the Fourteenth Century to the Present – A Cultural History* (Stanford, 1990)

Allworth, E. ed., *Central Asia: 130 Years of Russian Dominance* (3rd edn, Durham, N.C., and London, 1994)

Altay, A. 'Kirgiziya during the great purge', *Central Asian Review*, 12:2, 1964, 97–107

Aminov, A. *Ekonomicheskoe razvitie Srednei Azii* (Tashkent, 1959)

Aminov A. and A. Babakhodzhaev, *Ekonomicheskie i politicheskie posledstviya prisoedineniya Srednei Azii k Rossii* (Tashkent, 1966)

Anderson, J. 'Saving the union: The Soviet referendum of March 1991', in A. Macartney, ed., *Asking the People: The Referendum and Constitutional Change* (Edinburgh, 1992), pp. 47–53

Anderson, J. 'Out of the kitchen, out of the temple: Religion, atheism and women in the Soviet Union', in S. P. Ramet, ed., *Religious Policy in the Soviet Union* (Cambridge, 1993), pp. 206–28

Anderson, J. 'Islam in the Soviet archives: A research note', *Central Asian Survey*, 13:3, 1994, 383–94

Anderson, J. *Religion, State and Politics in the Soviet Union and the Successor States* (Cambridge, 1994)

Atkin, M. *The Subtlest Battle: Islam in Soviet Tajikistan* (Philadelphia, 1989)

Atkin, M. 'Islamic assertiveness and the waning of the old Soviet order', *Nationalities Papers*, 20:1, 1992, 55–73

Avezov, M. O. ed., *Istoriya Kazakhskoi SSR*, Volume 1 (Alma Ata, 1957)

Aydin, M. 'Turkey and Central Asia: Challenges of change', *Central Asian Survey*, 15:2, 1996, 157–77

Bairamsakhatov, N. *Dukhovnaya kul'tura naroda i ateizm* (Ashkhabad, 1981)

Baker, J. 'The position of women in Kazakhstan in the inter-war years', *Central Asian Survey*, 4:1, 1985, 75–114

Banuazizi A. and M. Weiner, eds, *The New Geopolitics of Central Asia and its Borderlands* (Bloomington and Indianapolis, 1994)

Barthold, V. V. *A Short History of Turkestan* (Leiden, 1956)

Becker, R. S. *Russia's Protectorates in Central Asia – Bukhara and Khiva* (Cambridge, 1968)

Bendrikov, K. E. *Ocherki po istorii narodnogo obrazovaniya Turkestana* (Moscow, 1960)

Bennigsen, A. 'Several nations or one people: Ethnic consciousness amongst Soviet Central Asian Muslims', *Survey*, 24:3, 1979, 51–64

Bennigsen, A. 'Soviet Muslims and the world of Islam', *Problems of Communism*, 29:2, 1980, 38–51

Bennigsen, A. ed., *Soviet Strategy and Islam* (London, 1989)

Bennigsen A. and C. Lemercier Quelquejay, 'The history of the Kazakh press', *Central Asian Review*, 13:2, 1966, 150–63

Bennigsen A. and C. Lemercier Quelquejay, *Islam in the Soviet Union* (London, 1967)

Bennigsen A. and S. Enders Wimbush, *Muslim National Communism in the Soviet Union* (London, 1979)

Bideleux, R. *Communism and Development* (London, 1985)

Blank, S. 'The contested terrain: Muslim political participation in Soviet Turkestan', *Central Asian Survey*, 6:4, 1987, 47–73

Bonner, A. 'Islam and the state in Central Asia: A comparative analysis', *Central Asian Monitor*, 1995, No. 6, pp. 27–37

Bourdeaux, M. A. ed., *The Politics of Religion in Russian and the New States of Eurasia* (New York, 1995)

Bremmer I. and R. Taras, eds, *Nations and Politics in the Soviet Successor States* (Cambridge, 1993)

Bremmer I. and C. Welt, 'The trouble with democracy in Kazakhstan', *Central Asian Survey*, 15:2, 1996, 179–99

Broxup, M. 'The basmachi', *Central Asian Survey*, 2:1, 1983, 57–81

Bushkov V. I. and D. V. Mikul'sky, *Tadzhikskoe obshchestvo na rubezhe tysyacheletii – etnopoliticheskaya situatsiya v nachale 1990x godov* (Moscow, 1992)

Buttino, M. 'Study of the economic crisis and depopulation in Turkestan, 1917–20', *Central Asian Survey*, 9:4, 1990, 59–74

Buttino, M. ed., *In a Collapsing Empire* (Milan, 1992)

Carlisle, D. 'Islam Karimov and Uzbekistan: Back to the future', in T. Colton and R. Tucker, eds, *Patterns in Post-Soviet Leadership* (Boulder, 1985), pp. 191–216

Carlisle, D. 'The Uzbek power elite: Politburo and Secretariat (1938–83), *Central Asian Survey*, 5:3, 1986, 91–132

Carlisle, D. 'Power and politics in Soviet Uzbekistan: From Stalin to Gorbachev', in W. Fierman, *Soviet Central Asia: The Failed Transformation*, pp. 93–130

Caroe, O. *Soviet Empire – The Turks of Central Asia and Stalinism* (London, 1967)

Cassen, R. ed., *Soviet Interests in the Third World* (London, 1985)

Conquest, R. *The Great Terror* (London, 1971)

Critchlow, J. *Nationalism in Uzbekistan: A Soviet Republic's Road to Sovereignty* (Boulder, 1991)

Curzon, G. *Russia in Central Asia in 1889* (London, 1889)

Dahl, R. *Democracy and its Critics* (New Haven and London, 1989)

Dannreuther, R. *Creating New States in Central Asia* (London, Adelphi Papers 288, 1994)

Danopolous C. and D. Zirker, ed., *Civil–Military Relations in the Soviet and Yugoslav Successor States* (Boulder, 1996)

Davis, H. C. *The Great Game in Asia, 1800–44* (London, 1918)

Demko, G. *The Russian Colonisation of Kazakhstan, 1896–1916* (Bloomington, Indiana, 1969)

d'Encausse, H. C. *Islam and the Russian Empire: Reform and Revolution in Central Asia* (London, 1988)

Diamond, L. 'Towards democratic consolidation', *Journal of Democracy*, 5:3, 1994, 4–17

Dienes, L. 'Pastoralism in Turkestan – Its decline and its persistence', *Soviet Studies*, 27:2, 1975, 343–65

Dienes, L. *Soviet Asia – Economic Development and National Policy Choices* (Boulder and London, 1987)

Dieter, H. 'Regional integration in Central Asia: Current economic position and prospects', *Central Asian Survey*, 15:3/4, 1996, 369–86

Eickelman, D. ed., *Russia's Muslim Frontiers* (Bloomington, 1993)

Ellis, C. H. *The British 'Intervention' in Transcaspia, 1918–19* (Berkeley and Los Angeles, 1963)

Ellman M. and V. Kontorovich, eds, *The Disintegration of the Soviet Economy* (London, 1992)

Fedorov, E. *Ocherki natsional'no osvoboditel'nogo dvizheniya v Srednei Azii* (Tashkent, 1925)

Ferdinand, P. ed., *The New Central Asia and its Neighbours* (London, 1994)

Fierman, W. 'The communist party, "Erk" and the changing Uzbek political environment', *Central Asian Survey*, 10:3, 1991, 55–72

Fierman, W. ed., *Soviet Central Asia: The Failed Transformation* (Boulder, 1991)

Foltz, R. 'The Tajiks of Uzbekistan', *Central Asian Survey*, 15:2, 1996, 313–16

Galuzo, P. G. *Turkestan – Koloniya* (Moscow, 1929, republished in Oxford, 1985)

Gellner, E. 'The importance of being modular', in J. Hall, ed., *Civil Society: Theory, History, Comparison* (Cambridge, 1995), pp. 32–55

Gidulianov, P. *Otdelenie tserkvi ot gosudarstva v SSSR* (Moscow, 1926, with 1928 supplement)

Gillard, D. *The Struggle for Asia, 1828–1914* (London, 1977)

Ginzburg, A. I. ed., *Russkie v novom zarubezh'e: Kirgiziya* (Moscow, 1994)

Gleason, G. 'The Pakhta programme – the politics of sowing cotton in Uzbekistan', *Central Asian Survey*, 2:2, 1983, 109–20

Gleason, G. 'Sharaf Rashidov and the dilemmas of national leadership', *Central Asian Survey*, 5:3, 1986, 133–60

Glebov O. and J. Crowfoot, eds, *The Soviet Empire – Its Nations Speak Out* (New York, 1989)

Greaves, R. *Persia and the Defence of India* (London, 1959)

Gross, J.-A. ed., *Muslims in Central Asia – Expressions of Identity and Change* (Durham, N.C., 1992)

Haghayeghi, M. *Islam and Politics in Central Asia* (London, 1995)

Hajda L. and M. Beissinger, eds, *The Nationality Factor in Soviet Politics and Society* (Boulder, 1990)

Huntington S. 'Democracy's third wave', in L. Diamond and M. Plattner, eds, *The Global Resurgence of Democracy* (Baltimore and London, 1993), pp. 17–18

Huskey, E. 'The politics of language in Kyrgyzstan', *Nationalities Papers*, 23:3, 1995, 549–72

Inoyatov, Kh. *Pobeda Sovetskoi vlasti v Turkestane* (Moscow, 1978)

Johnson L. and C. Archer, eds, *Peacekeeping and the Role of Russia in Eurasia* (Boulder and Oxford, 1996)

Khalfin, N. A. *Russia's Policy in Central Asia, 1857–1868* (Oxford, 1964)

Khodzhaev, F. ed., *Ocherki revolyutsionnogo dvizheniya v Srednei Azii* (Moscow, 1926)

Kinyapina, N. S. *Vneshnyaya politika rossii vtoroi poloviny XIX veka* (Moscow, 1974)

Kinyapina, N. S., M. M. Bliev and V. V. Degoev, *Kavkhaz i Srednyaya Aziya vo vneshnei politike Rossii* (Moscow, 1984)

Kolossov, V. *Ethno-Territorial Conflicts and Boundaries in the Former USSR* (Durham, 1992)

Konstitutsiya respubliki Kazakhstana (Alma Ata, 1993)

Konstitutsiya respubliki Uzbekistana (Tashkent, 1992)

Kostyukova, I. 'The towns of Kyrgyzstan change their faces: Rural–urban migrants in Bishkek', *Central Asian Survey*, 13:3, 1994, 425–34

Kunavina, G. S. *Formirovanie zheleznodorozhnogo proletariata v Turkestane, 1881–1914gg* (Tashkent, 1967)

Landa, R. G. 'Islamskii fundamentalizm', *Voprosi istorii*, 1993:1, 32–41

Landau, J. *The Politics of Pan-Islam: Ideology and Organisation* (Oxford, 1990)

Lapidus, I. *A History of Islamic Societies* (Cambridge, 1988)

Lavrent'ev, V. I. *Kapitalizm v Turkestane* (Leningrad, 1930)

Lewis, R. ed., *Geographic Perspectives on Soviet Central Asia* (London, 1992)

Linz J. and A. Valenzuela, eds, *The Failure of Presidential Democracy, Volume 1: Comparative Perspectives* (Baltimore, 1994)

Lowe, C. J. *Reluctant Imperialists* (New York, 1967)

Lubin, N. 'Assimilation and retention of ethnic identity in Uzbekistan', *Asian Affairs*, 12:3, 1981, 277–85

Lubin, N. *Labour and Nationality in Soviet Central Asia – An Uneasy Compromise* (Princeton, 1984)

Lubin, N. *Central Asians Take Stock: Reform. Corruption and Identity* (Washington, 1994)

Lunin, B. V. ed., *Revolyutsiya 1905–1907gg v Srednei Azii i Kazakhstane* (Tashkent, 1985)

McAuley, A. 'Economic development and political nationalism in Uzbekistan', *Central Asian Survey*, 5:3, 1986, 161–82

McAuley, A. 'The Central Asian economy in comparative perspective', in M. Ellman and V. Kontorovich, eds, *The Disintegration of the Soviet Economy* (London, 1992)

MacKenzie, D. *The Lion of Tashkent – The Career of General Cherniaev* (London, 1974)

MacKenzie, D. 'Turkestan's significance to Russia', *Russian Review*, 33:2, 1974, 167–88

McLean, F. *A Person from England* (Oxford, 1958)

Malik, H. ed., *Central Asia: Its Strategic Importance and Future Prospects* (New York, 1994)

Mandelbaum, M. ed., *Central Asia and the World* (New York, 1994)

Manz, B. ed., *Central Asia in Historical Perspective* (Boulder, 1994)

Masal'sky, V. I. *Turkestanskii krai* (St Petersburg, 1914)

Massell, G. *The Surrogate Proletariat – Muslim Women and Revolutionary Strategies in Soviet Central Asia, 1919–29* (Princeton, 1974)

Mavlani, A. I. *Mikhail Vladimirovich Morozov* (Tashkent, 1963)

Medlin, W. ed., *Education and Development in Central Asia – A Case Study of Social Change in Uzbekistan* (Leiden, 1971)

Melvin, N. *Forging the New Russian Nation* (London, 1994)

Melvin, N. *Russians Beyond Russia: The Politics of National Identity* (London, 1995)

Mints, A. ed., *Srednyaya Aziya – Ekonomiko-geograficheskaya kharakteristika i problemy razvitiya khozyaistva* (Moscow, 1969)

Morozova S. and M. Lashch, *Tadzhikistan: vesna i leto 1992* (Moscow, 1992)

Naumkin, V. ed., *State, Religion and Society in Central Asia* (Reading, 1993)

Nazarbaev, N. *Without Right or Left* (London, 1992)

Norton, A. R. ed., *Civil Society in the Middle East* (London, 1995)

Novak, Yu. 'Mezhetnicheskie otnosheniya v Uzbekistane', *Sotsiologicheskie issledovaniya*, 1994:4, 41–52

Nove A. and J. Newth, *The Soviet Middle East – A Model for Development*, (London, 1967)

Olcott, M. B. 'The basmachi or freemen's revolt in Turkestan, 1918–24', *Soviet Studies*, 33:3, 1981, 352–69

Olcott, M. B. *The Kazakhs* (Stanford, 1987)

Olcott, M. B. *Central Asia's New States: Independence, Foreign Policy and Regional Security* (Washington, 1996)

Olivier, B. 'Korenizatsiya', *Central Asian Survey*, 9:3, 1990, 77–98

Paksoy, H. B. ed., *Central Asian Reader* (New York, 1994)

Pal'vanova, B. P. *Emansipatsiya musul'manki* (Moscow, 1982)

Patniak, A. 'Agriculture and rural out-migration in Central Asia', *Europe–Asia Studies*, 47:1, 1995, 147–69

Pierce, R. *Russian Central Asia, 1867–1917 – A Study in Colonial Rule* (Berkeley, 1960)

Pipes, R. *The Formation of the Soviet Union: Communism and Nationalism, 1917–23* (Cambridge, 1954)

Poliakov, S. *Everyday Islam – Religion and Tradition in Rural Central Asia* (New York, 1992)

Ponomarev, V. *Samodeyatel'nye obshchestvennye organizatsii Kazakhstana i Kirgizii, 1987–91* (Moscow, 1991)

Ponomarev V. and S. Dzhukeeva, eds, *Dokumenty i materialy o sobytiyakh 1986 goda v Kazakhstane* (Moscow, 1993)

Pyaskovskii, A. V. *Revolyutsiya 1905–07gg v Turkestane* (Moscow, 1958)

Pyaskovskii A. V. ed., *Vosstanie 1916 goda v Srednei Azii i Kazakhstane – Sbornik dokumentov* (Moscow, 1960)

Rakowska-Harmstone, T. *Russia and Nationalism in Central Asia – The Case of Tadzhikistan* (Baltimore, 1970)

Razakov, T. *Oshskie sobytiya – na materialakh KGB* (Bishkek, 1993)

Rogger, H. 'D. M. Skobelev: The hero and his worship', *Oxford Slavonic Papers* No. 9, 1976

Roi, Y. 'Central Asian riots and disturbances, 1989–90', *Central Asian Survey*, 10:3, 1991, 21–54

Roi, Y. ed., *The USSR and the Muslim World* (London, 1984)

Roi, Y. ed., *Muslim Eurasia – Conflicting Legacies* (London, 1995)

Rumer, B. *Soviet Central Asia – A Tragic Experiment* (London, 1989)

Rumer, B. *Central Asia in Transition* (New York, 1996)

Rywkin, M. ed., *Russian Colonial Expansion to 1917* (London, 1988)

Sabol, S. 'The creation of Soviet Central Asia: The 1924 national delimitation', *Central Asian Survey*, 14:2, 1995, 225–42

Safarov, G. *Kolonial'naya revolyutsiya* (Moscow, 1921, republished in Oxford, 1985)

Shain Y. and J. Linz, eds, *Between States: Interim Governments and Democratic Transitions* (Cambridge, 1995)

Sheehy, A. 'The Andizhan uprising of 1898 and Soviet historiography', *Central Asian Review*, 13:2, 1966, 139–50

Shlapentokh, V. ed., *The New Russian Diaspora: Russian Minorities in the Former Soviet Republics* (New York, 1994)

Shugart M. and J. Carey, *Presidents and Assemblies: Constitutional Design and Electoral Dynamics* (Cambridge, 1992)

Sokol, E. *The Revolt of 1916 in Central Asia* (Baltimore, 1954)

Starr, S. F. 'Making Eurasia stable', *Foreign Affairs*, January–February 1996, 80–92

Suleimenov B. S. and V. Ya. Basin, *Vosstanie 1916 goda v Kazakhstane* (Alma Ata, 1977)

Sultan-Galiev, M. S. *Stat'i* (Oxford, 1984)

Sumner, B. H. *Tsardom and Imperialism in the Far East and the Middle East, 1880–1914* (London, 1942)

Szporluk, R. ed., *National Identity and Ethnicity in Russia and the New States of Eurasia* (New York, 1994)

Tillet, L. *The Great Friendship* (Chapel Hill, 1969)

Tismaneau, V. ed., *Political Culture and Civil Society in Russia and the New States of Eurasia* (New York, 1995)

Vambery, A. *The Life and Adventures of Arminius Vambery* (London, 1914)

Vambery, A. *Central Asia and the Anglo-Russia Frontier Question* (London, 1974)

Veksel'man, M. I. 'Rossiiskii monopolisticheskii i inostrannyi kapital v toplivnoi promyshlennosti Srednei Azii v kontse XIX–nachale XXv.', *Istoricheskie zapiski*, 113 (Moscow, 1986), 283–304

Webber, M. *The International Politics of Russia and the Successor States* (Manchester, 1996)

Werner, C. A. 'A preliminary assessment of attitudes towards the privatisation of agriculture in contemporary Kazakhstan', *Central Asian Survey*, 13:2, 1994, 295–304

Wheeler, G. *The Peoples of Central Asia* (London, 1966)

White, G. 'Civil society, democratisation and development (i): clearing the analytical ground', *Democratisation*, 1:3, 1994, 375–90

Winrow, G. *Turkey in Post-Soviet Central Asia* (London, 1995)

Wolfson, S. 'Oil fever in Kazakhstan: Environmental angle', *Environmental Policy Review*, 8:1, 1994, 6–13

Zenkovsky, S. *Pan-Turkism and Islam in Russia* (Cambridge, Mass., 1960)

Ziyaev, Kh. Z. *Revolyutsiya 1905–1907gg v Srednei Azii i Kazakhstane* (Tashkent, 1958)

Zviagelskaia, I. *The Russian Policy Debate on Central Asia* (London, 1995)

Newspapers and periodicals

Asian Affairs
BBC Summary of World Broadcasts
Central Asian Review
Central Asian Survey
Europe-Asia Studies (formerly *Soviet Studies*)
Foreign Affairs
International Affairs
Izvestiya
Journal of Democracy
Kazakhstanskaya pravda
Labyrinth
Middle East International
Moskovskie novosti
Narodnaya gazeta (formerly *Kommunist Tadzhikistana*)
Nationalities Papers
Nezavisimaya gazeta
Open Media Research Institute
Pravda
Pravda vostoka
Problems of Communism
Res publika
Segodnya
Slovo kyrgyzstana (formerly *Sovetskaya Kirgiziya*)
Survey
Transition
Turkestanskie vedomosti
Turkmenskaya iskra
World Politics

Index